T0301014

ANALYSIS OF THE
KOREAN
STOCK MARKET
Behavioral Finance Approaches

ANALYSIS OF THE
KOREAN
STOCK MARKET
Behavioral Finance Approaches

Keunsoo Kim

Kyung Hee University, South Korea

Jinho Byun

Ewha Womans University, South Korea

This work was supported by the National Research Foundation of Korea Grant
funded by the Korean Government (NRF-2012S1A6A4021437).

 **World Scientific**

NEW JERSEY · LONDON · SINGAPORE · BEIJING · SHANGHAI · HONG KONG · TAIPEI · CHENNAI · TOKYO

Published by

World Scientific Publishing Co. Pte. Ltd.

5 Toh Tuck Link, Singapore 596224

USA office: 27 Warren Street, Suite 401-402, Hackensack, NJ 07601

UK office: 57 Shelton Street, Covent Garden, London WC2H 9HE

Library of Congress Cataloging-in-Publication Data

Names: Kim, Keunsoo, author. | Byun, Jinho, author.

Title: Analysis of the Korean stock market : behavioral finance approaches / Keunsoo Kim
    (Kyung Hee University, South Korea), Jinho Byun (Ewha Womans University, South Korea).

Description: 1 Edition. | New Jersey : World Scientific, [2018] |
    Includes bibliographical references and index.

Identifiers: LCCN 2017056910 | ISBN 9789813236752

Subjects: LCSH: Capital market--Korea (South) | Corporate governance--Korea (South) |
    Money market--Korea (South)

Classification: LCC HG5780.5.A3 K523 2018 | DDC 332.64/25195--dc23

LC record available at https://lccn.loc.gov/2017056910

British Library Cataloguing-in-Publication Data

A catalogue record for this book is available from the British Library.

For any available supplementary material, please visit
http://www.worldscientific.com/worldscibooks/10.1142/10896#t=suppl

Desk Editor: Shreya Gopi

Typeset by Stallion Press
Email: enquiries@stallionpress.com

Printed in Singapore

Contents

Preface

The main ideas of this book were planned over fourteen years ago, when we were both working at the Korea Capital Market Institute as research fellows returning from the US after getting our PhD degrees. While analyzing the Korean stock market, we discovered that little research on the Korean stock market had been published in English. As a result, empirical findings using a Korean dataset are not well known to the international investment communities and academia. In 2004, we began to discuss the idea of writing a book that would introduce the Korean stock market with some more empirical analyses. In the meantime, we both started our professional careers at universities, and research pressure as junior professors pushed our plan to the backburner. Our long-time idea was finally started in 2012 and was financially supported by the National Research Foundation of Korea.

The pricing models, such as the capital asset pricing model (CAPM), suggest that a stock's performance should not ultimately depend on the stock's characteristics but on its risk. Academicians, however, have documented several anomalies related to the seasonal effect, size, book-to-market ratio, past returns, and so on. The investment industry has paid attention to these anomalies because the anomalies imply that certain categories of stocks based on their characteristics can consistently outperform others. According to Bernstein (1995), the investment community developed investment products to take advantage of anomalies long before the academic world agreed that anomalies even exist. However, styling investments based on size and book-to-market ratio began to spread rapidly within the investment community during the 1980s, when academic research confirmed the persistence and robustness of the anomalies.

Academic research has sometimes influenced the investment business world with its insightful intuition of investment strategies. For example, Dimensional Fund Advisors, which is recognized as a successful investment company, developed its investment strategy based on academic research. The strategy of Dimensional Fund Advisors is to achieve high expected returns by taking advantage of the size effect and the book-to-market effect. Applied Quantitative Research Capital Management, founded in 1998, has also achieved outstanding performance by adapting value and momentum strategies, which its founders researched in academia.

However, the Korean investment community does not seem to be interested in research-oriented investment strategies. Professional investors usually pursue short-term profits, likely because of short-term evaluation of their investment performance. Thus, they mainly focus on market timing and pick up theme stocks for short-term capital gains based on their own economic predictions, personal investment experiences, or technical analysis. Unfortunately, the academic literature has yet to document any reliable short-term profitable strategy because any abnormal returns easily disappear after considering transaction costs. This is one of the reasons why the Korean investment community is not interested in academic research. On the other hand, practical issues do not attract academicians, who mainly aim to publish their research in academic journals. As a result, the investment community has rarely interacted with academia. We want to bridge the academic and investment communities by providing empirical analyses of the Korean stock market that also contain practical value.

This book comprehensively analyzes anomalies in the Korean stock market, including time series anomalies, such as the January effect; cross-sectional anomalies, such as the size effect and book-to-market effect; and anomalies related to corporate events. Although most of these anomalies have previously been found in the Korean stock market, academic papers have sometimes provided different or even opposing results regarding the existence of the same anomaly, likely because of different samples, study periods, or methodologies. Because we employ the same long-term period of 1980–2013 and the same dataset in most of our studies, our research provides more consistent results.

In most analyses, we document anomalies without controlling risk. We focus on determining whether anomalies exist and persist in terms of raw returns. Instead of controlling for risk, we show how frequently anomalies have reversed over the sample period to understand the level of risk. Our approach is straightforward and easy to understand. In the absence of any convincing risk model, any risk-controlled abnormal returns related to anomalies cannot avoid the controversy of whether anomalies result from poor risk measurement or not. Such controversy may not be important to practitioners as much as to academicians. For example, Dimension Fund Advisors believe that the size and book-to-market effects are risk premiums but pursue high expected returns by holding risky stocks over long-term periods. If one pursues good investment performance from a long-term perspective, our research on anomalies will be attractive.

We employ two behavioral aspects throughout the book, which differentiates this work from other research or books. First, this book regards the market return predictability of the aggregate M/B (market-to-book) ratio, which is an aspect of the behavioral approach. We find that the aggregate M/B ratio, which is calculated monthly as the sum of all market capitalization values divided by the sum of all book values across all listed firms in the Korea Composite Stock Price Index (KOSPI) market, has predictive power for market returns in the Korean stock market. Only a few academic studies have investigated the predictive capability of the M/B ratio. The regression analyses of Kothari and Shanken (1997) and Pontiff and Schall (1998) suggest that as the aggregate M/B ratio rises, future stock returns tend to decline. Our book confirms the aggregate M/B ratio's ability to predict the market in a more practical way. Every month of the sample period is classified as either a high M/B month or a low M/B month. The creation of monthly aggregate M/B ratios and classification of high and low M/B months are carefully designed to avoid any look-ahead bias.

We find that, from 1989 through 2013, the average six-month equally weighted return is 15.6% following low M/B months, which is much higher than the 3.9% following high M/B months. The aggregate M/B months also have predictability for January returns. The average January return is 11.07% following low M/B months and 3.39% following high M/B months. We also investigate whether the market predictability of the aggregate M/B ratio influences major anomalies and market reaction to corporate events.

The second point of the behavioral approach used here is to examine the trading behavior of investor types with regard to anomalies and corporate events. Because a trading dataset stratified by investor types (individual, institutional, or foreign) is available in Korea, this book provides a distinctive opportunity to understand the real behavior of investor types. For example, although most research in the US stock markets uses the transaction records of retail investors at large brokerage firms, such a dataset usually covers less than 10 years, making it difficult to investigate the trading behavior of investor types. Such datasets fail to represent all individual investors in the US stock market. Other sources, like the New York Stock Exchange's Consolidated Auto Trail Data, are also limited to a few years, while the Trade and Quote and Institute for the Study of Securities Markets datasets do not contain any information about whether a trade is initiated by the buyer or seller or whether an individual investor or institutional investor participates in the trade. On the other hand, the dataset of the Korea Exchange (KRX) provides daily buying and selling value (in KRW) and volume (shares) of investor types for every stock listed on the KOSPI market. Thus, this book deals with a wide range of investment subjects with a unique data sample that is not available in the US.

We find that most small firms in the KOSPI market are predominantly traded by individual investors. It seems that foreign or domestic institutional investors hardly influence valuation of these stocks. In the case of stocks for which individual investors trade more than 90% (*Indp*>90%), low B/M stocks do not have higher profitability and sales growth than high B/M stocks for three years before and after sorting B/M stocks. Thus, low B/M stocks with $Indp>90\%$ appear to be neither growth nor profitable stocks. On the other hand, low B/M stocks with $Indp\leq90\%$ appear to be both growth and profitable stocks. Because individual investors value stocks in different ways, stock markets appear to be separated based on whether foreign investors or domestic institutional investors interact with individual investors. Such stock market separation may be a clue to understanding anomalies. For example, the market reaction to a firm's corporate events may also depend on whether individual investors trade its stocks dominantly. Furthermore, any study that investigates the trading behavior of investor types should carefully interpret their trading behavior. Our research indicates that small stocks are usually traded among individual investors rather than between different investor types. The trading behavior of different investor types for these stocks can easily be misleading if we ignore the large trading volume among individual investors. Different trading behavior of individual investors may be an important key to understanding the sources of anomalies, such as the size effect, January effect, book-to-market effect, and price momentum.

The book's structure reflects our behavioral finance approach: we analyze the trading behavior of investors and/or provide the market predictability of stock returns for major topics covered in the chapters, with the exception of some descriptive chapters. The book consists of six chapters, and a brief synopsis of each chapter follows.

Chapter 1 begins by introducing the history of the Korean stock market and gives an overview of the market's development. Furthermore, the current status of the Korean stock market is explained in this chapter, including the market trading system, daily price limit, circuit break, and side car. We also examine the performance of Korean market indices, and introduce market statistics including market capitalization, the number of listed stocks, IPOs, and SEOs over the time period.

Chapter 2 explains the two aspects of the behavioral approach used to analyze anomalies and corporate events in this book: trading behavior and market predictability. This chapter explains why the trading behavior of investor types is important in stock valuation and discusses the Korean trading dataset's advantage in analyzing trading behavior compared to other countries' datasets. In addition, the aggregate M/B ratio's ability to predict the market is explained.

Chapter 3 examines anomalies related to the seasonal effect. The January effect, January barometer, weekend effect, and holiday effect are analyzed. The January effect exists in Korea and is more significant. Interestingly, foreign investors are strong net buyers of stocks in January for which they account for at least 5% of trading value. However, the January effect is more prominent in stocks for which foreign investors account for less than 5% of trading value.

Chapter 4 comprehensively examines cross-sectional anomalies: size effect, B/M effect, long-term reversal, short-term price momentum, and turnover ratio effect. Although these anomalies have been intensively analyzed in the US, results using a Korean dataset are not well known to practitioners or academics. Furthermore, trading behaviors by investor types will be novel knowledge to readers interested in anomalies.

Chapter 5 considers corporate events, such as IPOs, SEOs, stock splits, stock repurchases, and dividend announcements. This book provides results on long-term performance after the events. In addition, this chapter examines the trading behavior of investors and market reaction to events that occurred in periods following high (or low) M/B months. The distinctive characteristics of the Korean regulation systems regarding corporate events are explained in this chapter.

Chapter 6 presents industry analyses. This chapter examines the sales revenue, profitability, valuation, and financial risk of companies listed on KRX at both the sectoral level and the industrial level. The number of listed firms and the sales revenue for the tertiary sector are much smaller than those for the secondary sector. Chapter 6 also examines 27 industries and their major firms by sector in terms of major financial ratios.

This book took longer than we had originally planned. The more we studied, the more questions we had to raise. This research attempts to summarize anomalies in the Korean stock market but also leads to many unresolved questions. The academic literature evolved rapidly while we were writing. There may be many subjects that we do not include. Nevertheless, it was a precious opportunity for us to spend many years investigating anomalies in the Korean stock market. This research will provide a broader picture of anomalies in the Korean stock market.

We would like to acknowledge the financial support of the National Research Foundation of Korea. Without their support, it would have taken much longer to finish this challenging job. We also greatly appreciate the constructive comments of unknown referees. In addition, special thanks go to Joshua K. Kim, who thoughtfully read the book and gave helpful comments. We also thank Miss Shreya Gopi for guiding us through publishing this book. Last but not least, we would like to express heartfelt thanks to our families, who are always giving us peace and vitality.

References

Bernstein, R., 1995, *Style Investing*, Hoboken, NJ: John Willey & Sons, Inc.

Kothari, S.P. and J. Shanken, 1997, Book-to-Market, Dividend Yield, and Expected Market Returns: A Time Series Analysis, *Journal of Financial Economics* 44, 169–203.

Pontiff, J. and L. Schall, 1998, Book-to-Market Ratios as Predictors of Market Returns, *Journal of Financial Economics* 49, 141–160.

About the Authors

Keunsoo Kim is a Professor at the Graduate School of Pan-Pacific International Studies, Kyung Hee University. He worked for five years in Korea Capital Market Institution (KCMI) after receiving Ph.D. degree of business from State University of New York at Buffalo in 2000. As a research fellow of KCMI, he published a number of research reports with regards to improvement of fund policy and regulation in Korea, the business strategy of securities companies, comparative analysis on Korean, Japanese, and Chinese institutional investors, and investor education.

He has been a Professor at the Graduate School of Pan-Pacific International Studies since 2005. He has researched on behavioral finance, anomalies, and the trading behavior of investor types in the Korean stock market. For example, he created a Korean version of the investment sentiment index and tested the effect of investment sentiment on market reaction to corporate events such as stock split and stock repurchase. He also surveyed academic studies related to behavioral finance in the Korean stock market.

Professor Kim continues to be interested in improving financial capability in Korea by publishing several books such as a guide to smart financial life and strategic plans for financial capability.

Jinho Byun is a Professor of Finance at Ewha Womans University, School of Business. He has a Master's degree in Finance from the University of Wisconsin-Madison and received his PhD in Finance from the School of Management, University at Buffalo (SUNY). Prior to joining Ewha in 2003, he worked at the Korea Capital Market Institute (KCMI) as a research fellow. At that time, he participated in research projects on improving the Korean stock market system. Professor Byun's research focuses on corporate finance, market anomalies, and investment strategies. He has published over twenty research articles in academic journals, including the *Journal of Finance*, *Asia-Pacific Journal of Financial Studies*, and *Asian Review of Financial Research* He also published several books such as *Guide to Smart Financial Life for 20s*, *Fundamentals of Investments*, and *Financial Management*.

Professor Byun has served as Vice President at the Korean Securities Association and as an editor in major Korean finance journals such as the *Korean Journal of Financial Studies* and *Korean Journal of Financial Management*. He has broad advisory experiences and has served as a committee member at government, Korean public funds, and major financial companies, including Financial Services Commission, Financial Supervisory Service, Korea Exchange, and National Pension Service.

Chapter 1

Korean Capital Market

1.1. History of Korean Capital Market

This chapter gives an overview of the history of Korean capital markets based on five sub-periods: the early stage (1945–1967), the development stage for securities infrastructure (1968–1979), the market liberalization and globalization stage (1980–1996), the Asian financial crisis and reform stage (1997–2003), and the globalized capital market stage (2004–). For each period, we explain the status of stock market development; the main issues encountered, such as a market crash; and the enactment or revision of major securitie-srelated legislation.

The Korean capital market was in a poor condition in its early stage because available capital was very limited. However, as the Korean economy rapidly developed, the capital market began to play a role in channeling capital to firms during the development stage. Because the Korean economy is characterized as a small open economy, the capital market also pursued the global trend of deregulation and liberalization of policy during the market liberalizing and globalizing stage. In a liberalized market, each economic unit is required to manage risk by itself. However, the Korean government, firms like *chaebols*, and financial institutions were left too vulnerable to the Asian currency crisis because of their poor risk management. The Asian currency crisis badly hurt the Korean economy in 1997–1999. Korea accelerated liberalization and globalization of the capital markets during the Asian financial crisis and reform stage. After Korea went through the structural changes of reforms, the risk management capability of each economic unit improved. However, the easy monetary policy during the global financial crisis sharply increased household debt, which has become a major risk for the Korean economy.

1.1.1. *Early Stage (1949–1967)*

The first Korean securities company, called Daehan securities company and later renamed Kyobo securities company, was founded in 1949. The number of securities companies increased to 33 by 1955 (Lee *et al.*, 2005). The Korea Stock Dealers Association was also founded to help Korean firms raise capital for investment. Their role, however, was limited to arranging over-the-counter (OTC) trading of government bonds until the Korea Stock Exchange (KSE) was incorporated in 1956, with joint contributions from banks, insurance companies, and securities companies. The KSE, now known as the Korea Exchange (KRX), initially listed 12 corporations and 3 government bonds.

The Korean government took over the assets of Japanese corporations in the process of Korea's liberation from Japan. In the 1950s, most corporations were state-owned companies. They did not want to issue stocks to the secondary market because the demand for stocks was limited as a result of the lack of capital. However, because the Korean government needed immediate and extensive capital to shore up the weak fiscal conditions of the country, it issued bonds in the KSE, and these government bonds were actively traded. According to Yoon (2015), government bonds were issued 17 times between January 1950 and January 1963, amounting to KRW 9.9 billion. In 1957–1960, the trading value of government bonds accounted for 70–80% in the KSE, compared with only 10–25% accounted for by stock trading.

The market conditions for stock trading were very poor. The number of listed firms and their floating stocks were extremely small, and the investor base was also very limited. Later settlements for securities trading were permitted in the KSE to activate securities trading at that time. Traders could purchase large amounts of securities by depositing a small margin of 10% in a clearinghouse. Such margin trading, however, led the market to be extremely speculative, causing a series of market crashes because of incomplete transaction settlements. Indeed, government bond transactions collapsed on January 16, 1958, because of settlement failure, an event referred to as the January 16 crash of the government's bond.

According to Yoon (2015), securities companies were divided into a buyer group that wanted the bond price to increase and a seller group that wanted the bond price to fall. These groups aggressively traded to move the government's bond in their preferred direction. The bond price soared by 2.5 times from June 1957 to December 1957, when the National Assembly announced the reduction of the government's bond. However, when the National Assembly passed the original plan of issuing the government's bond at the end of December 1957, the price crashed by 50% for 9 days. The trading volume irrationally increased at that time. The buyer group made ruinous buying orders while the seller group made selling orders without affordable government bonds. As most securities companies failed to pay the required margins, the Korean government nullified all transactions made on January 16, 1958. This incident shows how poorly the securities market in Korea worked at that time. Although the later settlement system caused speculative trading and the market crash, the government could not renounce this system because the market might not have been sustainable with thin trading. Because of the January 16 crash, several securities companies went bankrupt and many investors left, leaving the market in the doldrums for a few years.

In January 1962, the government legislated the Securities and Exchange Act (SEA), which established legal grounds for the organization structure and operation management of the KSE. Under the SEA, the KSE became a corporation whose stocks were listed on the KSE as well. The KSE stocks were attractive to investors because the KSE was expected to develop rapidly, and securities companies wanted to have majority shares to control the KSE. The price of the KSE soared into the sky, increasing by more than 60 times from January to April 1962 and by 136 times from July 1961 to April 1962. Other stocks, such as shares of the Korea Securities Finance Corporation and the Korea Electric Power Corporation (KEPCO) experienced dramatic price increases as well.

The irrational rise of the KSE price at that time could not be explained without the later settlement system. Later settlement made it easy for a number of securities companies to manipulate stock prices even with a small amount of funds because stock buyers could delay payment for stock purchases for 1 month with penalty fees. Under the SEA of 1962, the KSE was required to make proxy payment for stock purchases for stock buyers who delayed payment. Such a proxy payment system made it possible to buy an enormous amount of stock without the funding to afford it.

At that time, people colluded in stock price manipulation. Yoon (2015) wrote, "Since early May 1962, Mr. Yoon Ensang had initiated daily meetings for a stock purchasing group to make buying strategy plans. Tongil and Ilheung securities companies that Mr. Yoon owned were leading buyers for the KSE stocks. The selling group, whose leader was Taeyang securities company, also had meetings to plan their selling strategy. On May 23, twenty-three securities companies met together and decided on the full-scale attack for selling the KSE stocks on May 25. After hearing the attack plan, many buyers switched to sellers." It was possible to manipulate stock price at that time because of the small number of floating stocks, the narrow investor base, and the later settlement system. Such price manipulation may be the case of market failure. Many investment practitioners at that time believed they could control stock prices when they purchased or sold in cohort. Such a belief still remains in the Korean investment community.

The aggressive buying and selling of the KSE stocks reached the peak of trading volume in May 1962. Table 1.1 shows the extent of the trading volume increase. The proportion of stock trading volume increased from 17.13% in 1960 to 99.17% in 1962. The irrational price level of the KSE stocks was not sustainable, and the stock price of the KSE began to decrease in May. Furthermore, the later settlement system was not sustainable as proxy payments by the KSE excessively accumulated. Indeed, some securities companies failed to pay

Table 1.1.   Securities Trading Amount in Korea from 196 to 1962 (unit: KRW million)

Year	Stock	Government Bond	Total Amount	Stock Proportion (%)
1960	275	1,330	1,605	17.13
1961	438	911	1,345	32.57
1962	98,375	821	99,196	99.17

Source: Korea Exchange (1963), Securities Statistics Year Book (cited by Lee *et al.*, 2005).

for stock purchases. This incident, called the Security Crisis of May 1962, resulted in the suspension of the KSE and the bankruptcy of several securities firms. The government redenominated the currency in June 1962, and the KSE reopened in July 1962, but faced serious doldrums. The stock price of the KSE decreased to less than 1% of its peak in February 1963. After experiencing the stock market collapse, many investors lost trust in the securities market and left the market. A deep downturn arrived.

In 1963, the Korean government revised the SEA to create legal grounds for the sound development of the securities market. The government reorganized the KSE from a corporation into a state-owned entity in response to the Security Crisis of May. In addition, the government mandated that securities firms hold an adequate level of equity to ensure their financial stability and improved the securities transaction systems. Nevertheless, the later settlement system was still allowed in the KSE.

The trading value of securities plummeted after the Security Crisis of May, as Table 1.2 reports. The trading value of stocks decreased from KRW 98.3 billion in 1962 to KRW 26.0 billion in 1963 and then continued to decrease, indicating difficulty in recovering investor confidence in the securities market. The trading value of bonds also decreased substantially, and stock trading accounted for more than 95% of activity in this period. The number of listed firms was still very small during 1962–1968, although it increased to 34 listed firms in 1968.

The equity market did not play a major role in channeling capital to corporations during this period. According to the Capital

Table 1.2.   Securities Trading Value (KRW million) from 1962 to 1968

| | Stock | | | | Proportion |
Year	Number of Listed Companies	Trading Value	Bond	Total	of Stock (%)
1962	16	98,375	821	99,196	99.2
1963	15	26,000	1,103	27,103	95.9
1964	17	27,039	708	27,747	97.4
1965	17	9,271	166	9,437	98.2
1966	24	11,160	86	11,246	99.2
1967	24	24,917	36	24,953	99.9
1968	34	19,984	26	20,010	99.9

Source: Korea Financial Investment Association (KFIA), (2009), Capital Market in Korea.

Cycle of Korea (Bank of Korea, 1976, as cited in Korea Financial Investment Association, 2009), corporations raised capital amounting to KRW 36.2 billion in 1966 and KRW 67.7 billion in 1968 via equity issues. International loans, which were a major source of corporate investment, amounted to KRW 48.8 billion in 1966 and KRW 108.7 billion in 1968. Although equity capital increased between 1966 and 1968, the proportion of equity capital decreased from 23.9% in 1966 to 18.8% in 1968.

1.1.2. *Development Stage for Securities Infrastructure (1968–1979)*

As demand for domestic capital surged, the Korean government, which desperately needed a large amount of capital for economic development, recognized the stock market as an efficient tool for collecting capital from investors. Beginning in the late 1960s, the government's policy was oriented to promote Korea's securities market. In November 1968, the government enacted the Capital Market Promotion Act (CMPA), which was designed to provide tax relief to corporations when they became publicly listed on the KSE. Under the CMPA, the state-owned Korea Investment Corporation (KIC) was established to take responsibility for undertaking initial public offerings (IPOs) because securities firms at that time did not have enough capital to undertake IPOs. Thus, the foundation of CMPA was critically important in facilitating IPOs (Lee *et al.*, 2005).

The government undertook several measures to strengthen the securities market and boost the demand for stock investment. The strongest incentive it offered for going public was providing financial benefits to listed firms by decreasing their corporate tax rate compared to non-listed firms: The corporate tax rate was 20 percentage point lower for a listed firm than for a non-listed firm when taxable income was over KRW 5 million (Lee *et al.*, 2005). In addition, a listed firm could pay taxes or deposits via shares to the central or local government. Several measures were undertaken to increase the demand for stocks: Firms were encouraged to guarantee a certain dividend ratio to all shareholders except the government; shareholders were exempt for the dividend tax; the entry barrier for securities firms was lowered by substituting the registering system for the approval system; and the Securities Investment Trust Business Act (SITBA) was introduced in August 1969. Under SITBA, investment trust businesses were permitted to increase demand for stocks through the indirect investment of retail investors. In December 1971, the government finally abolished the later settlement system to discourage overspeculative investment and to activate cash transactions.

Although the CMPA was designed to encourage corporations to go public and become listed on the KSE, only one corporation did so (Lee *et al.*, 2005). Corporations could receive corporate tax benefits without actually being listed on the KSE because the requirements for going public were too loose. In addition, firms wanted to avoid going public because they worried about losing their corporate control or revealing corporate secrets.

As of June 1971, interest on a bank loan was 22% per year (Korea Bank, 1974), but corporations had difficulty in obtaining bank loans because available loans were so limited for them. Corporations with growth opportunities therefore had to rely on private loans as a source of capital, but the interest rates on private loans was two or three times higher than that on bank loans. Economic real growth stayed above 10% between 1968 and 1971; however, as it decreased to 7.2% in 1972, many corporations could not pay the high interest of private loans and became financially distressed.

In August 1972, the government announced the Emergency Order for Economic Development and Stability, the main measure of which was to freeze private loans and encourage debt–equity swaps of private loans. This order was designed to rescue financially distressed corporations with high private loans. Private loan providers, however, had to bear serious losses as a result of this order, essentially violating the principle of capitalism. The government also promulgated the Short-Term Finance Business Act, the Credit Unions Act, and the Mutual Savings and Financing Act to institutionalize private financing (KFIA, 2009). In 1973, Securities Exchange Act regulations were revised with new stipulations to enhance the external audit system and introduce a book-entry clearing system to reduce transaction costs and risk related to exchange of securities with cash.

In December 1972, the government legislated the Public Corporation Inducement Law (PCIL), the main purpose of which was to force firms to go public. The PCIL designated requirements for public firms and provided additional financial benefits to them. If firms refused to go public, they were subject to financial and tax restrictions. Furthermore, the government privatized state-owned companies and implemented securities market promotion policies designed to boost demand for stock investment.

Although the first oil shock occurred in the mid-1970s, the annual growth rate of the Korean economy stayed above 10% from 1971 to 1978. With the successful economic growth of the 1960s and 1970s, new acts in the 1970s like PCIL triggered the development of the securities market. The number of listed firms dramatically increased from 42 in 1969 to 274 in 1976. The number of shareholders also increased from 54,300 to 568,000, resulting in a great expansion of the Korean stock market's investor base. In particular, high returns on IPO stocks increased individual investors' interest in stock investment.

Market capitalization in the Korean stock market has also shown amazing growth, as seen in Table 1.3. The capitalization value

Table 1.3. Growth of Securities Market from 1968 to 1976

Year	No. of Listed Companies	No. of Shareholders (thousand)	Market Capitalization (KRW billion)	Trading Value (KRW billion)	Capital Mobilization (KRW billion)
1969	42	54	86.6	41.9	6.1
1970	48	76	97.9	41.1	7.2
1971	50	82	108.7	33.8	2.9
1972	66	103	246.0	70.3	24.7
1973	104	200	426.2	160.1	54.5
1974	128	200	532.8	178.9	74.3
1975	189	291	916.1	333.5	156.3
1976	274	568	1,436.1	628.2	262.2
1977	323	395	2,350.8	NA	362.4
1978	356	963	2,892.5	NA	653.1

Source: Korea Exchange, Securities Statistics Year Books (cited in Korea Financial Investment Association, 2009).

increased from KRW 86.6 billion in 1969 to KRW 1,436 billion in 1976; the trading value was KRW 628.2 billion in 1976, almost 14 times as high as that in 1969. Strong incentives and forced requirements for going public led firms to raise capital and be listed on the stock market, as Table 1.3 illustrates.

In November 1976, the SEA was revised substantially in response to the sudden growth of the securities market in the 1970s. First, demand for a self-regulatory system increased to ensure efficient regulation and investor protection. The Securities and Exchange Commission (SEC) and its executive body, the Securities Supervisory Board (SSB), were established as Korea's principal securities regulators in 1976 (KFIC, 2009). The SEC, which was composed of the president of KSE, the president of Korea Bank, the vice-minister of Finance, and three other persons, had the power to oversee and investigate securities issuances; illegal trading, such as stock price manipulation; and securities-related organizations. Several measures were added to support and stabilize the corporate control of listed firms, including tender offers, regulation of total equity investment, and limits on proxy votes. In addition, regulations on disclosure and insider trading and restrictions on securities transactions by executives of securities companies were introduced to promote fair transactions. The Korea Securities Computer Corporation (Koscom) was also founded in September 1977 to provide an electronic computer service for securities market transactions under the permission of the Ministry of Finance.

The first oil boom provided great opportunities to Korean construction firms in the middle of the 1970s. The construction contract with the Middle East amounted to USD 7.9 billion in 1978, an enormous sum compared to Korea's economic size — Korean export value only reached USD 10 billion in 1977. The construction firms' stocks dramatically rose between 1975 and 1978, and the average annual returns on construction stocks were above 100% for the same period. Although some construction firms exhibited extremely poor profitability, their stocks soared nonetheless because they belonged to the construction industry. However, stock performance in other industries was poor. For example, electricity and electronics, chemicals, and finance stocks experienced negative returns on average from 1976 to 1977 (Yoon, 2015). The second oil shock overshadowed the global economy in 1979, causing high inflation and global economic recession in the early 1980s.

Construction stocks began to plummet beginning in late July 1978. The stock prices of major construction firms decreased by more than 70% until December 1978. In particular, many financially distressed firms in the construction industry, whose prices have surged during the period of 1975–1978, went bankrupt or were delisted from the KSE. For example, Bumwha construction corporation, whose sales and net income were estimated as KRW 6.5 billion and KRW 210 million, respectively, in 1978 turned out to have KRW 1.7 billion of sales and KRW −60 million of net income (Lee *et al.*, 2005).

1.1.3. *Market Liberalization and Globalization Stage (1980–1996)*

The second oil shock, the global recession, and the political instability of Korea resulted in poor economic growth in the early 1980s. The average economic growth was 5.6% between 1979 and 1982.

The Korean economy maintained double-digit growth in most of the mid- and late-1980s. Beginning in the 1970s, several developed countries pursed deregulation and financial liberalization to establish a more efficient and productive economic system. Because the Korean economy pursued an open economic policy with free trading, the Korean government could not look away from the global trend of financial liberalization and deregulation; it began to deregulate capital markets so that foreign investors could participate in the Korean capital market and businesses in the 1980s. Korean funds and financial organizations also began to participate in the international markets.

The government announced a four-phase Capital Market Globalization Plan in 1981 that ultimately aimed to completely globalize the Korean capital markets by the early 1990s. Accordingly, Korea Investment Trust (later renamed Korea Investment & Securities) and Daehan Investment Trust (later renamed Hana Financial Investment) launched the Korea International Trust (KIT) and Korea Trust (KT), respectively, in 1981. These funds were the first indirect investment vehicles through which foreign investors began to invest in Korean stocks and bonds. After successful distribution of these funds, several investment trust funds were issued for foreign investors.

The government pursued deregulation to allow foreign investors to invest in the domestic market and domestic investors to invest in overseas markets. Nomura Securities established the first foreign representative office in Seoul in 1981, followed by Merrill Lynch in 1985 and later by other foreign securities companies. Large Korean securities companies also established overseas offices. Daewoo and Daishin securities companies founded branch offices in Tokyo and New York in 1984. Other securities companies also established branches in major cities (KFIA, 2009).

The second oil shock, the bubble burst of construction stocks, the political instability, and low Korean economic growth led to a bearish stock market from 1978 to 1985. The Korean Composite Stock Price Index (KOSPI), a value-weighted average index including all firms listed on the KSE, started with 100 on January 4, 1980. KOSPI increased from 100 in 1980 to 163 in 1985. The aggregate

M/B ratios stayed very low, between 0.4 and 0.6, for the period of 1980–1985.[1]

In 1982, the SEA was further revised to promote fair trading by strengthening its regulations on insider trading and market price manipulation, increasing its disclosure requirements, and introducing an investment advisory system. The capital gains tax exemption, temporarily granted under the Regulation Law on Tax Reduction and Exemption, was reinstated under the Corporate Income Tax Law of 1985.

From the mid-1980s, the Korean economy grew at a rate of more than 10% per year. Low international raw material price, low valuation of Korean currency, and a low interest rate helped the Korean economy successfully grow with a large trade surplus. With successful economic growth, the Korean securities market aggressively expanded in terms of IPOs, number of listed firms, and investor base. In the mid-1980s, firms began to go public voluntarily and rushed to increase their capital through public offering. As a result, the number of listed firms increased from 342 in 1985 to 669 in 1990. Capital collected through IPOs amounted to KRW 4,723 billion from 1986 to 1990, whereas capital collected through SEO totaled KRW 22,879 billion, about 3.8 times higher than IPOs (Lee *et al.*, 2005). Direct financing through the capital market exceeded private loans as a means of supplying capital. According to Yoon (2015), investors numbered approximately 770,000 as of 1985 and increased to 19 million at the end of 1989, which accounts for 45% of the Korean adult population.

As the investor base sharply increased, securities companies began to flourish, with the average amount of capital per company reaching about KRW 100 billion by the end of 1989 (KFIA, 2009). The KOSPI reached 1,000 in March 1989, up from 163 in 1985, and the aggregate M/B ratio increased from 0.69 in 1985 to 2.21 in 1989, The finance, trading, and construction industries were the main sources of the KOSPI rise. The prices of securities companies

---

[1]The aggregate M/B ratio is defined as the sum of all market capitalization values divided by the sum of all book values across all firms listed on the KOSPI market.

soared as the average net income of securities companies grew 150.2% for 4 years since 1985 (Yoon, 2015). Hot investor sentiment toward the securities industry expanded to other financial sectors, such as banking, short-term investment finance, and insurance; these financial industries were expected to reap the benefits of financial liberalization. Stock prices of trading companies also rose sharply because trade with communist countries was expected to grow substantially. In addition, construction stock prices rapidly increased as presidential candidate Noh Taewoo promised a plan to construct 2 million house in 1987.

In 1987, the SEA was revised, changing from a state-owned entity to a membership system for the KSE. The OTC stock trading system was introduced to allow venture companies and small- and medium-sized enterprises (SMEs) to participate in the securities market in 1988. Brokerage commissions were liberalized, and autonomy in securities companies' business was permitted in 1988.

As the international stock market plummeted in the second half of 1989, the Korean securities market also turned bearish. Because many retail investors neither understood the risk of stock investing nor experienced investment losses, some staged protests against the government, urging the government to control stock prices through market intervention. In response, the government announced an unprecedented measure to support stock prices on December 12, 1989, and promised unlimited financial support to investment trust companies so that they could purchase stocks. Three major investment companies aggressively purchased stocks and generated a short-term rally in December. However, the KOSPI continued to decrease, from 909.7 in December 1989 to 688.7 in April 1990 in terms of the monthly index. The Korean government was not able to discern the difference between consumption and financial products at that time, and it treated the stock market as it did the agricultural market: The government believed that market prices of stocks could be made to rise simply by purchasing stocks with huge amounts of money. Three major investment trust companies became financially distressed as a result of investment losses when the government's measures to increase stock demand failed.

In 1992, foreign investors were allowed to directly invest in the stocks of firms listed on the Korean stock market with a 10% ceiling of ownership for a privately owned firm and an 8% ceiling of ownership for a state-owned firm. The ceiling of ownership gradually declined, and foreign investors were allowed to hold up to 100% of stocks in privately owned companies by 1998. There were restrictions on stock investment in state-owned companies, although such ceilings have gradually been weakened; for example, foreign investors were allowed to invest in up to 10% of stock in state-owned companies in 1995 and up to 40% in 2000. Korean securities firms also began to invest in foreign securities in 1988 with a ceiling of investment amount that gradually increased from USD 30 million in 1988. The ceiling of investment finally disappeared in 1996. Overseas investment by both institutional and individual investors was fully liberalized by 1996.

Korean firms began to be listed on foreign stock exchanges. Formerly Pohang Iron and Steel Company (POSCO) and Korea Electronic Power Corporation (KEPCO) were the first firms listed on the New York Stock Exchange (NYSE) through IPOs in 1994. Afterward, the number of Korean firms listed on foreign stock exchanges gradually increased. As of 2005, eight Korean firms were listed on the NYSE and four on the NASDAQ stock market (KRX, 2016). In addition, a number of Korean firms were also listed on European exchange markets such as the London Stock Exchange and the Luxembourg Stock Exchange.

The Korea Securities Dealers Association began to manage the OTC market for venture companies and SMEs beginning in April 1987. The Korea Securities Dealers Automated Quotation (KOSDAQ) market was established in July 1996 based on the OTC market for direct financing of venture companies and SMEs. In addition, in July 1997, the stock index option trading system was introduced with the Korea Futures Exchange (KOFEX), established in April 1999.

After the KOSPI reached its peak of 1,003.3 in March 1989, it gradually decreased and then fluctuated between the 600s and 700s in early 1990. Foreign investors became major investors soon after they were allowed to directly invest in the Korean stock market in 1992.

They tended to purchase blue chips exhibiting excellent fundamental value and large capitalization. The KOSPI reached 1,145 points in November 1994, its highest point until that time. However, only large blue chips experienced a high price increase. Most small stocks failed to join in the price increase (Yoon, 2015).

1.1.4. *Asian Financial Crisis and Reform Stage (1997–2003)*

The short-term lending rate began to be liberalized in 1991; thereafter, interest rates were gradually liberalized so that they could be determined in the market. Before the liberalization of interest rates, financial resources were allocated to export-oriented firms at lower lending interest rates to encourage exports. In the early 1990s, while the government still controlled the direct foreign borrowing of domestic firms, domestic banks were permitted to borrow money from foreign financial institutions (Cho, 2000). When the stock market turned bearish after 1994, firms tended to rely on short-term foreign loans through domestic financial institutions to finance long-term investment projects.[2] At that time, the interest rates of short-term foreign loans were much lower than domestic interest rates. The short-term external debts of the banking sector were USD 61.1 billion in 1996 and USD 49.2 billion in 1997; long-term debts were USD 38.3 billion in 1996 and USD 41.8 billion in 1997 (Kim, 2006). As commercial and merchant banks failed to roll over short-term debts in late 1997, the Korean government was forced to deplete its foreign reserves to help Korean financial institutions pay short-term debt. However, the Korean government officially requested help from the International Monetary Fund (IMF) on November 21, 1997, as foreign reserves dried up.

Macroeconomic variables looked better in the mid-1990s than in the early 1990s. According to the Economic Statistics System of the Bank of Korea, the annual economic growth was stably high, between

---

[2]Merchant banks heavily relied on cheap short-term Japanese funds from Hong Kong to finance long-term investment projects. *Chaebols* used their own merchant banks for their investments (Park *et al.*, 2004).

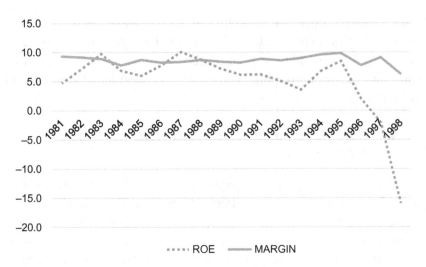

Figure 1.1.   ROE (%) and Operating Margin (%) in the Manufacturing Sector from 1981 to 1998

ROE (%) is calculated as the sum of all net income divided by the sum of all book values across all listed firms in the KOSPI market. Operating Margin (%) is the percentage of the sum of all operating income divided by all sales revenue across all listed firms in the KOSPI market.

Source: KOCOinfo of the Korea listed companies association (KLCA).

7.6% and 9.6%, during 1994–1996, while the annual growth rate was lower than 6% in 1992 and 1993. The inflation rate was below 5% in 1995 and 1996, lower than the 6.2% rate in 1994.

The manufacturing sector in the KOSPI market did not show any serious downturn in profitability ratio until 1995. Figure 1.1 shows that the return on equity (ROE) of the manufacturing sector in the KOSPI market tended to decrease, moving from 10.1% in 1987 to 3.6% in 1993. However, its ROE bounced back to 6.8% in 1994 and 8.5% in 1995 before lowering to 1.9% in 1996, 1 year before the Asian financial crisis. The overvalued Korean won relative to Japanese yen might be partially responsible for poor profitability in 1996.[3] The

---

[3]The strong dollar policy from mid-1995 resulted in the strong Korean won against Japanese yen because the value of the Korean won heavily relied on the US dollar under the managed floating system (Kim, 2006). A strong Korean won against Japanese yen led Korean exporting firms to suffer as a result of losing price competitiveness. Thus, Korean exporting firms had poor profitability.

debt–equity ratio of the manufacturing sector gradually increased from 182% in 1989 to 257% in 1996,[4] but it sharply increased to 330% in 1997. Nevertheless, the debt–equity ratio of the manufacturing sector was not high at all before the Korean currency crisis, compared to the 1980s when the debt–equity ratio of the manufacturing sector stayed higher than 350%. These profitability and debt ratios may not be accurate because window dressing in accounting was not unusual at that time. Nevertheless, the fundamental performance of the Korean economy did not appear to be responsible for the Korean currency crisis.

The Korean currency crisis seems to be due to poor risk management by the Korean government, firms, and financial institutions. Korean firms like *chaebols* were exposed to unnecessary short-term exchange risk because they used short-term foreign debts to finance long-term investment projects. Furthermore, they were overly vulnerable to external shocks like a currency or economic crisis because of high leverage. Korean financial institutions did not have a well-established credit evaluation system because the government used to allocate limited capital to exporting firms like *chaebols*. In addition, they had poor risk management of assets because they tended to finance long-term loans with short-term external debt, exposing themselves to unnecessary exchange rate risk and interest rate risk. The poor management of the exchange rate under the managed floating system was attributed to the Korean government. Because the Korean currency was strong, exporting firms lost their price competitiveness beginning in late 1995. The strong Korean won resulted in an increasing current account deficit, deteriorating the profitability of Korean firms and accelerating their credit risks. In addition, the Korean government sold USD 9.5 billion in the exchange market to prevent a sharp currency depreciation in 1997 just before the currency crisis. Because the government did not have any available foreign reserve to bear the currency risk, it had to request rescue funds from the IMF. In summary, although

---

[4]The debt–equity ratio is calculated as the sum of total debts divided by the sum of total book equity across all listed firms in the KOSPI market.

financial liberalization demands risk management capability from each economic organization, Korea was not able to deal properly with the currency liquidity risk in 1997.

The IMF program included macroeconomic measures and financial structure reforms. The IMF asked the Korean government to keep a maximum deficit of 0.8% of gross domestic product (GDP) and to maintain a tight monetary policy, resulting in high interest rates. The call market rate increased from 14.1% in November 1997 to 25.6% in January 1988 (Cho, 2000). The currency crisis along with the tight fiscal policy and high interest rates resulted in the sudden shrinkage of the Korean economy: negative economic growth, bankruptcies of many firms, and high unemployment. GDP growth was –5.5% in 1998, and the unemployment rate rose from 2.1% in October 1997 to 7.0% in June 1998. Even many financially good firms went bankrupt or experienced financial distress because of their partners' failure to meet their financial arrangements at that time. The system risk of the crisis spread throughout the Korean economy.

The Asian financial crisis of 1997 harshly shook the Korean capital market as well. At that time, the capital market faced a historical downturn. The KOSPI had declined since early 1996. As shown in Figure 1.2, KOSPI was 647 in September 1997 and plunged to 376 in December 1997; it immediately bounced back to 567 in January 1998 but afterward collapsed again to 298 in June 1998, its lowest level since 1987. However, the KOSPI recovered over several months and returned to 883 in June 1999 as the international IT boom began to approach its peak.

Facing the financial crisis, the government undertook corporate restructuring based on five principles: enhancement of management transparency, elimination of mutual debt guarantee between subsidiaries of *chaebols*, improvement of capital structure by reducing the debt–equity ratio, a focus on core business by selling off other businesses, and improvement of corporate governance. Five major *chaebols* undertook major deals of exchanging business with each other to concentrate on their core businesses. The other *chaebols* went through the workout program with their main banks. Under this

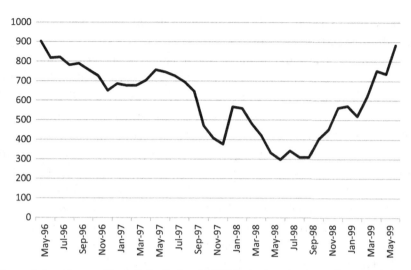

Figure 1.2.   Korean Stock Price Index (KOSPI) during the Asian Financial Crisis

program, final support was provided to viable firms making self-restructuring efforts. However, non-viable firms had to be merged, sold, or liquidated through the restructuring process.

According to Cho (2000), 20% of financial assets were nonperforming assets of Korean financial institutions in early 1998, and nonperforming assets were estimated to be more than one-third of GDP at that time. The government provided KRW 155 trillion of public funds to rehabilitate financial institutions. Four major banks became state owned, and five small banks were closed. Many other banks had been restructured through diverse methods, such as mergers, downsizing and raising additional capital (Cha, 2010). The business approval of 22 merchant banks was dismissed, and 7 merchant banks were merged (KRX, 2016).

The Korean government reorganized legal and regulatory infrastructure to conduct necessary financial reforms. In April 1998, the Financial Supervisory Commission (FSC) was established as a consolidated supervisory organization. The FSC encompasses formerly separate securities, banking, and insurance regulators. The FSC is responsible for overseeing the entire financial sector to enhance the regulatory system and its effectiveness. The Financial

Supervisory Service (FSS) was founded in January 1999 to serve as an administrative body for the FSC.

Following the agreement between the Korean government and the IMF, Korean capital markets were aggressively liberalized and globalized. In December 1997, immediately after the Asian financial crisis, foreign portfolio investments were allowed to make stock investments of up to 50% in a single issue and up to 55% of the total amount. In May 1998, the ceiling of foreign investment was completely removed for private companies' stocks. Furthermore, the foreign ownership restriction for investment trust companies and securities companies was abolished as well. As the capital market was globalized, foreign investors became key investors in the Korean market. Foreign investor ownership gradually increased from 21.7% in 1999 and has stayed over 30%. Although foreign investor ownership has fluctuated, foreign investors have been major investors with the largest proportion of ownership, followed by individual investors and domestic institutional investors.

The bond market and the money market were also globalized. Regulations on foreign investment in listed bonds were rescinded in December 1997. In February 1998, foreign investors were permitted to invest in corporate-issued money market products such as commercial paper, commercial bills, and trade bills, among others, issued by financial institutions, including certificates of deposit (CDs), covered bills, merchant bank bills, and repurchase agreements.

In 1998, the Securities Investment Company Act was enacted, allowing both company-type investment trusts called mutual fund-type and contract-type investment trusts. In 2001, wrap accounts were introduced to meet the needs of customers in an aging society by providing comprehensive asset management services. New indirect investment products such as real estate investment trusts (REITs) and exchange-traded funds (ETFs) were launched in the early 2000s. The Securities Investment Company Act, SITBA, and the Trust Business Act were merged to form the Indirect Investment. Asset Management Business Act in May 2005 to encourage fund investment.

To promote transparency in the accounting system, the Korea Accounting Standards Board was established in 1999 under the

Korea Accounting Institute to meet international standards of accounting. In addition, to prevent window dressing of accounting and to enhance the credibility of accounting information, the 30 largest *chaebols* were required to prepare consolidated financial statements.

Korea completely redeemed all IMF loans in August 2001, which amounted to USD 19.5 billion. It took approximately 3 years and 8 months to repay all rescue loans, almost 3 years faster than the original payment schedule. The quick recovery of the Korean market was partially attributed to the global boom of the Internet Communication Technology (ICT) industry.

Figure 1.3 shows the price movements of the KOSPI and KOS-DAQ markets when their prices are set to 100 in January 1997. The monthly value-weighted returns in the KOSPI and KOSDAQ markets are compounded to examine time series price movements. The price of the KOSPI market decreases more than that of the KOSDAQ market during the Asian financial crisis because *chaebols* exhibited

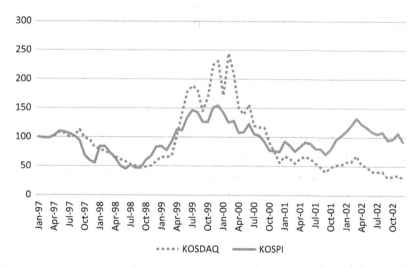

Figure 1.3. KOSPI and KOSDAQ Price Movement between January 1997 and December 2002

The prices of the KOSPI and KOSDAQ markets are set to 100, and compounded returns are calculated by using monthly value-weighted returns.
Source: FnGuide.

poorer performance than small and medium listed firms; at that time, the *chaebols* had much higher leverage and lower profitability. However, the price of the KOSPI market appears to recover faster than that of the KOSDAQ market in late 1998.

The price of the KOSDAQ market began to soar from early 1999 until early 2000 during the global ITC boom period. The KOSDAQ price soared by 259.9% just for 1 year, between March 1999 and February 2000, although the NASDAQ composite rose by 284.4% for more than 3 years, between January 1997 and February 2000. Most firms listed on the KOSDAQ market were small and young with new technology. The listing requirements for the KOSDAQ market were much lower than those for the KOSPI market. The KOSDAQ firms were expected to have great growth opportunities, although their profitability was still low at that time.

In particular, the ICT-related industry had an extremely high price increase in the KOSDAQ market between March 1999 and February 2000: 907% for the computer programing and consultancy industry and 1,087.4% for the information service industry. At the end of 1999, the M/B ratio of the computer programing and consultancy industry was 10.7, and the M/B ratio of the information service industry was 46.5. After their prices peaked, they plummeted badly. Although the market might expect high profitability from these industries, their ROEs rapidly decreased. For example, the average ROE of computer programing and consultancy was −12% from 1999 to 2002.

The KOSDAQ market premium existed in other industries as well during the ICT bubble period. In the case of the electronics industry, the KOSDAQ firms were small and young but had no cutting-edge technology compared to the KOSPI firms. However, the M/B ratio of the electronics industry in the KOSDAQ market was 8.24 at the end of 1999, whereas that in the KOSPI market was 3.1. Such high valuation of the KOSDAQ firms was not supported by financial performance. The operating margin rate for the KOSPI firms was 9.2% between 1996 and 1999, whereas that for the KOSDAQ firms was 5.8%.

As the NASDAQ market turned bearish in mid-2000, the KOS-DAQ market also plummeted. As of December 2002, the average price level of the KOSDAQ stocks was only 30% of their prices in January 1997 just after the KOSDAQ market was launched. Because the KOSDAQ stocks were predominantly owned by individual investors, most were victims of the ICT bubble burst. In particular, several KOSDAQ firms were detected as being involved in embezzlement of firms' money, window dressing in accounting, price manipulation, and illegal loans. As stock market confidence waned, individual investors left the KOSDAQ market. The original purpose of the KOSDAQ market was to channel capital to young and small firms like venture companies, companies that naturally are much riskier than established companies. Thus, professional investors are more appropriate investors in the KOSDAQ market because they are well aware of investment risk. However, individual investors, who were dominant in the KOSDAQ market, suffered from the ICT bubble burst and several illegal incidents, probably because of the relatively loose system of the KOSDAQ market in terms of list and exit requirements, information transparency, and so on.

The KOSDAQ stocks continued to fall until July 2004 when their price level was only 9% of the highest level. After the ICT bubble burst, the international stock markets turned into bear markets. Each country lowered interest rate to prevent the economic recession. Low interest rate eventually boosted the world economy. According to the World Bank, the world economic growth rate was 2.33% between 2001 and 2003 but it increased to 4.22% between 2004 and 2007. However, the low interest rate not only stimulated the economic recovery but also triggered real estate bubble in many developed countries.

1.1.5. *Globalized Capital Market Stage (2004–)*

The KRX, which integrated the operations of the KSE, KOSDAQ, and KOFEX markets, was launched in 2005 pursuant to the Korea

Securities and Futures Exchange Act of January 2004. The consolidated exchange was established to strengthen the global competitiveness of the capital market by enhancing the market's operation efficiency. The transaction system of the KOSPI market was equally applied to the KOSDAQ market. The liquidity provider (LP) program was introduced to increase trading volume and improve trading quality for less-liquid stocks by making arrangements between listed firms and securities firms. The operation management of the stock option market and the futures market was transferred from the KSE to the KOFEX market. The FreeBoard, an OTC stock trading market for non-listed firms, was established in July 2005 to support promising venture companies and SMEs. The Korea New Exchange (KONEX), replacing the FreeBoard, was created in 2013 to activate trading and supply funds for high-potential small- and medium-sized venture companies. In December 2007, the Bond Quotation System (BQS) was introduced to enhance transparency and liquidity in the OTC bond market.

In contrast to KOSDAQ stocks, KOSPI stocks underwent a gradual increase in price for 2001–2004. Afterward, their prices sharply rose with high economic growth, from 895.9 in December 2004 to 2,006.8 in October 2007. Such a bullish stock market and low interest rates contributed to the rapid expansion of the indirect investment market in Korea. According to the Korea Financial Investment Association,[5] assets under management (AUM) of equity funds amounted to KRW 8.6 trillion in December 2004 and dramatically increased to KRW 140.2 trillion in December 2008. Although AUM of equity funds gradually decreased to KRW 73.7 trillion in December 2016 after the global financial crisis, it is obvious that the indirect investment culture has successfully matured into an important choice for stock investment since the mid-2000s. AUM of foreign equity funds accounted for about 52% AUM of total equity funds as of the end of 2007 (KRX, 2016). Thus, Korean investors invested about half of indirect investment funds in international stocks.

---

[5] AUM was retrieved from the KFIA website (http://freesis.kofia.or.kr/stat/eng Main.do).

The Framework Act on Fund Management, enacted in 2004, allows the National Pension Fund to invest in the stock market. In 2005, the Trust Business Act was revised to permit securities companies to engage in trust business, and retirement pension plans (similar to US 401(k) plans) were introduced, with pension funds permitted to invest in the stock market pursuant to the Employee Retirement Benefit Security Act (KFIA, 2015). As of the end of 2014, pension funds amounted to KRW 107 trillion. The proportion of defined benefits (DB) accounted for 75.5%, and defined contributions (DC) accounted for 22.4%. DB remains the dominant retirement pension type in Korea (KRX, 2016).

The government enacted the Financial Investment Services and Capital Market Act (FSCMA) in 2007. FSCMA is comprehensive legislation that integrated the six previously separate acts governing Korea's capital market, including the SEA, the Futures Trading Act, and the Indirect Investment Asset Management Business Act. It can be regarded as the most significant and comprehensive reform of the financial market's legal framework, and it created a foundation for the Korean capital market to compete in the global markets.

The main feature of the FSCMA is to systematically regulate financial investment products in the capital markets based on classification of financial investment services, financial investment products, and investor types. Financial investment business has six types: investment dealing, brokerage, collective investment, investment advisory business, discretionary investment business, and trust business. Investors are classified as professional investors who do not need strong investor protection or non-professional investors. If investment business is the same, the same regulation must be applied to all financial institutions, regardless of the different types of financial institutions, such as commercial banks or securities companies.

Another feature of the FSCMA is that it permits financial institutions to have an expanded scope of financial investment business to compete with different types of financial institutions. In principle, a financial institution is permitted to conduct any financial investment business unless the FSCMA has a prohibition clause for that specific financial investment business. The Chinese wall is required to protect against conflicts of interest between financial institutions and investors.

The global financial crisis of 2007–2008 was triggered by the real estate bubble in the United States. The Community Reinvestment Act (CRA), a US federal law, was designed to help low- and moderate-income American households buy houses via mortgage loans. The enforcement of CRA contributed to the rapid expansion of sub-prime mortgage loans, along with the low-interest-rate policy meant to prevent a US economic downturn. Financial institutions like investment banks created new liquid securities backed by underlying bundled sub-prime mortgage loans and sold these securities to US and European financial institutions. Collateralized debt obligation (CDOs) were sometimes sold as low-risk securities by combining them with credit default swaps (CDSs), usually issued by insurance companies. Thus, mortgage banks, investment banks, commercial banks, and insurance firms were all interconnected by sub-prime mortgage loans.

The financial crisis began in 2007 with a crisis of the sub-prime mortgage market in the United States. High default rates ruined the value of sub-prime mortgage loans, rapidly devaluating MBS and CDOs. As the value of toxic assets evaporated, financial institutions owning those toxic assets faced serious financial distress. The financial crisis began as Lehman Brothers, the fourth largest investment bank, filed for bankruptcy in September 2008. AIG, which sold numerous CDSs, was obliged to pay tens of billions of dollars as CDOs were about to default. The US government bailed out AIG with USD 85 billion, but the financial crisis rapidly spread to other US financial institutions and European financial institutions as well.

The global financial crisis heavily hit the Korean financial market, although Korean financial institutions were not exposed to the toxic assets infected by the default of sub-prime mortgage loans. According to Kim (2009), the Korean won depreciated against the US dollar by over 25.4% from September 2008 until the end of November 2008 as a result of the bankruptcy of Lehman Brothers. The 25.4% depreciation was the largest fall among major Asian countries, excluding Turkey.

Furthermore, stock prices plummeted by 27.2% in the same period. After the Asian financial crisis, most firms listed on the KOSPI or KOSDAQ market gradually reduced their leverage. Their financial risk was much lower during the global financial crisis than during the Asian financial crisis. Thus, their financial risk could not explain the unexpected sharp depreciation of the Korean won during the global financial crisis.

The severe depreciation of the Korean won can be attributed to the capital inflow problem (Kim, 2009). The Korean economy has moved toward closer integration with the global market by liberalizing the capital market. The liberalized market in Korea has attracted foreign capital inflows. During the global financial crisis, however, foreign investors had to rebalance their international portfolios by transferring their financial assets to safer currencies or hard currencies. According to Kim (2009), USD 42.8 billion of assets were withdrawn from Korea between the fourth quarter of 2008 and the first quarter of 2009. Foreign capital outflows were concentrated in the banking sector, although the Korean government guaranteed banking sector debt at that time. The sudden depreciation of Korean currency during the global financial crisis shows that currency risk management is essential for a small economy with a highly globalized capital market.[6]

The abrupt depreciation of Korean currency seriously damaged the financial soundness of Korean SMEs that mistakenly hedged currency risk with *knock-in knock-out* (KiKo) derivatives. KiKo was designed for currency hedging for exporters. For example, KiKo in Korea enables its holder to sell one US dollar at the predetermined Korean won if the US dollar moves within a certain range of the Korean won. Suppose that the market price of the US dollar against the Korean won is M and the predetermined Korean won is S. If M falls below the lower bound of the range, a KiKo contract is worth

---

[6]Other currencies in southeast Asian countries did not significantly depreciate during the global financial crisis compared to the Korean won, probably because the international portfolios of foreign investors had small weights for investment in these countries.

nothing, called a *knock-out*. However, if M rises above the upper bound, the option holder must sell two US dollars at S, instead of one dollar. Such a *knock-in* position forces its holder to have losses of $2 \times (M - S)$. As a result, the sharp depreciation of local currency resulted in heavy losses, especially for SMEs that overhedged with KiKo contracts. The direct costs to the SMEs resulting from KiKo contracts were estimated at USD 2 billion in Korea, and 776 firms suffered from losses of KiKo (Dodd, 2009). The substantial losses from similar currency derivatives occurred in 12 emerging countries, mostly in Asia and South Latin America.

Although it is questionable whether KiKo was originally designed for currency hedging, it is more curious that such exotic derivatives could be successfully sold in many developing countries. Firms with serious losses from KiKo were in an overhedged position because they made too many KiKo contracts. Such overhedging might be due to their poor financial capability or their currency speculation.[7] On the other hand, distributors have a strong incentive to sell KiKo for their own interests. Thus, sales representatives can understate the currency risk of KiKo by only emphasizing its selling points. Thus, mis-selling of complicated financial products like KiKo is not only an ethical issue but also a conflict of interest between distributors and financial consumers.

In deregulated or liberalized capital markets, financial consumers should usually take responsibility for all outcomes of their own decisions about selection of financial products. Financial consumers can make an unwise decision because of their poor financial capability or mis-selling by distributors. In either case, it is a daunting task for

---

[7]If firms made KiKo contracts without clearly understanding the potential risk, they should have poor financial capability. On the other hand, KiKo distributors claimed that firms intentionally took the overhedged position because of the expected gains of KiKo with the high probability that the market price of the US dollar against the Korean won would not rise above the upper bound. Thus, firms might be currency speculators because they were willing to take the risk of serious potential risk for expected gains.

a government authority to prevent financial consumers from exposing themselves to unwanted financial risk.

As the global capital markets became more integrated, the financial crisis triggered by the US sub-prime mortgage default quickly spilled over to Europe. The European sovereign debt crisis began at the end of 2009. Greece, Portugal, Ireland, Spain, and Cyprus were unable to pay or roll over their government debt without the assistance of the European Central Bank or the IMF. The global financial crisis decreased world economic growth significantly. World economic growth averaged 4.22% per year between 2004 and 2007 before the global financial crisis but averaged 2.27% from 2008 to 2015.[8] Korean economic growth was 4.86% between 2004 and 2007, but 3.1% between 2008 and 2015. Thus, the Korean economy has performed better than the world economy, although not impressively so. The global financial crisis did, however, hurt the Korean stock market as well. The KOSPI decreased to 1,124 in December 2008 from 2,065 in October 2007. Afterward, it gradually increased and exceeded 2,000 in 2010. However, the KOSPI has fluctuated between 1,900 and 2,000 since 2010.

The easy monetary policy after the global finance crisis sharply increased household debt in Korea. According to the Economic Statistical System of the Korean Bank, household debt increased from KRW 858 trillion in 2008 to KRW 1,566 trillion in 2016. The percentage of household debt out of household disposable income increased from 143.2% in 2008 to 179.0% in 2016. As of 2015, Korea ranked ninth in the ratio of household debt to disposable income (OECD, 2015).[9] However, the consistent rise of household debt has become the most important risk factor in the Korean economy. The burdens of interest and principal payment can sharply shrink domestic consumption in the future when interest rates on loans begin to increase.

---

[8]GDP growth data were retrieved from http://data.worldbank.org/indicator/ NY.GDP.MKTP.KD.ZG.

[9]The source of household debt and disposable income is OECD data (https:// data.oecd.org/hha/household-debt.htm).

1.2.   Current Status of Korean Stock Markets

1.2.1.   *Market Trading System*[10]

Regular trading in the KRX begins at 9:00 and ends at 15:30. The opening price is determined based on cumulative quotations between 8:00 and 9:00. Trading orders received from 8:00 to 9:00 are assumed to be placed at the same time, which is referred to as simultaneous quotations. The opening price is determined as a single price to match the demand of cumulative bids with the supply of cumulative asks. Trading orders during regular hours are executed based on the continuous auction method with price and time priority from 9:00 to 15:20. The closing price is determined like the opening price based on cumulative quotations from 15:20 to 15:30. The closing price of the trading day is also applied to the trading orders between 15:30 and 16:00. The auction method for a single periodic price is applied for the off-hours session from 16:00 to 18:00. The single price is determined every 10 minutes for which orders are received. As a result, the price is determined 12 times for 16:00–18:00. The closing price of the last trading day is applied during the off-hours trading from 7:30 to 8:30.

1.2.1.1.   *Trading unit and tick size*

The trading unit for stocks, including equities, and ETFs, in the KRX markets is one share, but the trading unit for equity linked warrants (ELWs) is 10 shares. Tick size refers to the smallest price movement in the market. For the KOSPI market, different tick sizes are applied to the securities based on their base price, as shown in Table 1.4. Although the minimum tick size varies according to the base price, KRW 5 is the single tick size applied for all listed ETFs and ELWs.

---

[10]The information about trading mechanism is retrieved from KRX website: http://global.krx.co.kr/main/main.jsp.

Table 1.4. Tick Size and Base Price of Securities in the KOSPI Market

Base Price of Securities (in KRW)	Tick Size (in KRW)
Less Than 1,000	1
1,000–5,000	5
5,000–9,990	10
10,000–49,950	50
50,000–99,900	100*
100,000–499,500	500
greater than or equal to 500,000	1,000

Note: *The maximum tick size is KRW 100 in the case of KRW 50,000 or above in the KOSDAQ market.

1.2.1.2. *Daily price limit*

The daily price limit has gradually increased from ±6% of the base price (normally the previous day's closing price) in 1995 to ±30% in 2015. The daily price limit refers to both the upper and lower bound to which the price of an issue can move in a day. Thus, no investors or member firms can place orders exceeding the upper or lower price limits. The price limit for off-hours trading is ±10%, which is much smaller than the daily price limit.

1.2.1.3. *Safety devices*

Two safety devices can warn of or smooth severe fluctuations in security prices: circuit breakers and side cars. Three stepwise circuit breakers are triggered to suspend trading of all equities and relevant futures/options for 20 min when the KOSPI falls by 8%/15%/20% or more from the previous day's closing value for at least 1 min. The first step of the circuit break is triggered when the KOSPI falls by 8% or more, while the second step occurs when the KOSPI falls by 15% or more. Each step of the circuit break is limited to once per day. If the KOSPI falls by 20% or more than the previous day's closing value and 1% or more than the KOSPI value at the time of the second step, all transaction orders in the KOSPI market are canceled without transaction.

The side car is triggered to suspend the validity of program trading orders for 5 min after sudden fluctuations in the market. The side car of the KOSPI market is triggered especially when the price of the KOSPI 200 index futures deviates by more than 5% from the base price for at least 1 min. The side car is limited to once per day.

1.2.2. *Price of KOSPI and KOSDAQ*

The KOSPI is calculated as $\frac{\text{Current Market Capitalization}}{\text{Base Market Capitalization}} \times 100$, where the base market capitalization is market capitalization as of January 4, 1980. To maintain consistency in the index, the current market capitalization and base market capitalization are readjusted when a change in the number of listed shares results from security offerings with or without a capital increase, stock dividend, or merger.

Figure 1.4 shows price movements of KOSPI and KOSPI size-indices from 2001 to 2014. KOSPI Large Cap is composed of the 100 largest stocks ranked in order of market capitalization.

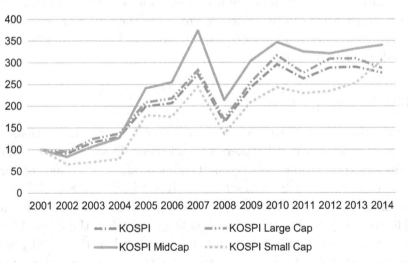

Figure 1.4.   Price of KOSPI, KOSPI Large, Mid-, and Small Caps from 2001 to 2014

KOSPI and KOSPI size-indices are rescaled to 100 in 2001 to compare their price performance.
Source: KRX.

KOSPI Mid-Cap includes 200 stocks ranking from 101 of market capitalization through 300. KOSPI Small Cap includes the remaining stocks.

The price levels of KOSPI and KOSPI size-indices are similar in 2000. KOSPI Small Cap is 531.16 at the end of 2000, which is the highest price level among the indices, while KOSPI Mid-Cap is 432.9, the lowest price level. The price levels of these indices are rescaled to 100 in 2001 to compare their performance. According to Figure 1.4, the KOSPI increases by 176% from 2001 to 2014. The movement of KOSPI Large Cap is similar to that of KOSPI because KOSPI has more weights for large stocks. The KOSPI Mid-Cap rises by 240% from 2001 to 2014, which is the highest increase among KOSPI size-indices. The KOSPI Small Cap, however, increases by 207% from 2001 to 2014. As such, the size effect does not appear in the KOSPI market for 2001–2014. The standard deviation of KOSPI Small Cap's annual return is 41.0% while that of KOSPI Large Cap's yearly return is 26%. This result confirms that small stocks tend to be more volatile than large stocks. The standard deviation of KOSPI Mid-Cap's annual return is 33%.

KOSDAQ size-indices have been published since July 29, 2002. The top 100 stocks in terms of market capitalization are classified as Large Cap, referred to as the KOSDAQ 100. KOSDAQ Mid 300 includes 300 stocks ranked from 101 to 400 in order of market capitalization. KOSDAQ Small is composed of the remaining stocks. The levels of these indices are not similar in the early 2000s. For example, the price level of KOSDAQ is 722.1 in 2001, while KOSDAQ 100 is 1,421.4 in the same year. The price levels are rescaled to 100 in 2001, as shown in Figure 1.5.

The price performance of KOSDAQ size-indices differs from that of KOSPI size-indices. All KOSDAQ indices declined for 13 years from 2001 to 2014. KOSDAQ Mid 300 shows the worst price performance, with a 39% decrease between 2001 and 2014, while KOSPI Mid-Cap achieves the best performance for the same period. KOSDAQ Small loses only 4.8% for the period of 2001–2014. All KOSDAQ indices decline for 13 years. KOSDAQ's poor performance

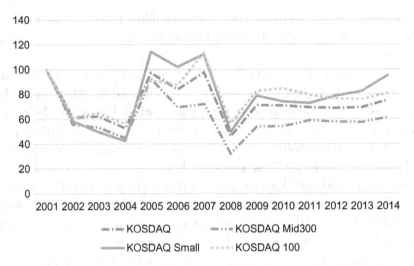

Figure 1.5.   Price Level of KOSDAQ and KOSDAQ 100, Mid 300, and Small from 2001–2014

The KOSDAQ index and KOSDAQ size-indices are rescaled to 100 in 2001 to compare their performance.
Source: KRX.

is mainly attributed to the collapse of the information technology (IT) bubble.

1.2.3.   *Market Capitalization*

Capitalization of shares for major exchanges is reported in Table 1.5. Although the global financial crisis still shadows the world economy, market capitalization in the world's major exchanges tends to increase. However, the market capitalization values of the Tokyo Stock Exchange, BME Spanish, and Deutsch Borso tend to be stagnant from 2008 to 2011.

Capitalization in the KRX more than doubled from 2008 to 2011, although it decreased between 2010 and 2011. The ranking of the KRX also improved from 19th in 2009 to 15th in 2011 in terms of market capitalization. NYSE Euronext (US) has the largest exchange market capitalization at \$11.8 trillion and NASDAQ OMX has the second largest market as of 2011. The Tokyo Stock Exchange, which was the second largest until 2009, became the third largest after 2009.

Table 1.5. Market Capitalization of Major Exchanges from 2008 to 2011 (Billion USD)

Exchange	2008	2009	2010	2011
NYSE Euronext (US)	9,209	11,838	13,394	11,796
	(192.7)	(120.0)	(119.9)	(138.5)
NASDAQ OMX	2,249	3,239	3,889	3,845
	(1,143.5)	(716.4)	(295.2)	(300.6)
Australian Securities Exchange	684	1,262	1,454	1,198
	(93.0)	(73.8)	(77.8)	(94.2)
Hong Kong Exchange	1,329	2,305	2,711	2,258
	(77.7)	(66.9)	(54.9)	(63.6)
KRX	471	835	1,092	996
	(261.2)	(149.0)	(149.3)	(194.2)
Shanghai Stock Exchange	1,425	2,705	2,716	2,357
	(193.2)	(207.3)	(169.4)	(159.5)
Tokyo Stock Exchange	3,116	3,306	3,827	3,325
	(128.5)	(119.2)	(106.5)	(123.7)
BME Spanish Exchange	948	1,435	1,172	1,031
	(143.8)	(132.2)	(117.3)	(109.4)
Deutsche Borso	1,111	1,292	1,430	1,185
	(239.1)	(98.8)	(104.5)	(132.8)
London SE Group	1,868	2,796	3,613	3,266
	(98.7)	(68.0)	(69.9)	(69.2)
NYSE Euronext (Europe)	2,102	2,869	2,930	2,447
	(107.5)	(68.1)	(69.9)	(80.4)

Source: World Federation of Exchanges; figures in parentheses indicate annual turnover velocity (%).

Figure 1.6 presents the market capitalization of the top 15 exchanges in the world as of January 2015. The capitalization rankings of most exchanges have not changed substantially, although the market capitalization of the major exchanges soars from 2011 to 2015. For example, the capitalization value of NYSE, the largest exchange market, increases by 62.9% from 2011 to January of 2015, while that of the KRX rises by 25.6% in the same period. The KRX remains ranked at 15[th]in market capitalization.

Figure 1.7 displays the 15 major exchanges in descending order of turnover velocity, defined as $100 \times \frac{\text{Monthly Average Trading Value} \times 12}{\text{Month-end Market Capitalization Value}}$. The turnover velocity of the major stock exchanges appears to vary. The Shenzhen Stock Exchange has the highest turnover velocity

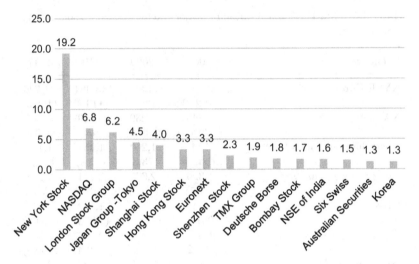

Figure 1.6. Market Capitalization of Top 15 Exchanges in the World (USD Trillion) as of January 2015

Source: Wikipedia (https://en.wikipedia.org/wiki/List_of_stock_exchanges).

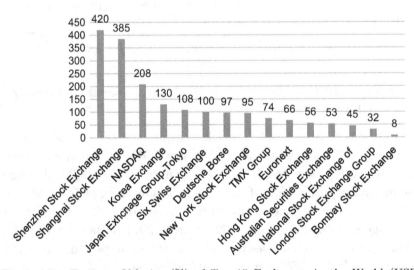

Figure 1.7. Turnover Velocity (%) of Top 15 Exchanges in the World (USD Trillion) as of January 2015

Source: Wikipedia (https://en.wikipedia.org/wiki/List_of_stock_exchanges).

among the major exchanges as of January 2015 at 420%. The Shanghai Stock Exchange has the second highest turnover velocity at 385%. NASDAQ, which had the highest turnover velocity in 2011, turns out to have the third highest turnover velocity. The turnover velocity of the KRX declines from 194.2% in 2011 to 130.5% in January 2015 and its rankings drops to the fourth.

1.2.4. *Number of Listed Companies in the KOSPI Market and the KOSDAQ Market*

The KOSDAQ market was established on July 1, 1996, by the Korea Securities Dealers Association and securities companies. The KOSDAQ market was created based on the NASDAQ market model so that small companies had easier access to capital markets. Entry barriers to the KOSDAQ market have been much lower than those to the KOSPI market. Although the number of listed companies in the KOSDAQ market was much less than that of the KOSPI market during the early period, it has increased to over 1,000 since 2007. As of 2013, the number of listed companies was 1,009 in the KOSDAQ market, while the KOSPI market had 777.

Compared to the KOSPI market, the KOSDAQ market is characterized by small stocks and low stock prices, as Table 1.6 indicates. Total market capitalization in the KOSPI market is usually more than 10 times as large as that in the KOSDAQ market. In 2013, the average stock price was KRW 8,767 in the KOSDAQ, while the average price per share was KRW 47,050 in the KOSPI. The number of shares in the KOSPI market was about 9 billion shares in 1997, which is 12.6 times more than in the KOSDAQ market. However, the number of listed shares in the KOSDAQ market sharply increased to 21 billion shares in 2013, which is almost 0.6 times as large as that in the KOSPI market.

1.2.5. *IPO and Seasoned Offering*

The major role of the stock market is to provide capital to companies. New capital raised by shares in Korea's primary market has fluctuated over time. Table 1.7 reports capital amounts raised from

Table 1.6. Major Characteristics of KOSPI and KOSDAQ Markets

Year	Number of Listed Companies		Number of Listed Shares (million)		Market Capitalization (KRW trillion)		Average Price (KRW)	
	KOSPI	KOSDAQ	KOSPI	KOSDAQ	KOSPI	KOSDAQ	KOSPI	KOSDAQ
1995	721	N.A.	7,609.4	N.A.	141.15	N.A.	18,550	N.A.
1996	760	N.A.	8,598.4	N.A.	117.37	N.A.	13,650	N.A.
1997	776	359	9,030.7	719.5	70.99	7.07	7,861	9,825
1998	748	331	11,443.7	1,167.1	137.80	7.89	12,042	6,762
1999	725	453	17,325.8	4,089.9	349.50	98.70	20,173	24,134
2000	704	604	19,638.7	7,048.8	188.04	29.02	13143	25,428
2001	689	721	19,578.3	8,414.1	255.85	51.82	10682	11,432
2002	683	843	26,463.4	10,517.6	258.68	37.40	14,764	7,678
2003	684	879	23,662.1	12,129.5	355.36	37.37	13,081	4,892
2004	683	890	23,426.9	12,175.9	412.59	31.15	15,513	4,075
2005	702	918	23,235.7	14,051.2	655.07	70.90	23,310	6,045
2006	731	963	24,560.5	16,602.0	704.59	72.14	29,785	7,103
2007	746	1,023	28,244.1	19,555.4	951.92	99.98	40,466	8,977
2008	765	1,038	29,097.3	22,374.0	576.93	46.19	35,160	6,520
2009	770	1,028	31,377.1	23,695.3	887.94	86.10	31,486	5,884
2010	777	1,029	33,706.3	23,370.7	1,141.89	97.97	37,553	6,845
2011	791	1,031	35,402.9	21,440.5	1,042.00	105.99	43,394	7,432
2012	784	1,005	35,323.0	21,012.2	1,154.29	109.12	42,574	7,901
2013	777	1,009	35,217.3	21,335.1	1,185.97	119.29	47,050	8,767

Source: Korea Exchange.

Table 1.7. New Capital Raised by Shares (KRW billions)

Year	KOSPI Market			KOSDAQ Market		
	IPO	Seasoned Offering & BW	Total	IPO	Seasoned Offering & BW	Total
1995	644.3	2,148.2	2792.5	N.A.	N.A.	N.A.
1996	1,391.4	3,651.5	5,043.0	N.A.	N.A.	N.A.
1997	479.3	2,676.3	3,155.6	197.6	1.5	199.1
1998	36.8	13,452.1	13,488.9	262.4	181.3	443.7
1999	1,720.1	33,426.9	35,147.0	2,122.1	2,420.0	4,542.1
2000	0.0	5,788.9	5,788.9	2,568.6	4,574.8	7,143.5
2001	217.8	5,097.8	5,315.6	1,313.3	1,259.1	2,572.4
2002	1,227.4	6,207.1	7,434.5	1,115.6	515.2	1,630.9
2003	560.3	7,166.4	7,726.7	577.6	1,115.3	1,692.9
2004	641.3	4,526.2	5,167.6	436.3	822.7	1,259.0
2005	451.7	1,876.8	2,328.5	849.8	1,637.3	2,487.1
2006	116.7	2,389.5	3,506.2	589.1	2,069.2	2,658.3
2007	1,525.3	10,479.9	12,005.2	776.9	3,812.0	4,588.9
2008	320.4	1,468.3	1,788.7	396.4	2,286.0	2,682.4
2009	472.7	5,659.9	6,132.6	1,201.4	3,562.9	4,764.3
2010	2,938.6	3,138.7	6,077.3	1,365.3	1,223.8	2,589.1
2011	1,358.9	8,803.9	10,162.8	1,079.6	606.3	1,685.9
2012	205.9	1,355.8	1,561.7	260.5	438.7	699.2
2013	661.5	2,877.4	3,538.9	627.6	766.6	1,394.2

Source: Korean Statistical Information Service.

IPOs, seasoned offerings, and the exercise of warrants in both the KOSPI and KOSDAQ markets. Before the Asian financial crisis, capital raised by equity issues is not large. Instead of stocks, Korean companies used to heavily rely on bank loans for new investment, resulting in high debt–equity ratios. According to Table 1.7, the capital raised from equity issues tends to increase but fluctuate over time.

It is acknowledged that equity issues are positively related to stock price performance. For example, when the stock price goes up, equity issues tend to increase. Table 1.7 confirms the positive relationship between stock price and equity issues. KOSPI decreased from 882.94 in 1995 to 376.31 in 1997 when the Asian financial crisis occurred. For these years, capital raised from IPOs, seasoned offerings, and bond warrants (BWs) is small as well. Capital raised from equity issues, however, is huge in both 1998, and 1999 when KOSPI rises by 173%. Korean firms were vulnerable to financial risk because of high debt ratios during the Asian financial crisis. After the Asian financial crisis, many listed firms increase their equity value through seasoned offerings to lower their debt ratios. Thus, the seasoned offering has been more active in the Korean stock market since the Asian financial crisis.

References

Cha, D. S., 2010, The Structure Adjustments of Korea After Crisis, In K. J. Sung, (eds.), *Korea Development Experience of the Korean Economy*, Kyung Hee University Press, Seoul.

Cho, Y. J., 2000, The Financial Crisis in Korea: Causes and Challenges, A Study of Financial Markets. Retrieved from https://aric.adb.org/pdf/aem/exter nal/financial_market/Republic_of_Korea/korea_mac.pdf.

Dodd, R., 2009, Exotic Derivatives Losses in Emerging Markets: Questions of Suitability, Concerns for Stability, IMF Working Paper. Retrieved from http://www.financialpolicy.org/kiko.pdf.

Lee, Y., K. Park, M. Lee, and S. Choi, 2005, The Centennial History of Stocks and Bonds in Korea (in Korean), Korea Securities Depository, Seoul.

Kim, K., 2006, The 1997–1998 Korean Financial Crisis: Causes, Policy Response, and Lessons, Seminar by the International Monetary Fund and the Government of Singapore. Retrieved from https://www.imf.org/external/np/semi nars/eng/2006/cpem/pdf/kihwan.pdf.

Kim, K., 2009, Global Financial Crisis and the Korean Economy, In R. Glick and M. Spiegel (eds.), *Asia Global Financial Crisis*, The Federal Reserve Bank of San Francisco, pp. 277–284.

Korea Exchange (KRX), Market data. Retrieved from https://global.krx.co. kr/main/main.jsp.

Korea Exchange (KRX), 2016, Korea Exchange 60 Year History. Retrieved from http://open.krx.co.kr/contents/OPN/04/04010000/ebook/ebook.html.

Korea Financial Investment Association, 2014, Capital Market in Korea, Seoul.

Park, Y. C., W. Song, and Y. Wang, 2004, Finance and Economic Development in Korea, Working Paper 04-06, Korea Institute for International Economics Policy.

Yoon, J., 2015, *100-Year History of Korean Stock Investment (in Korean)*, Gilbert, Seoul.

Chapter 2

Behavioral Approaches

The efficient market hypothesis does not imply that all investors are rational decision makers. Many irrational investors participate in capital markets. However, the impact of their trading on securities prices can be negligible for two reasons. First, irrational investors may be simple noise traders whose trading is not systematic. For example, some of them may irrationally buy stocks with hopes for a bull market, while others may irrationally sell them with the expectation of a bear market. As a result, the aggregated trading of these noise traders will not strongly influence stock returns. Second, rational informed arbitrageurs play an important role in eliminating price errors caused by noise traders. Since arbitrage activities wind up with profits for the arbitrageurs and losses for irrational investors, the market power of arbitrageurs will rise, thus diminishing the power of irrational investors.[1]

The large number of studies in financial literature, however, suggest that the trading behavior of noise traders can be systematic and consistently influence stock prices. Several psychological biases and common propensities of irrational decision making have been found since Kahneman and Tversky (1979) provided experimental

---

[1]The role of rational arbitragers can be limited because of fundamental risk (Barber and Thaler, 2003), limits of arbitrage (DeLong and Shleifer, 1990a; Shleifer and Vishny, 1993), destabilizing rational speculation (DeLong and Shleifer, 1990b), and market restriction such as transaction costs and short sale constraints.

survey results against the rationality of people's decision making. For example, investors are subject to overconfidence, representativeness, conservativeness, biased-self attribution, mental accounting, attention-grabbing, and anchoring biases. These biases induce investors to make similar sub-optimal judgments or exhibit trading patterns in the same direction under certain circumstances. Thus, a cohort of investors may display systematic trading patterns and influence stock prices. Therefore, it is interesting to examine how the trading behavior of different investor clienteles and their interaction are associated with anomalies such as seasonality of stock returns and short-term momentum.

In this regard, the financial literature typically regards individual investors as noise or irrational investors, while it sees institutional investors as informed rational investors. Individual investors are more prone to psychological biases since they do not clearly understand the relation between stock valuation and the major factors influencing the valuation such as the prospect and risk of a stock's fundamental value. Many studies examine the trading behavior of individual or institutional investors. For example, Barber and Odean (2011) survey papers about the trading behavior of individual investors.

Examining the trading behavior of investor types requires trading records of individual and institutional investors. However, information about trading records is limited in the US stock markets. For example, most research in the US stock markets uses the transaction records of retail investors at large brokerage firms. Although such data include large numbers of individual investors, they do not represent the trading behavior of individual investors in the entire stock market. In addition, since these data cover less than 10 years, it is difficult to investigate the trading behavior of investor types, which sometimes requires a long-term sample period. Another source of trading data is the NYSE's Consolidated Auto Trail Data (CAUD) files which list all orders executed on the exchange with identification of investor type. This sample, however, is also limited to only a few years. Trade and quote (TAQ) data are also important for analyzing investor behavior. TAQ provides detailed information about all transactions and quotes for all firms listed on the NYSE,

NASDAQ, and regional exchanges and covers 1993 to the present. In addition, the Institute for the Study of Securities Markets (ISSM) data set provides similar information from 1983 to 1992. Thus, these data sets cover a long-term period compared to others. However, these data sets do not contain any information about whether the trade is initiated by the buyer or the seller and whether an individual investor or institutional investor participates in the trade. Buy- or sell-initiated trade and identification of investor type must be inferred based on trade size and comparison of transaction price to the quote midpoint, which does not guarantee accuracy.

Other markets such as the Taiwanese and Finnish stock markets provide more complete information about transactions and identity of investor type. However, these data sets also cover a short-term sample period. For example, Baber *et al.* (2009) analyze the trading records of the Taiwanese data set from 1995 to 1999 to ascertain the investment performance of individual investors. Grinblatt and Keloharju (2000) examine 2 years of trading in Finland for investment performance of individual investors.

On the other hand, Korean transaction data are unique and comprehensive in that they can be used to measure the trading behavior of individual, foreign, and institutional investors from 1995 to the present. The Korea Exchange (KRX) data set provides daily buying and selling value (KRW) and volume (shares) of investor types for every stock listed on the Korean Stock Price Index (KOSPI) market. Such a comprehensive data set allows us to examine the trading behavior of investor types for anomalies. Investigation of the trading behavior with such a unique trading data set will provide a distinctive opportunity to comprehend the anomalies of the Korean stock markets.

Behavioral finance suggests that investor sentiment influences the market predictability of stock returns. It is commonly claimed that stock returns tend to be low following a high investor sentiment period, while they tend to be high following a low investor sentiment period. Since stock prices tend to be overvalued (undervalued) during high (low) investor sentiment periods, high (low) investor sentiment is followed by low (high) subsequent stock returns. Following Baker and Wurgler (2007), Kim and Byun (2010) create a sentiment index in the Korean stock market by using six individual investor proxies and find that the investor sentiment index has predictability for subsequent returns in the Korean stock market. However, we cannot create a consistent investor sentiment index since some individual investor proxies are no longer available. Furthermore, the investor sentiment index is subject to look-ahead bias. Instead, we test and find the predictability of the aggregate market-to-book (M/B) ratio on market returns. We examine whether the anomalies in the Korean stock market are associated with the market predictability of the aggregate M/B ratios.

Two behavioral approaches, trading behavior and market predictability of the aggregate M/B ratios, will provide new insights into the source of anomalies. This chapter will show basic empirical results for these two approaches.

2.1. Trading Behavior

The Korea Exchange (KRX) classifies major investors as government and public bodies, domestic institutional investors, individual investors, foreign investors, and other corporations. Domestic institutional investors include insurance companies, securities companies, asset management companies, pension funds, banks, and merchant and mutual saving banks. Foreigners began to invest in stocks in the KRX through funds in the early 1980s and were allowed to directly invest in stocks in the 1990s due to that era's financial liberalization policy. In the early 1990s, foreign stock investment was limited to up to 10% of stock market capitalization but was gradually increased. In 1998, the foreign investment limit was eliminated in principle.

2.1.1. *Ownership of Investor Types*

Table 2.1 shows how individual, domestic institutional, and foreign investors' stock ownership varies over time. The ownership among individual investors drops sharply after 1999, likely because of the foreign investment limit being lifted. The individual investor's ownership tends to be positively related to the stock-price movement.

Table 2.1. Ownership Proportion of Investor Types in the KOSPI Market:
1997–2013

Year	Capitalization (KRW trillion)	Individual Investor (%)	Institutional Investor (%)	Foreign Investor (%)	Turnover
1997	78.06	29.59	26.23	13.73	—
1998	145.69	28.87	13.65	17.98	—
1999	448.21	31.68	14.26	21.69	—
2000	215.97	23.47	16.43	26.98	—
2001	307.94	26.42	15.35	32.17	220.66
2002	296.08	25.55	15.28	32.79	248.86
2003	392.74	23.29	18.56	37.67	193.18
2004	443.74	20.80	17.01	40.10	148.25
2005	725.97	22.59	18.56	37.17	154.40
2006	776.72	21.98	20.80	35.16	128.74
2007	1,051.78	25.25	19.98	30.94	156.70
2008	621.68	29.96	11.69	27.25	172.64
2009	972.53	34.57	12.04	30.44	199.60
2010	1,236.34	24.09	13.45	31.17	146.32
2011	1,144.65	24.40	12.97	30.60	152.25
2012	1,263.41	23.99	15.84	32.47	107.43
2013	1,305.27	23.64	16.08	32.91	86.39

Source: Korea Exchange.

For example, the ownership of individual investors increases from 28.87% in 1998 to 31.68% in 1999 when the KOSPI increases by 82.8%. Likewise, their ownership increases from 29.96% in 2008 to 34.57% in 2009 when the KOSPI rises by 49.7%. Exceptions also exist. For example, the ownership of individual investors increases by only 1.79% points in 2005 when the KOSPI rises by 54%. The ownership of institutional investors varies in the range of 10% to 20%. The ownership of foreign investors peaks at 40.11% in 2004. After 2004, the stock ownership of foreign investors in the KOSPI market tends to decline gradually but remain above 30%. In short, foreign investors have become major investors in the Korean stock market since the financial liberalization period of the 1990s.

Table 2.2 shows that individual investors dominate the KOSDAQ market in comparison to the KOSPI market. The lowest ownership of individual investors is 44.93% in 2000, while the highest ownership is 71.49% in 2009. Institutional investors' ownership peaks at 20.16%

Table 2.2. Ownership Proportion of Investor Types in the KOSDAQ Market: 1999–2013

Year	Capitalization Value (KRW trillion)	Individual Investor (%)	Institutional Investor (%)	Foreign Investor (%)
1999	98.70	51.56	5.20	7.48
2000	29.76	44.93	20.16	6.89
2001	52.09	46.51	13.40	10.31
2002	37.40	47.82	11.38	10.50
2003	37.37	57.44	6.19	14.43
2004	31.15	57.94	8.70	15.41
2005	70.90	61.06	8.99	13.51
2006	72.14	61.40	9.44	14.64
2007	99.83	58.22	8.52	17.30
2008	46.12	66.24	3.38	8.17
2009	85.21	71.49	7.05	7.37
2010	97.53	57.90	6.91	10.15
2011	105.60	61.25	6.57	7.86
2012	109.12	63.47	6.33	8.20
2013	119.29	62.90	6.15	9.85

Source: Korea Exchange.

in 2000, but their ownership usually remains below 10%. Foreign investors tend to own much less stock in the KOSDAQ market than in the KOSPI market. Their ownership peaks at 17.3% in 2007 but afterward decreases to the range of a one-digit percentage.

2.1.2. *Trading Behavior by Investor Types*

Although the individual investor's stock ownership tends to be smaller than that of foreign investors in the KOSPI market after 1999, as seen in Table 2.1, the proportion of their trading value dominates the KOSPI market. According to Table 2.3, individual investors' trading value accounts for 66.6% of the total trading value in 1995. The proportion of individual investors' trading value increases until 1998 and afterward tends to decrease. However, the proportion of their trading value is usually more than 50%. Since their ownership tends to be in the range of 20%, the high proportion of individual investors trading indicates that they are frequent traders.

Table 2.3. Trading Value of Investor Types in the KOSPI Market: 1995–2014 (unit: KRW trillion)

Year	Individual Investor	Institutional Investor	Foreign Investor	Government	Total
1995	90.2 (66.6)	35.3 (26.1)	6.6 (4.8)	3.3 (2.5)	135.4
1996	95.7 (70.3)	29.5 (21.7)	8.2 (6.0)	2.7 (2.0)	136.2
1997	119.4 (73.9)	28.2 (17.4)	10.8 (6.7)	3.1 (1.9)	161.6
1998	148.9 (77.3)	23.7 (12.3)	14.3 (7.4)	5.6 (2.9)	192.6
1999	660.1 (76.1)	139.3 (16.1)	44.7 (5.2)	22.8 (2.6)	866.9
2000	451.1 (71.9)	102.5 (16.4)	57.5 (9.2)	16.0 (2.6)	627.1
2001	359.7 (73.2)	69.2 (14.1)	51.5 (10.5)	11.0 (2.2)	491.4
2002	531.1 (71.9)	101.4 (13.7)	84.7 (11.5)	21.8 (3.0)	739.1
2003	357.5 (65.3)	86.9 (15.9)	84.8 (15.5)	18.4 (3.4)	547.5
2004	321.2 (57.8)	88.3 (15.9)	125.6 (22.6)	20.8 (3.7)	555.8
2005	478.5 (60.9)	120.1 (15.3)	162.6 (20.7)	25.1 (3.2)	786.3
2006	434.8 (51.2)	162.3 (19.1)	220.5 (26.0)	30.9 (3.6)	848.5
2007	724.5 (53.2)	253.6 (18.6)	335.9 (24.6)	48.9 (3.6)	1,362.9
2008	637.5 (49.5)	279.5 (21.7)	329.0 (25.6)	41.1 (3.2)	1,287.2
2009	855.8 (58.4)	323.3 (22.1)	252.5 (17.2)	34.6 (2.4)	1,466.3
2010	770.1 (54.6)	307.0 (21.8)	286.9 (20.3)	46.6 (3.3)	1,410.6
2011	943.9 (55.5)	362.0 (21.3)	315.1 (18.5)	81.1 (4.8)	1,702.1
2012	608.0 (51.5)	253.8 (20.9)	276.9 (22.9)	40.3 (4.7)	1,490.4
2013	458.7 (50.8)	223.0 (21.2)	283.2 (28.7)	9.3 (0.9)	986.4
2014	437.4 (44.8)	221.9 (22.7)	292.9 (30.0)	8.7 (0.9)	976.0

Note: The parentheses indicate the trading value percentage of investor types.

Source: Korea Exchange.

On the other hand, foreign investors usually account for less than 25% of the total trading value while their ownership is usually higher than 30%, suggesting that they are not frequent traders. Institutional investors' ownership is always less than that of foreign investors after 1997 but their trading value is similar to foreign investors', indicating that institutional investors trade more frequently than foreign investors.

2.1.3. *Preferences of Investor Types over Stock's Characteristics*

Falkenstein (1996) shows that US mutual funds tend to prefer stocks with large market capitalization and high trading volume in a cross-sectional analysis of stock holdings of US mutual funds in 1991–1992. According to Gompers and Metric (2001), the institutional demand for large stocks gradually increases with major ownership shifts from individual investors to institutional investors. As a result, large stocks significantly outperform small stocks, resulting in the disappearance of the small stock premium after 1980.

With respect to foreign investors' preference, Kang and Stulz (1998) examines stock ownership of non-Japanese investors in Japan by using the Pacific-Basin Capital Market Research Center (PACAP) files from 1975 to 1991. They find that foreign investors prefer large stocks in the manufacturing industry that have good operating performance. Similarly, according to Dahlquist and Robertsson (2001) who analyze the Swedish market, foreign investors are typically institutional investors, and foreign investors, like institutional investors, are more likely to hold stocks with larger capitalization, higher cash flows, high liquidity and high recognition in the international market. In contrast, institutional investors avoid firms with high risk, high leverage, high dividend yields and high ownership concentration. Thus, they insist that foreign investors' preference represents an institutional bias. On the other hand, Merton (1987) argues that rational investors prefer stocks about which they have better information under conditions of information asymmetry. Thus, foreign investors may prefer large stocks because of asymmetric information.

In the Korean stock market, Ko *et al.* (2007) analyze the relation between the ownership of investor types and firm characteristics. They find that both institutional and foreign investors prefer stocks with large capitalization and high return on equity (ROE). Furthermore, foreign ownership is negatively related to the B/M ratio, indicating that foreign investors prefer growth stocks. Bae *et al.* (2011) report that foreign investors tend to buy stocks that have previously been highly profitable but sell stocks that have previously been less profitable. However, they argue that a firm's profitability is not a major determinant of foreign investors' buying or selling stocks.

Table 2.4 reports the relation between the characteristics of stocks and the trading proportion of investor types from 1996 to 2013. We eliminate financial companies but include firms with negative

Table 2.4. Characteristics of Stocks and Trading Activity of Investor Types from 1996 to 2013

Investor Type	Quintiles	B/M	Margin (%)	ROA (%)	Debt/ Assets	Size (KRW billion.)	Indp (%)	Insp (%)	Forp (%)
Ind. Investor	IND1	0.88	8.05	4.86	0.50	3,067.5	52.9	24.4	17.7
	IND2	1.31	4.10	0.05	0.62	581.7	74.5	14.5	7.0
	IND3	1.09	3.19	−1.21	0.68	172.8	86.8	7.3	3.2
	IND4	1.15	2.84	−2.89	0.67	73.1	94.0	2.8	1.6
	IND5	0.72	1.13	−3.95	0.72	36.7	97.0	1.1	0.9
Inst. Investor	INS1	0.79	1.19	−3.22	0.73	35.6	96.5	1.1	1.0
	INS2	0.87	2.07	−2.89	0.70	75.4	93.6	2.8	1.8
	INS3	1.31	4.16	−1.18	0.66	194.0	86.4	6.9	3.9
	INS4	1.21	4.95	1.07	0.60	841.7	73.3	14.2	8.9
	INS5	0.89	7.69	4.64	0.50	2,704.7	55.5	24.9	14.9
Foreign Investor	FOR1	1.27	3.19	−1.22	0.63	48.4	93.0	3.6	0.1
	FOR2	1.36	3.28	−1.06	0.62	75.2	93.2	3.6	1.4
	FOR3	1.30	3.49	−0.88	0.63	146.5	87.6	7.1	2.7
	FOR4	1.19	4.08	0.23	0.64	476.0	76.1	14.1	6.5
	FOR5	0.91	7.67	4.38	0.51	3,236.7	55.4	21.7	18.9

Notes: Stocks are divided into quintiles in ascending order of the proportion of each investor type's annual trading value out of the total annual trading value. For example, IND1 is composed of stocks for which the proportion of individual investors' annual trading value is below the 20th percentile, while IND5 is above the 80th percentile. B/M is average ratio of the total book value of equity to the total market value of equity for the quintile portfolio. The book value is available at the end of the fiscal year and the market value is measured at the end of the calendar year. ROA is a percentage of total net income divided by total assets. The margin rate is a percentage of total operating earnings divided by total sales. Debt/Asset is the ratio of total debt to total assets. *Indp, Insp,* and *Forp* are the proportion of individual investors', institutional investors', and foreign investors' trading value out of the total trading value.

book value of equity. Stocks are divided into quintiles in ascending order of the trading proportion of investor type. For example, IND1 indicates the lowest proportion of individual investors' annual trading value out of the total annual trading value, while IND5 indicates the highest proportion. According to Table 2.4, individual investors trade broadly in stocks and their proportion of trading value is much higher than other investors' even for IND1. The proportion of individual investors' trading value for IND1 is 52.9%, while the proportions for IND4 and IND5 are 94.0% and 97.0%, respectively. Thus, the valuation of stocks for IND4 and IND5 may be decided mainly by individual investors since individual investors are the predominant traders for these stocks.

On the other hand, both domestic institutional and foreign investors trade a limited selection of stocks in the Korean stock market. In particular, foreign investors concentrate on trading a relatively small number of stocks, although their average ownership tends to be greater than 30% after 2000. The proportion of foreign investors' trading value is less than 3% for stocks of FOR3, which means that foreigners do not trade in many stocks.

B/M, margin (operating margin rate), return on assets (ROA), the total debt to total asset ratio (Debt/Assets), and size in Table 2.4 are averages for the 18 years from 1996 to 2013. All variables in Table 2.4 are calculated by summing the corresponding individual variables across all firms of the same quintile in the year following the quintile portfolio formation. For example, the B/M ratio for IND1 is the ratio of the total book value of equity to the total market value of equity, where the total book value of equity for IND1 is the sum of all book values of equity across all firms in IND1 and the total market value for IND1 is the sum of all market values across all firms in IND1 in the year following IND quintile portfolio formation.

Consistent with earlier studies, both foreign and institutional investors actively trade large stocks. Size in Table 2.4 is positively related to the trading proportion of both institutional and foreign investors but negatively related to the trading proportion of individual investors. In addition, both foreign and institutional investors focus on trading stocks with low leverage, while individual investors trade stocks with high leverage.

Table 2.4 also shows that stocks with active trading of domestic institutional investors tend to have a high margin rate and ROA. ROA of INS1 is -3.22% and that of INS5 is 4.62%. The operating margin shows a similar relation with the quintile portfolio of INS. The preference of foreign investors is similar to that of institutional investors. Thus, the ROA and operating margin tend to be positively related to the quintiles of foreign investors' trading proportion. The higher the trading proportion of foreign investors, the higher the ROA and margin. It is important to note that profitability ratios such as ROA and margin rates are measured 1 year after the quintile portfolios of investor types' trading proportion are constructed. Thus, stocks traded actively by both foreign and domestic institutional investors tend to have better profitability ratios in 1 year than other stocks. In contrast, stocks with a high trading proportion of individual investors tend to perform worse in 1 year than those with a low trading proportion of individual investors. However, the high trading proportion does not necessarily mean net buying.

B/M ratio does not show any consistent pattern with IND quintiles. For example, the average B/M ratio of stocks with IND2 is highest and thereafter decreases. Table 2.4 shows that the stocks with IND5 have a 0.72 B/M ratio, while they have a 1.13% ratio for the operating margin. It is interesting that the stocks individual investors predominantly trade have the lowest B/M ratio but also the lowest profitability ratios in terms of the margin rate and ROA. Low B/M stocks are usually called growth stocks. Growth stocks are believed to have high future cash flows and low risk. Low B/M stocks with following poor profitability for IND5 cannot be reconciled with the common understanding of growth stocks.

On the other hand, both institutional investors and foreign investors predominantly trade low B/M stocks. In addition, these stocks have the highest margin rate and ROA as well. Thus, the stocks that both foreign and institutional investors actively trade are characterized as typical growth stocks which usually exhibit excellent profitability.

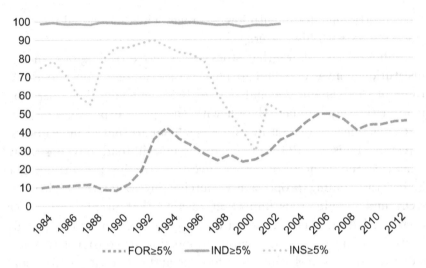

Figure 2.1. Proportion of Firms with at Least 5% Ownership of Investor Types in the KOSPI Market from 1984 to 2013

Note: FOR ≥5% indicates the proportion of KOSPI firms for which foreign investors have at least 5% ownership. INS (IND) represents institutional (individual) investors.

Source: KOCOinfo of Korea Listed Companies Association.

The Korea Listed Companies Association's KOCOinfo, a database website, provides information about each investor type's ownership for each stock until fiscal year 2003. Afterward, only information about foreign investor ownership is provided. Figure 2.1 shows how broadly each investor type holds the stocks listed on the KOSPI market. The proportion of firms for which individual investors have at least 5% ownership (IND ≥5%) is almost 99% Thus, individual investors hold most listed firms' KOSPI stocks with at least 5% ownership. However, foreign investors hold a limited number of firms' stocks with 5% or more ownership. As of 2013, firms with FOR ≥5% account for less than 50% listed firms in the KOSPI market Therefore, foreign investors' ownership concentrates on a limited number of firms, although foreign investors' ownership in the KOSPI market is more than 30%. On the other hand, the proportion of firms with INS ≥5% tends to decline but is much higher than the proportion of firms with FOR ≥5%.

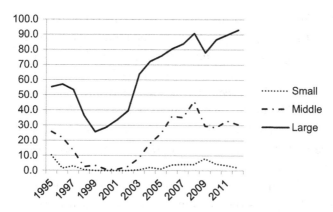

Figure 2.2. Percentage of Stocks with More than 5% Proportion of Foreign Investors' Trading Value (*Forp* ≥5%) in the KOSPI Market from 1995 to 2012

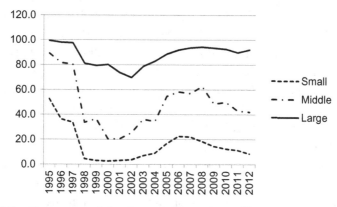

Figure 2.3. Percentage of Stocks with More than 5% Proportion of Domestic Institutional Investors' Trading Value (*Insp* ≥5%) in the KOSPI Market from 1995 to 2012

In the case of KOSDAQ firms, the proportion of firms with FOR ≥5% is less than 20% from 1997 to 2013 and the proportion of firms with INS ≥5% is about 31% as of 2003. However, firms with IND ≥5% account for more than 99.4% as of 2003. KOSDAQ firms also appear to be dominantly owned by individual investors.

In Figures 2.2 and 2.3, stocks are divided into three groups as small, middle and large portfolios. The criteria are the 30th and 70th percentiles of market capitalization at the end of every year.

If the market capitalization of a stock belongs to less than the 30th percentile, the stock belongs to the small portfolio. Stocks with market capitalization between the 30th percentile and 70th percentile belong to the middle portfolio. Stocks with market capitalization larger than the 70th percentile are classified into the large portfolio. Stocks with $Forp{\geq}5\%$ are defined as stocks for which foreign investors' annual trading value accounts for more than 5% of the total annual trading value. Stocks with $Insp \geq 5\%$ ($Indp \geq 5\%$) represent stocks with more than a 5% proportion of domestic institutional investors' (individual investors') annual trading value.

Figure 2.2 reports the percentage of stocks with $Forp \geq 5\%$ among stocks of each size portfolio. According to Figure 2.2, stocks with $Forp \geq 5\%$ are far less than 10% of small stocks except for 1995. This result confirms that foreign investors usually do not trade small stocks. Even in the case of the middle portfolio, stocks with $Forp \geq 5\%$ never account for more than 50% of stocks. Stocks with $Forp \geq 5\%$, are on average about 20% of middle stocks from 1995 to 2012. However, stocks with $Forp \geq 5\%$ of the large portfolio are, on average, 63.6% for the same period. The percentage of stocks with $Forp \geq 5\%$ tends to increase and is greater than 80% after 2005. This demonstrates that foreign investors prefer to trade large stocks, which is consistent with earlier studies.

Figure 2.3 displays the percentage of KOSPI stocks within size portfolios in which domestic institutional investors trade more than 5% in terms of trading value. Compared to foreign investors, stocks with $Insp \geq 5\%$ include more firms' stocks than stocks with $Forp \geq 5\%$ for all portfolios. The average proportion of stocks with $Insp \geq 5\%$ is 48.6% for the middle portfolio and 15.6% for the small portfolio. Note that the proportion of stocks with $Insp \geq 5\%$ sharply decreases particularly for both the middle and small portfolios after the Asian financial crisis and then gradually increases beginning in 2002. However, the proportion of stocks with $Insp \geq 5\%$ for small portfolios after 2002 never fully recovers to a level above 30% for 1995–1997. Thus, domestic institutional investors like foreign investors also tend to focus on trading limited stocks after the Asian financial crisis.

In contrast, stocks with *Indp* $\geq 5\%$ are basically all firms' stocks in the KOSPI market. For the middle stock portfolio, there is only one firm's stock in 1995 and 2003 in which individual investors do not trade more than 5%. Thus, individual investors trade most stocks regardless of their capitalization value.

In conclusion, many stocks are in the KOSPI market that individual investors predominantly trade without interaction of either institutional or foreign investors. As Table 2.4 indicates, the valuation of IND5 stocks that individual investors predominantly trade differs from that of INS5 and FOR5 in that IND5 has low B/M ratio but poor profitability. We conjecture that most stocks in the small portfolio are valued by individual investors since the trading value of foreign investors and institutional investors is negligibly small. Such market segmentation is also related to a stock's market capitalization. Furthermore, investigation of investor types' trading behavior is only meaningful for stocks that individual, domestic institutional, and foreign investors interactively trade. For example, since the stocks of the small portfolio are mostly traded among individual investors, studying the trading behavior of investor types for the small portfolio may result in misleading interpretations.

2.1.4. *Measurement of Trading Behavior*

In the next two chapters, we will report anomalies in the Korean stock exchanges such as return seasonality, size, and B/M effect. The trading behavior of different investor types with respect to these anomalies will be examined. The trading behavior of investor types can provide valuable information about the source of stock price movement. First, private information reflects a stock price in the market through the trading behavior of investors. For example, if foreign investors have positive private information about a firm, the information may be revealed to the market through purchases of the firm's stock. Public information does not necessarily provoke trading activity. However, if investor types have different interpretations of public information, their different interpretations will result in different trading behaviors. From the behavioral finance perspective, since individual investors may be more vulnerable to psychological biases, they can exhibit systematic trading behavior, resulting in price errors of securities.

For example, we will examine the seasonal trading pattern of each investor type since the trading patterns of investor types across calendar months may influence seasonal returns. The trade imbalance of investor types' buying and selling value is measured as their trading behavior. FnGuide provides daily trading volume and value of investor types for every stock listed on the KOSPI market since 1995.[2] The daily trading value (KRW) is summed to the monthly trading value (KRW).

The trade imbalance (*IMB*) of individual investors for stock i is defined as follows:

$$IndIMB_{it} = 100 \times \frac{(IndB_{it} - IndS_{it})}{MV_{it-1}} \qquad (1)$$

where *IndB* (*IndS*) is buying (selling) value of individual investors and MV_{it-1} is the market value, defined as the number of shares outstanding multiplied by the close price of stock i at $t-1$. This trade imbalance of individual, domestic institutional, and foreign investors can proxy buying/selling pressure of different investor types. This trade imbalance enables us to understand whether the systematic trading behavior of investor types exists with respect to anomalies.

Although the interaction of investor types' trading behavior is an important key to understanding the source of anomalies, such an interaction must be carefully interpreted. As we report, most small stocks are traded among individual investors. Although the ownership of foreign investors is, on average, higher than 30% after the Asian financial crisis, stocks for which the trading value of foreign investors accounts for 5% of total trading value constitute far less than 10% among small stocks. Domestic institutional investors also do not actively trade small stocks. Furthermore, the valuation of stocks that individual investors predominantly trade differs from the valuation of other stocks. Thus, stocks in the Korean stock markets appear to be segmented into two types of stocks: stocks

---

[2]Daily trade volume is not available in the KOSDAQ market.

for which three investor types actively trade and stocks for which only individual investors actively trade.

2.2. Predictability

2.2.1. *Investor Sentiment*

Many academicians of behavioral finance claim that investor sentiment can influence valuation of securities. High (low) investor sentiment will cause widespread overvaluation (undervaluation) in the securities markets, resulting in lower (higher) subsequent market returns. Thus, investor sentiment may have predictive power for future market returns. Many studies suggest individual proxies as measures of investor sentiment. Some of these individual proxies are directly related to the trading behavior of retail investors or their views of current and future economic activity: the trade imbalance of retail investors (Kumar and Lee, 2006), mutual fund flows (Frazzini and Lamont, 2008; Ben-Rephael *et al.*, 2012), and consumer confidence (Lemmon and Portniaguina, 2006; Schmeling, 2009).

Kumar and Lee (2006) find that buy–sell imbalance of retail investors has incremental power in explaining monthly returns. Their time series factor model suggests that the buy–sell imbalance of retail investors is positively related to simultaneous monthly returns, especially for stocks with high concentration of retail investors such small firms, lower priced firms, firms with lower institutional ownership, and value (high B/M) firms. They claim that the trade imbalance of retail investors may be a proxy of retail sentiment.

Frazzini and Lamont (2008) argue that individual investors can indirectly affect stock prices via inflow of mutual funds. When individual investors purchase mutual funds that own a high proportion of a company's stock, the investors indirectly buy more stocks of the company, resulting in overvaluation of this stock. As a result, the future performance of mutual funds becomes poor in process of correcting the overvaluation of the stock. Frazzini and Lamont find that net increase in mutual fund inflows predicts low future returns by using mutual fund flow as a measure of investor sentiment. In addition, Ben-Rephael *et al.* (2012) use net exchanges between bond funds and equity funds as an investor sentiment proxy. They find that this net exchange is positively related to the contemporaneous aggregate market return but negatively related to the subsequent market returns for 1984–2008.

Lemon and Portniaguina (2006) employ the two surveys of consumer confidence such as the index of Consumer Confidence by the Conference Board and the University of Michigan Consumer Confidence Index. These two indices do not directly reflect consumers' views on securities prices. However, they find that the consumer confidence indices play a role in forecasting the returns of small stocks and stocks with low institutional ownership as a measure of investor sentiment. Consumer confidence as a proxy for investor sentiment is also supported by Schmeling's (2009) empirical results of international stock markets. Schmeling examines the relation between consumer confidence and future stock returns for 18 industrialized countries and finds that consumer confidence tends to predicts prominently expected returns between 1 and 6 months and its predictability dwindles between 12 and 24 months. The predictive power of consumer confidence is stronger for countries that are culturally more prone to herd-like investment behavior and for countries that have less efficient regulatory institutions or less market integrity.

On the other hand, some researchers argue that investor sentiment can be measured from market activities or market reaction to the specific events: Liquidity, IPO volume, the first day returns on IPO stocks, the proportion of new equity issues, closed-end fund discount (CEFD), and dividend premium. Although some of these variables appear to have the predictive power for the future market returns, it is controversial whether the predictive power results from either variation in risk factors or sentiment-related price errors.

It is well known that higher liquidity tends to forecast lower subsequent returns in the cross section analysis of the firm level (Amihud and Mendelson, 1986; Brennan and Subrahmanyam, 1996) and in the time series analysis of aggregate market level (Chordia *et al.*, 2000; Huberman and Halka, 2001; Amihud 2002). Amihud and Mendelson (1986) and Vayanos (1998) claim that the source of the negative relation between liquidity and subsequent returns is liquidity risk premium. In contrast, Baker and Stein (2004) interprets market liquidity as a sentiment indicator. Their model has two critical assumptions: the existence of irrationally overconfident investors and short sales constraints. Irrational investors overreact to positive private signals about future fundamentals by excessively buying stocks in the market. Active participation of irrational investors provides high liquidity when their valuations are higher than those of rational investors. Thus, high liquidity in the market indicates high sentiment, generating overvaluation of the market. On the other hand, the short sale constraint keeps irrational investors out of the market when their valuations are lower. Baker and Stein find that share turnover as a measure of liquidity has predictive power for future market returns.

According to Ritter (2016), the average first-day return is 18.5% for 1980–2015 and 13.9% for 2001–2015 in US, respectively. Ritter (1991) finds the poor long-term performance of IPO stocks and substantial variation in the underperformance which is consistent with periodic optimism of investors.[3] In regards to the IPO market, Baker and Wurgler (2007) argue that IPO issues and its first day returns can be measures of investor sentiment in the stock market.

Stocks tend to underperform in the few years following both initial and seasoned offerings (Ritter, 1991; Loughran and Ritter, 1995; Speiss and Affleck-Graves, 1995; Brav and Gompers, 1997). Baker and Wurgler (2000) document that the proportion of new equity issues to total new equity and debt issues has predictive power for US stock market returns between 1928 and 1997. In particular, firms tend to issue relatively more equity than debt just before the bear market and avoid equity in favor of debt before the bull market. Thus, the higher (lower) share of new equity issues in total new equity and debt issues predicts lower (higher) subsequent market returns. Graham and Harvey (2001) find that managers tend to issue equity

---

[3]However, the underperformance of IPO stocks is controversial since Brav and Gompers (1997) and Brav *et al.* (2000) show that the poor performance of IPO stocks may be due to their characteristics such as small and high growth stocks.

when the stock price rises. Their study offers evidence that the stock market as a whole may be inefficient and managers may exploit this inefficiency with their financing decision. Thus, the higher proportion of new equity issues to total new equity and debt issues may represent higher investor sentiment.

Lee *et al.* (1991) argue that fluctuation of CEFD may depend on change in individual investor sentiment. They view individual investors as noise traders whose trading indicates market sentiment. Since individual investors hold high proportion of closed-end funds, CEFD reflects expectation of individual investors. For example, CEFD will be smaller when individual investors become optimistic. They document that CEFD becomes smaller when small stocks, on average, perform better. However, Chen *et al.* (1993) and Doukas and Milonas (2004) provide evidence to the contrary. Neal and Wheatley (1998) find that CEFDs and net mutual fund redemptions forecast the size premium, especially for long horizons. Qui and Welch (2006), however, provide evidence that CEFDs do not appear to be correlated with direct sentiment measures such as UBS/Gallup surveys of investor sentiment. Thus, whether CEFDs reflect investor sentiment is still controversial in behavioral finance.

According to Baker and Wurgler (2004), dividend premium is defined as the difference between the average M/B ratios of dividend-paying stocks and non-dividend paying stocks. The dividend premium basically depends on investors' preference for safe cash flows. When investors prefer safe cash flows to risky cash flows, the dividend premium tends to increase and vice versa. Baker and Wurgler show that investor demand for safe case flows such as dividend appears to spring from sentiment. Since dividend paying stocks are priced at a premium in the low sentiment period, higher dividend premium represents lower sentiment.

Baker and Wurgler (2006, 2007) develop the investor sentiment index by employing principal component analysis to draw a common sentiment component from six individual component proxies: share turnover, IPO volume, first-day returns of IPO stocks, the equity share in new issues, CEFD, and the dividend premium. The first four variables are positively related to the sentiment level, while the last two are negatively related. Following the methodology of Baker and Wurgler (2006, 2007), Kim and Byun (2010) create the sentiment index in the Korean stock market. They employ two individual sentiment proxies from Baker and Wurgler's six proxies and four additional proxies because of the limited data availability. The six individual proxies are turnover ratio (*TURN*), relative equity issuance (*SR*) (Baker and Wurgler 2006, 2007), the monthly trade imbalance of individual investors (Kumar and Lee 2006), monthly stock fund flow ratio (Coval and Stafford 2005; Frazzini and Lamont 2005), customers' deposits for stock investment (CD), and the customer expectation index (CEI) for the business cycle (Kim and Byun, 2010).

Figure 2.4 shows two sentiment indices SENT and BSENT from 1999 to 2010. *SENT* is the first principal component of levels or changes in six investor sentiment proxies, while *BSENT* is another sentiment index after controlling business cycle components. These two indices move similarly although *SENT* changes more smoothly. They are high in 1999 when the information technology (IT) bubble rises to a peak and low in late 2000 when the IT bubble bursts.

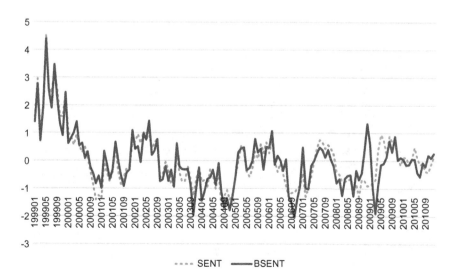

Figure 2.4.   Monthly Sentiment Index: 1999–2010

Sentiment levels, however, are not necessarily high when a stock price has risen over time. For instance, the KOSPI gradually increases from 535.7 in March 2003 to 1,295 in November 2006 when *BSENT* reaches its lowest level. Afterward, the KOSPI rises sharply to over 2,000 at the end of October 2007, suggesting that the low sentiment index may have predictive power regarding high stock returns in the future.

Behavioral finance claims that investor sentiment has the power to predict future returns in securities markets. Since high (low) investor sentiment generates overvaluation (undervaluation) of securities, the subsequent returns on securities will be lower (higher) in the process of price error correction. Figure 2.5 indicates the predictability of the sentiment index quartile on the equally weighted (EW) average monthly return for the subsequent 6 months in the KOSPI market. *SENTQ (BSENTQ)* is formed on the basis of the monthly sentiment index in ascending order from January 1999 to December 2010. For example, *SENTQ (BSENTQ)* = 1 is the lowest quartile and *SENTQ (BSENTQ)* = 4 is the highest. Likewise, *P6* is the EW average return in the KOSPI market for the past 6 months and P6Q is the quartile group in ascending order on the basis of P6.

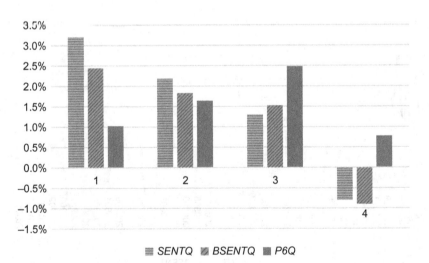

Figure 2.5. Predictability of the Sentiment Index Quartiles on EW Monthly Return for the Subsequent 6 Months in the KOSPI Market from 1999 to 2010

When *SENTQ* (*BSENTQ*) = 1, the EW monthly return for 6 months is, on average, 3.21% (2.44%). On the contrary, when *SENTQ* (*BSENTQ*) = 4, the subsequent EW monthly return is −0.8% (0.90%). These results are consistent with Baker and Wurgler's (2007) empirical result suggesting that the monthly sentiment index has predictability for future stock returns. However, P6Q, the quartile based on 6-month past returns, does not display any consistent relationship with the subsequent EW returns.

Although the sentiment index has predictable power for subsequent returns, it has its own weaknesses. First, the principal component analysis requires the entire period of data to capture common components from individual proxy variables. Thus, the analysis reflects look-ahead bias. Second, it is difficult to obtain consistent individual proxy variables in Korea since the definition and calculation methods of some variables change over time.

2.2.2. *Alternative Individual Proxy: Aggregate Market-to-Book Ratio*

It is well known that the book-to-market ratio can account for a substantial portion of cross-section variation in stock returns. Stocks with high B/M ratios, called value stocks, tend to have higher abnormal returns than those with low B/M ratio, called growth stocks. Fama and French (1993, 1996) suggest that the B/M ratio is a proxy for distress risk. Distressed firms may be more sensitive to certain business cycle factors and investors may not be able to hedge such distress-related risk. Thus, the distress-related risk is a systematic risk. On the other hand, Lakonishok *et al.* (1994) argue that value (growth) stocks tend to be undervalued (overvalued) because investors incorrectly extrapolate firms' past earnings growth rate. As a result, value stocks with poor earnings or low sales growth tend to be undervalued. Subsequent high returns can be obtained in the process of correcting undervaluation of these value stocks since their future cash flows are, on average, unexpectedly favorable.

These controversial arguments can be explained by using the simple model derived from the dividend growth model. According to the dividend growth model, $P_0 = \frac{\text{div}_1}{r-g}$ where P_0 is the current stock price and div_1 is the next period's dividend; r is a required return on the stock, which is related to a stock's systematic risk, and g is dividend growth. If the dividend payout ratio is k, $\text{div}_1 = k\,E_1$ where E_1 is the next period's earnings per share. Thus, the dividend growth model can be changed to $\frac{P_0}{E_1} = \frac{k}{r-g}$. $\frac{P_0}{E_1}$ is the ratio of price to the next period's earnings. Since ROE can be defined as E_1/b where b is the book value per share, $E_1 = b\,\text{ROE}$. Therefore, the equation $\frac{P_0}{E_1}$ can be rearranged to $\frac{P_0}{b} = \frac{k\,\text{ROE}}{r-g}$ which is the ratio of the market price of a share to the book value per share. P_0/b is same as M/B where M is the market price multiplied by outstanding shares of equity and B is b multiplied by outstanding shares of equity. As a result, the M/B ratio depends on ROE, r, and g where ROE and g are related to the next period's profitability and the growth rate of long-term cash flows, respectively,[4] while r represents the risk of equity. Thus, the M/B ratio depends on future profitability (ROE), future cash flow growth (g), and risk (r). Instead of the M/B ratio, financial literature usually employs the B/M ratio in a cross-sectional analysis which is an inverse of the M/B ratio. However, since the aforementioned equation describes the relation between the M/B ratio and other factors, we will use the M/B ratio especially when the M/B ratio is applied to the predictability on market returns.

According to the risk-based hypothesis, high M/B stocks have strong future cash flows and/or low risk. In other words, high M/B stocks tend to have high g and low r. In contrast, the overreaction arguments claim that high M/B stocks have neither strong future cash flows nor low risk. Since high M/B ratios, on average, cannot be justified by high g and low r, these stocks are overvalued. Their subsequent returns will be low in the process of correcting such overvaluation.

---

[4]Since the dividend growth rate relies on earnings growth, g can be interpreted as earnings growth or a sustainable cash flow growth rate. Since the dividend policy cannot influence a firm's value in the perfect market, as Modigliani and Miller (1961) argue, k (dividend payout ratio) will not affect the valuation of a share.

On the other hand, Kothari and Shanken (1997) and Pontiff and Schall (1998) extend the cross-sectional analysis of the book-to-market effect to a time series analysis. For example, Pontiff and Schall examine the predictability of the aggregate M/B ratio on future returns from 1926 to 1994. Their regression methodology shows that the subsequent market return tends to decline, as the M/B ratio of the Dow Jones Industrial Average (DJIA) rises. They argue that the DJIA M/B ratio contains information about future returns that is not captured by interest rate yield spreads and dividend yields. The source of the M/B's predictability can also be explained by the aforementioned equation, $\frac{M}{B} = \frac{k\,\text{ROE}}{r-g}$.

According to the above M/B equation, the aggregate M/B ratio can vary over time since both market risk and expected cash flows in the stock market change over time. For example, a rise in economic uncertainty increases market risk, resulting in increased r, the expected market return. Higher r decreases the aggregate market capitalization and thus reduces the aggregate M/B ratio. The aggregate M/B ratio also decreases if g is expected to be lower; g can be interpreted as the market portfolio's future cash flow growth. Therefore, the aggregate market-to-book ratio contains information about expected market return as well as future cash flow growth at the level of the market portfolio. Thus, the risk-based hypothesis can claim that the low aggregate M/B ratio can predict the high expected returns on the market portfolio and/or the low growth rate of future cash flows. However, the low (high) M/B ratio can serve as a proxy of under(over)valuation from the perspective of the overreaction hypothesis. According to the overreaction hypothesis, the low or high aggregate M/B ratio may not be justified by the market risk or future cash flow growth. The low (high) M/B ratio may be followed by high (low) subsequent market returns as a result of correcting under(over)valuation. Thus, both approaches have the same predictability regarding the aggregate M/B ratio and future returns: Lower (higher) aggregate M/B ratio level predicts higher (lower) subsequent market returns. We will examine the predictability of the M/B ratio in more practical way by sorting time series M/B ratios into quartiles.

We employ all listed firms in the KOSPI market, excluding financial companies, to create monthly aggregate M/B ratios. The book value of a fiscal year ending the calendar year t for all firms is summed to the aggregate book value of the stock market. Since a firm's financial statement is available to the market at most 5 months after the firm's fiscal year-end in Korea, information about the book value of the fiscal year ending calendar year t will be revealed in May of calendar year $t + 1$. Thus, we use the aggregate book value of a fiscal year ending the calendar year t to create the aggregate M/B ratio from May of year $t + 1$ to April of year $t + 2$. A firm's market capitalization is summed monthly to produce the aggregate market value for one year beginning with May of year $t + 1$. Finally, dividing the monthly aggregate market value by the annual aggregate book value yields the monthly aggregate M/B ratio from May of year $t + 1$ to April of year $t + 2$.[5]

Figure 2.6 presents the monthly aggregate M/B ratios, which are standardized with a 0 mean and 1 standard deviation. The standardized M/B ratios display a pattern similar to *SENT* although the M/B ratios appear to follow *SENT*'s pattern with lags. For example, *SENT* peaks in May 1999, while the M/B ratio reaches its peak in December 1999. However, it is more important to compare the levels. Since the mean of *SENT* is 0, investor sentiment may be interpreted as high if *SENT* is larger than 0. Likewise, if the M/B ratio measures over- or undervaluation of the stock market, stocks tend to be overvalued if the M/B index is larger than 0. Investor sentiment is extremely high in the early months of 1999, while the M/B ratio is far below 0 during the same period, indicating undervaluation. Thus, when investor sentiment becomes high in

---

[5] Our method of calculating the aggregate M/B ratios suggests that the book value of equity precedes the market value of equity by at least 5 months. The number of outstanding shares for the market value of equity may be larger than for the book value of equity if seasoned equity offerings or initial public offerings occur during the time gap between the book value and market value of equity. Thus, the aggregate M/B ratio can be high not only because of high market valuation of equity but also because of increases in shares on stock markets. In particular, the aggregate M/B ratios will be higher when seasoned equity offerings or initial public offerings are actively issued in stock markets.

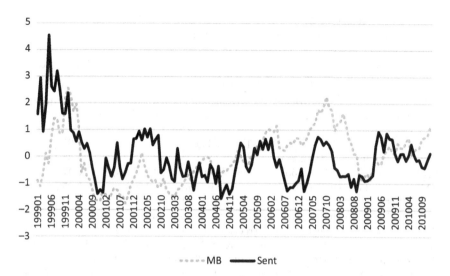

Figure 2.6. Monthly M/B Ratio in the KOSPI Market and Investor Sentiment Indices (*SENT*) from 1990 to 2010

early 1999, stock undervaluation may be serious. However, stock undervaluation turns into overvaluation in July 1999 and reaches a peak in December 1999.

If the M/B ratios shown in Figure 2.6 indicate the degree of over- or undervaluation, the degree of overvaluation during the pre-global financial crisis period is as high as during the IT bubble in the Korea stock market. On the other hand, investor sentiment is much higher during the IT bubble period than during the pre-global financial crisis.

Table 2.5 presents EW and valued weighted (VW) average monthly returns in the KOSPI market for 6 months immediately after quartiles are decided in ascending order of all time-series monthly *SENT* (aggregated M/B ratios). For example, Q1 indicates that *SENT* (M/B ratio) belongs to the lowest quartile. EW and VW monthly returns are averaged for the 6 months immediately after Q1 is decided. Q1 of *SENT* has the highest EW monthly return of 3.26%, while Q4 of *SENT* has the lowest. With respect to EW returns, *SENT* quartiles have reliable predictability. However, Q2 of *SENT* has the highest VW returns but the order of *SENT* quartiles

Table 2.5. Predictability of *SENT* and Aggregate M/B Ratios on EW and VW Monthly Average Returns for 6 Months from 1999 to 2010

		SENT		Aggregate M/B Ratio	
Quartiles	No	EW Returns (%)	VW Returns (%)	EW Returns (%)	VW Returns (%)
Q1	36	3.26 (3.06)	1.75 (2.11)	2.72 (2.88)	2.81 (4.23)
Q2	36	2.23 (2.28)	1.96 (2.23)	2.85 (2.81)	1.35 (1.58)
Q3	36	1.32 (2.55)	0.85 (1.26)	2.13 (2.65)	1.47 (2.43)
Q4	35	−0.71 (−0.76)	−0.13 (−0.11)	−1.68 (−1.99)	−1.25 (−1.48)

Notes: The parentheses indicate the t value calculated based on Newey and West's (1987) standard error correction method with five lags. *SENT* and aggregate monthly M/B ratios in the KOSPI market are divided into quintiles in ascending order of M/B ratios and *SENT*, respectively. Thus, Q4 indicates months with the highest M/B ratios or highest *SENT*, respectively. VW and EW monthly returns in the KOSPI market are calculated for the 6 months immediately after sorting M/B ratios or *SENT*.

tends to have a negative relation with VW monthly returns. For example, Q4 of *SENT* has negative VW monthly returns, while Q1 of *SENT* has positive returns.

On the other hand, the quartiles of aggregate M/B ratios have relatively weak relationships with both EW and VW monthly returns. Q2 of M/B ratios, rather than Q1, has the highest EW monthly returns although the difference is not significant. In regard to VW monthly returns, Q3 of M/B ratios has the second highest VW monthly returns, although the difference between Q2 and Q3 is only 0.12%. Nevertheless, the quartiles of M/B ratios have useful predictability for subsequent monthly returns since the difference in monthly average returns between Q1 and Q4 of M/B ratios is at least as high as that between Q1 and Q4 of *SENT*s. For example, the average monthly return of Q1 of M/B ratios minus that of Q4 of M/B ratios is higher than 4.0% in terms of both EW and VW returns, while Q1 of *SENT* minus Q4 of *SENT* has 3.97% of EW monthly returns and 1.88% of VW monthly returns. Specifically, Q4 of M/B ratios has the lowest VW and EW average monthly returns, which are lower than VW and EW monthly returns for Q4 of *SENT*.

2.2.2.1. *M/B ratios in the KOSPI and KOSDAQ markets*

Most players in the KOSDAQ market are individual investors. According to the academic literature, individual investors are more likely to be vulnerable to psychological effects and their trading behavior may cause more price errors than that of institutional investors. Thus, the aggregate M/B ratios obtained using KOSDAQ stocks may capture misvaluation of stocks better than those obtained using KOSPI stocks, if the M/B ratio measures the degree of misvaluation. Therefore, it is interesting to examine whether the aggregate M/B ratios in the KOSDAQ market have better predictability for future returns.

We compare the predictability of KOSPI M/B ratio quartiles on the subsequent 6-month EW and VW returns in the KOSPI market with that of KOSDAQ M/B ratio quartiles. Since monthly KOSDAQ M/B ratios are available beginning in August 1997, the test period for comparing the predictability of both M/B ratio quartiles covers September 1997–December 2013. Figure 2.7 shows that the 6-month EW and VW returns in the KOSPI market tend to have a negative relationship with KOSPI M/B ratio quartiles as well as KOSDAQ

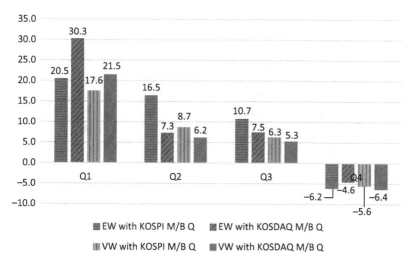

Figure 2.7. Predictability of KOSPI and KOSDAQ M/B Quartiles on 6-Month EW and VW in the KOSPI Stock Market from 1997 to 2013

M/B ratio quartiles. Thus, both M/B quartiles appear to have predictable power for subsequent returns in the KOSPI market. Q1 of KOSDAQ M/B ratios has higher EW and VW returns than Q1 of KOSPI M/B ratios. All Q4s of KOPSPI and KOSDAQ M/B ratios have negative EW and VW returns in the KOSPI market. However, their Q2 and Q3 do not yield significantly different returns except for EW returns with KOPSI M/B ratio. In addition, Q1 minus Q4 of KOSDAQ M/B ratios has higher EW and VW returns in the KOSPI market than Q1 minus Q4 of the KOSPI M/B ratios. Thus, the KOSDAQ M/B ratios appear to have superior predictability on KOSPI stock returns.

Figure 2.8 presents 6-month EW and VW returns in the KOS-DAQ market for KOSPI and KOSDAQ M/B ratio quartiles. The quartiles of monthly M/B ratios also tend to have a negative relationship with EW and VW returns in the KOSDAQ market. However, the negative relationship in the KOSDAQ market is not as strong as in the KOSPI market. For example, Q1, Q2, and Q3 of KOSPI M/B ratios do not provide significantly different VW returns in the KOSDAQ market, which are around 4%. Q4 of KOSDAQ

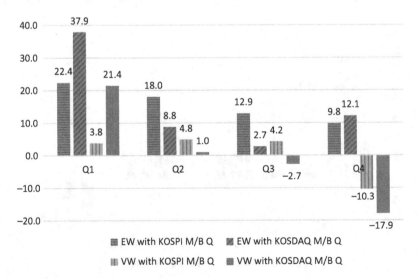

Figure 2.8.   Predictability of KOSPI and KOSDAQ M/B Quartiles on 6-Month EW and VW in KOSDAQ Stock Market from 1997 to 2013

M/B ratios has 12.1% of EW returns, which is higher than Q2 and Q3. However, Q1 of KOSPI and KOSDAQ M/B ratios has much higher EW and VW returns than Q4. In particular, Q1 minus Q4 of KOSDAQ M/B ratios has much higher EW and VW returns than for the KOSPI M/B ratios. For example, Q1 of KOSDAQ M/B ratios has 21.4% VW returns, while Q4 has −17.9%.

In short, both KOSPI and KOSDAQ M/B ratio quartiles have predictive power for subsequent returns. KOSDAQ aggregated M/B ratios result in a larger difference in both EW and VW returns between Q1 and Q4 than KOSPI M/B ratios. Both KOSPI and KOSDAQ M/B ratios have a more stable negative relationship with EW and VW returns in the KOSPI market than in the KOSDAQ market. KOSDAQ ratio quartiles have a more consistent and stronger negative relationship with VW returns in the KOSDAQ market. In general, KOSDAQ aggregate M/B ratios appear to have stronger predictability on market returns than KOSPI aggregate M/B ratios. However, since KOSPI M/B ratios cover a longer period than KOSDAQ M/B ratios, KOSPI M/B ratios will be used to predict future stock returns.

2.2.2.2. *Iterative sorting of M/B ratios to avoid look-forward bias*

To avoid look-ahead bias, predictability should be tested based only on information available at the time of sorting the time series M/B ratios. We develop iterative sorting of M/B ratios to avoid look-ahead bias. In the first step, we sort M/B ratios into quartiles by using 90 months' data from June 1981 to December 1988. In the next step, the M/B ratio quartile in January 1989 is determined on the basis of all available M/B ratios from June 1981 to January 1989. We repeat this step every month beginning with January 1989. The M/B ratio in month t after December 1988 is classified into one of four quartiles by sorting all available M/B ratios from 1981 through the latest month t. The M/B ratio quartile determined in month t is used to predict EW returns from $t + 1$ to $t + 6$. This method avoids look-ahead bias but does not guarantee that the four groups of M/B ratio have the same number.

Table 2.6. Predictability of the Aggregate M/B ratio on 6-Month EW Cumulative Return in the KOSPI Market

	Jan. 1989–Dec. 2013		Jan. 1989–Jan. 2001		Feb. 2001–Dec. 2013	
Group	N	6-Month EW Return	N	6-Month EW Return	N	6-Month EW Return
G1	7	66.28 (2.81)	7	66.28 (2.81)	0	N.A.
G2	87	11.76 (2.25)	41	9.63 (0.95)	46	13.74 (4.28)
G3	122	8.17 (3.12)	51	3.97 (1.55)	71	11.33 (2.94)
G4	84	−2.41 (−0.65)	46	−3.85 (−0.89)	38	−0.68 (−0.11)

Note: ( ) indicates t value calculated based on Newey and West's (1987) standard error correction method with five lags.

Table 2.6 shows the 6-month EW returns based on the aggregate M/B ratios of KOSPI stocks by using the iterative sorting method. G1 (G4) indicates the lowest (highest) M/B ratio group. G1 has only seven observations covering the period of December 1997–October 1998, when the Asian financial crisis overshadowed the stock markets. For these 7 months, M/B ratios were below 0.62. Such low M/B ratios were also found in the KOSPI market in the early 1980s. According to Table 2.6, 6-month EW returns are negatively related to aggregate M/B ratio quartiles. Even excluding the EW returns of G1, G2 has the second highest EW returns and G4 the lowest. The negative relation holds for both the entire test period of 1989–2013 and the two sub-periods.

Since the number in each group differs and G1 has only seven observations for the entire period, we sort these four groups into high M/B months (G3 and G4) and low M/B months (G1 and G2). Figure 2.9 reports 6-month EW returns following low or high M/B months in the KOSPI market. To avoid overlapping months of the holding period, we sort M/B months every 6 months. Sorting months are December and June of every year beginning with December 1988. If the M/B ratio ranking belongs to G1 or G2, we measure the subsequent 6-month return as the return following the low M/B month. Otherwise, the subsequent 6-month return is classified as the return following a high M/B month. For example, if a M/B ratio ranking belongs to G1 in December 1997, 6-month returns are

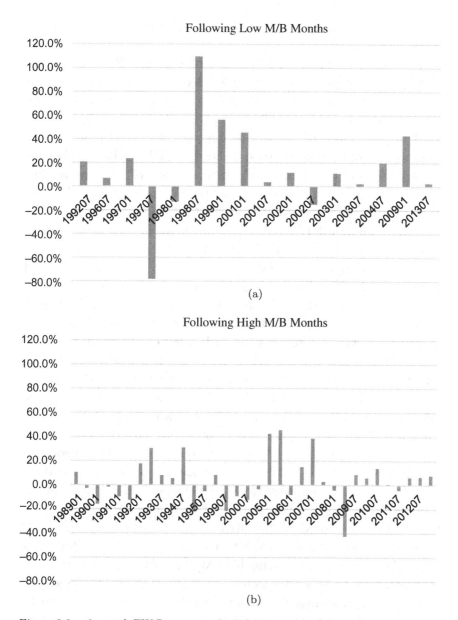

Figure 2.9. 6-month EW Returns in the KOSPI Market Following Low and High M/B Months: 1989–2013

measured from January 1998 to June 1998 as returns following the low month.

According to Figure 2.9, the lowest 6-month EW return was −78.2% for the period of July 1997–December 1997 following the low M/B month, while the highest 6-month EW return was 109.5% for the period of July 1998–December 1998 following the low M/B month. Three of 16 periods following low M/B months have negative 6-month EW returns. Following high M/B months, the negative 6-month EW returns number 15 out of 34 periods. The relative frequency of negative 6-month EW returns following low M/B months is 18.8%, but it is 44.1% following high M/B months. The average 6-month EW return is 15.6% following low M/B months, which is much higher than the 3.9% following high M/B months. The standard deviation of the EW months is 39.5% following low M/B months and 18.8% following high M/B months.

Figure 2.10 reports 6-month VW returns in the KOSPI market following low or high M/B months. According to Figure 2.10, negative 6-month VW returns appear in 4 out of 16 periods following low M/B months. On the other hand, the negative 6-month VW returns number 16 out of 34 periods following high M/B months. Thus, the relative frequency of negative 6-month returns is 25.0% following low M/B months and 47.1% following high M/B months. Therefore, there is a greater chance of having positive VW returns following low M/B months than high M/B months. The average 6-month VW return is 11.4% following low M/B months and 0.1% following high M/B months. However, the standard deviation of the VW return is 19.6% following low M/B months, which is a little higher than the standard deviation of 16.4% following high M/B months. In short, the average VW return is much higher following low M/B months than following high M/B months, although the VW returns appear to be a little more volatile following low M/B months.

In summary, average 6-month returns following low M/B months are much higher than following high M/B months, regardless of VW or EW returns. These results confirm that the aggregate M/B ratio has predictive power for future returns. On the other hand, the

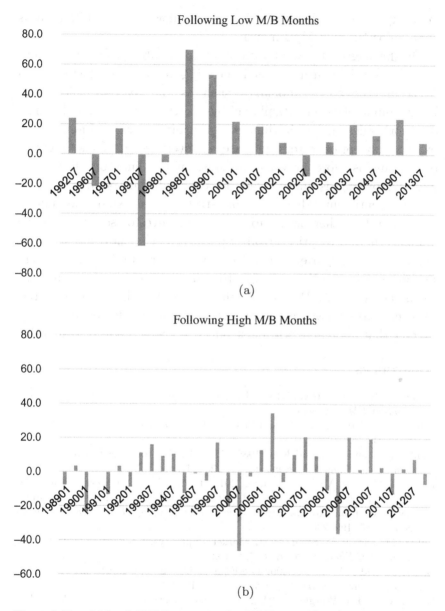

Figure 2.10.   6-Month VW Returns in the KOSPI Market Low and High M/B Months: 1989–2013

volatility of 6-month returns is higher following low M/B months than following high M/B months.

If the aggregate M/B ratio has predictability for subsequent 6-month stock returns, it is interesting to see how low or high M/B months affect anomalies such as the seasonal effect and book-to-market effect. Stambaugh *et al.* (2011) argue that the limit on short sales makes it difficult for arbitrageurs to immediately exploit any price errors in case of overpricing. Thus, security overpricing is more prevalent because of the limit on short sales and overpricing is more likely to occur during periods of high investor sentiment. The long–short strategy that exploits anomalies will generate higher profits following high investor sentiment if the anomaly is due to price errors. Specifically, the short-leg strategy, defined as shorting overvalued stocks, will be profitable following high investor sentiment. We can apply the same logic of investor sentiment to the aggregate M/B ratio. To the extent that the aggregate M/B ratio captures misvaluation, the limit on short sales enables us to predict that anomalies will be stronger following high M/B months.

References

Aggarwal, R. and P. Rivoli, 1990, Fads in the Initial Public Offering Market? *Financial Management* 19, 45–57

Amihud, Y., 2002, Illiquidity and Stock Returns, *Journal of Financial Markets* 5, 31–56.

Amihud, Y. and H. Mendelson, 1986, Asset Pricing and the Bid-Ask Spread, *Journal of Financial Economics* 17, 223–249.

Bae Sung C., J. H. Min, and S. Jung, 2011, Trading Behavior, Performance, and Stock Preference of Foreigners, Local Institutions, and Individual Investors: Evidence from Korean Stock Market, *Asia-Pacific Journal of Financial Studies* 40, 199–230.

Baker, M. and J. C. Stein, 2004, Market Liquidity as a Sentiment Indicator, *Journal of Financial Markets* 7, 271–299.

Baker, M. and J. Wurgler, 2000, The Equity Share in New Issues and Aggregate Stock Returns, *Journal of Finance* 55, 2219–2257.

Baker, M. and J. Wurgler, 2004, A Catering Theory of Dividends, *Journal of Finance* 59, 1125–1165.

Baker, M. and J. Wurgler, 2006, Investor Sentiment and Cross-Section of Stock Returns, *Journal of Finance* 61, 1645–1680.

Baker, M. and J. Wurgler, 2007, Investor Sentiment in the Stock Market, *Journal of Economic Perspective* 21, 129–152.

Barber, B. M., Y. Lee, Y. Liu, and T. Odean, 2009, Just How Much Do Individual Investors Lose by Trading? *Review of Financial Studies* 22, 609–632.

Barber, B. M. and T. Odean, 2011, The Behavior of Individual Investors, Working Paper. Retrived from http://ssrn.com/abstract=1872211.

Barberies, N. and R. Thaler, 2003, A Survey of Behavioral Finance, In G. Constantinides, M. Harris, and R. Stulz, (eds.), *Handbook of Economics of Finance*, North-Holland, Amsterdam.

Ben-Rephael, A., S. Kandel, and A. Wohl, 2012, Measuring Investor Sentiment with Mutual Fund Flows, *Journal of Financial Economics* 104, 363–382.

Brav, A. and P. A. Gompers, 1997, Myth or Reality? The Long-Run Underperformance of Initial Public Offerings: Evidence from Venture and Non-venture Capital-Backed Companies, *Journal of Finance* 52, 1791–1821.

Brav, A., C. Geczy, and P. Gompers, 2000, The Role of Lockups in Initial Public Offerings, *Review of Financial Studies* 16, 1–29.

Brennan, M. and A. Subrahmanyam, 1996, Market Microstrcutre and Asset Pricing: On the Compensation for Illiquidity in Stock Returns, *Journal of Financial Economics* 41, 441–464.

Brown, S., W. Goetzmann, T. Hiraki, and M. Watanabe, 2005, Investor Sentiment in Japanese and U.S. Daily Mutual Fund Flows, Working Paper.

Chen, N., R. Kan, and M. Miller, 1993, Are the Discounts on Closed-End Funds a Sentiment Index? *Journal of Finance* 48, 795–800.

Chui, A., S. Titman, K. Wei, 2010, Individualism and Momentum around the World, *Journal of Finance* 65, 361–392.

Coval, J. and E. Stafford, 2007, Asset Fire Sales (and Purchases) in Equity Markets, *Journal of Financial Economics* 86, 479–512.

Dahlquist, M. and G. Robertsson, 2001, Direct Foreign Ownership, Institutional Investors, and Firm Characteristics, *Journal of Financial Economics* 59, 413–440.

DeLong, J. B., Shleifer A., Summers L. and R. Waldmann, 1990a, Noise Trader Risk in Financial Markets, *Journal of Political Economy* 98, 703–738.

DeLong, J. B. and Shleifer A., Summers L. and R. Waldmann, 1990b, Positive Feedback Investment Strategies and Destabilizing Rational Speculation, *Journal of Finance* 45, 375–395.

Derrien F., 2005, IPO Pricing in "Hot" Market Conditions: Who Leaves Money on the Table?, *Journal of Finance* 60, 487–521.

Doukas, J. and N. Milonas, 2004, Investor Sentiment and the Closed-End Fund Puzzle: Out-of-Sample Evidence, *European Financial Management* 10, 235–266.

Falkenstein, E. G., 1996, Preferences for Stock Characteristics as Revealed by Mutual Fund Portfolio Holdings, *Journal of Finance* 51, 111–135.

Fama, E. and K. French, 1993, Common Risk Factors in the Returns on Stocks and Bonds, *Journal of Financial Economics* 33, 3–56.

Fama, E. and K. French, 1995, Multifactor Explanations of Asset Pricing Anomalies, *Journal of Finance* 51, 55–84.

Frazzini, A. and O. Lamont, 2008, Dumb Money: Mutual Fund Flows and the Cross-Section of Stock Returns, *Journal of Financial Economics* 88, 299–322.

Gompers, P. A., P. G. J. O'Connell, and M. S. Seasholes, 2001, Institutional Investors and Equity Prices, *Quarterly Journal of Economics* 116, 229–259.

Gompers, P. A. and A. Metrick, 2001, Institutional Investors and Equity Prices, *Quarterly Journal of Economics* 116, 229–259.

Graham, J. and C. Harvey, 2001, The Theory and Practice of Corporate Finance: Evidence from the Field, *Journal of Financial Economics* 60, 187–243.

Grinblatt, M. and M. Keloharju, 2000, The Investment Behavior and Performance of Various Investor Types: A Study of Finland's Unique Data Set, *Journal of Financial Economics* 55, 43–67.

Gruber, M. J., 1996, Another Puzzle: The Growth in Actively Managed Mutual Funds, *Journal of Finance* 51, 783–810.

Huberman, G. and T. Stein, 2001, Systematic Liquidity, *Journal of Financial Research* 24, 161–178.

Hvidkjaer, S. 2006, A Trade-Based Analysis of Momentum, *Review of Financial Studies* 19, 457–491.

Kahneman, D. and A. Tversky, 1979, Prospect Theory: An Analysis of Decision under Risk, *Econometrica* 47, 263–291.

Kang, J. and R. M. Stulz, 1997, Why is there a Home Bias? An Analysis of Foreign Portfolio Equity Ownership in Japan, *Journal of Financial Economics* 46, 3–28.

Kim, K. and J. Byun, 2010, Effects of Investor Sentiment on Market Response to Stock Split Announcement, *Asian-Pacific Journal of Financial Studies* 39, 687–719.

Ko, K., K. Kim, and S. H. Cho, 2007, Characteristics and Performance of Institutional and Foreign Investors in the Japanese and Korean Stock Market, *Journal of the Japanese and International Economics* 21(2), 195 213.

Kothari, S. P., and J. Shanken, 1997, Book-to-Market, Dividend Yield, and Expected Market Returns: A Time Series Analysis, *Journal of Financial Economics* 44, 169–203.

Kumar A. and C. Lee, 2006, Retail Investor Sentiment and Return Comovements, *Journal of Finance* 61, 2451–2486.

Lamont, O. and J. Stein, 2006, Investor Sentiment and Corporate Finance: Micro and Macro, *American Economic Review* 96, 147–151.

Lee, C., A. Shleifer, and R. Thaler, 1991, Investor Sentiment and the Closed-end Puzzle, *Journal of Finance* 46, 75–109.

Lemmon, M. and E. Portniaguina, 2006, Consumer Confidence and Asset Prices: Some Empirical Evidence, *Review of Financial Studies* 19, 1499–1529.

Loughran, T. and J. Ritter, 1995, The New Issues Puzzle, *Journal of Finance* 50, 23–51.

Lowry, M., 2003, Why Does IPO Volume Fluctuate So Much? *Journal of Financial Economics* 67, 3–40.

Merton, R. C., 1987, A Simple Model of Capital Market Equilibrium with Incomplete Information, *Journal of Finance* 42, 483–510.

Modigliani, F. and M. Miller, 1961, Dividend Policy, Growth, and the Valuation of Shares, *Journal of Business* 34, 411–433.

Neal, R. and S. Wheatley, 1998, Do Measures of Investor Sentiment Predict Returns? *Journal of Financial and Quantitative Analysis* 33, 523–547.

Pontiff, J. and L. Schall, 1998, Book-to-Market Ratios as Predictors of Market Returns, *Journal of Financial Economics* 49, 141–160.

Qui, L. and I. Welch, 2006, Investor Sentiment Measures. Retrieved from http://ssrn.com/abstract_589641.

Ritter, J., 1991, The Long-Run Performance of Initial Public Offerings, *Journal of Finance* 46, 3–27.

Ritter, J., 2016, Initial Public Offerings: Updated Statistics, Retrieved from (https://site.warrington.ufl.edu/ritter/files/2016/03/Initial-Public-Offerings -Updated-Statistics-2016-03-08.pdf).

Sapp, T. and A. Tiwari, 2004, Does Stock Return Momentum Explain the "Smart Money" Effect? *Journal of Finance* 59, 2605–2622.

Schmeling, M., 2009, Investor Sentiment and Stock Returns: Some International Evidence, *Journal of Empirical Finance* 16, 294–408.

Stambaugh, R., J. Yu, and Y. Yuan, 2012, The Short of It: Investor Sentiment and Anomalies, *Journal of Financial Economics* 104, 288–302.

Speiss, K. and J. Affleck-Graves, 1995, The Long-Run Performance of Stock Returns Following Debt Offerings, *Journal of Financial Economics* 54, 45–73.

Vayanos, D., 1998, Transaction Costs and Asset Prices: A Dynamic Equilibrium Model, *Review of Financial Studies* 11, 1–58.

Zheng, L., 1999, Is Money Smart? A Study of Mutual Fund Investors' Fund Selection Ability, *Journal of Finance* 54, 901–933.

Chapter 3

Seasonal Anomalies

3.1. January Effect

3.1.1. *Literature Review*

It is a stylized fact that the month of January has systematically higher returns than any other calendar month. This phenomenon is referred to as the January effect. Rozeff and Kinney (1976) provided the first empirical evidence of the January effect in the United States, which has gained much attention from both academicians and practitioners. Keim (1983) and Reinganum (1983) demonstrate that the January effect is primarily concentrated in small firms. Roll (1983) and Keim (1989) argue that market microstructure effects, such as the bid–ask spread and thin trading, which are more pronounced for small and low priced stocks, are important factors in explaining the abnormally high returns in January.

Many studies have also documented significant January effects in major EU countries, Canada, and Japan (Gultekin and Gultekin, 1983; Berges *et al.*, 1984; Kato and Schallheim, 1985). However, once any anomaly is found and revealed to the market, the efficient market hypothesis suggests that rational investors would arbitrage the anomaly away. For example, the strategy of buying stocks in December and selling them in late January or in February will have the January effect disappear. Mehdian and Perry (2002), Gu (2003), and Schwert (2003) provide empirical results that the January effect becomes weaker. However, Easterday *et al.* (2009) suggest that the average January return becomes smaller after 1963–1979 not because investors attempt to exploit the January effect but because the period of 1963–1979 has abnormally higher January returns. They claim that there are no active arbitrage activities related to the January anomaly since trading volume in December and January is not higher for small stocks than in any other calendar months.

The literature on the January effect offers several explanations for the abnormally high returns in January. The first one is the tax-loss selling hypothesis, which depends on the tax-motivated trading of individual investors. Prior to the calendar year-end, individual investors sell stocks that have declined in value to realize tax losses. Such selling results in a tendency for late December transactions to close at bid prices. Thus, recorded returns over the last few days of December are small or negative. Without pressure to sell stocks immediately after the calendar turn, the closing prices move, on average, from the bid toward the midpoint of the spread. As a result, a positive recorded return appears in the early days of January. However, small stocks with capital gains do not have abnormally high returns in January of the following year. Many studies support or are consistent with the tax-loss selling hypothesis (Ritter, 1988; Dyl and Maberly, 1992; Poterba and Weisbenner, 2001; D'Mello et al., 2003; Stark et al., 2006).

Although the tax-loss selling hypothesis may be the most likely explanation for the January effect, it is not sufficient to explain the abnormally large returns observed in many other countries where the tax year for individuals is not the calendar year (Keim and Ziemba, 2000; Fountas and Segredakis, 2002). The Korean stock market is a case in which the tax-loss selling hypothesis cannot be applied since there is no capital gains tax for stock trading in Korea.

Another promising explanation for the January effect is the window-dressing hypothesis. According to this hypothesis, institutional investors have incentives to rebalance portfolios at the end of the calendar year when they want their portfolios to look great in the year-end report. Thus, just prior to the calendar year-end, they buy stocks with good return performance and sell stocks with poor return performance to present respectable year-end portfolio holdings. Many studies (Haugen and Lakonishok, 1988; Ackert and Athanassakos, 2000; O'Neal, 2001; Ng and Wang, 2004) provide empirical evidence of institutional investors' trading behavior during the turn of the year, which is consistent with the window-dressing hypothesis. The literature, however, casts doubt on the role of institutional window dressing in determining the seasonality in stock returns. The research into window dressing has mostly used quarterly or even semi-annual portfolio disclosures. Ortiz *et al.* (2012) point out that a low frequency of portfolio disclosure may not show actual change in portfolio holdings because the disclosed portfolio holdings may already be the result of window dressing. This possibility casts doubt on the accuracy of such previous results. Furthermore, it is also questionable why the January effect is prominent among small stocks rather than large stocks if window dressing is a major source of its effect.

The January effect is also found in the Korean stock market. Choi and Kim (1994) report the January effect by using the Korea Composite Stock Price Index (KOSPI) and size indices from 1980 to 1992. They find that the January effect of middle-cap and small-cap indices is prominent especially in the first 10 days of January. Yoon and Lee (2009) examine whether the January effect exists in both KOSPI and Korea Securities Dealers Automated Quotations (KOSDAQ) stocks by using the KOSPI and size indices from 1980 to 2002 and the KOSDAQ and size indices from 2002 to 2006. Although the January effect is found in the Korean stock markets, only the January return on the small-cap index is statistically significant in the KOSPI market. However, the authors do not find any statistically significant January return in the KOSDAQ market, likely because of the short sample period.[1]

In summary, the January effect in the Korean stock market cannot be explained by the tax-loss selling hypothesis. Consistent with earlier findings, the January effect is prominent for small stocks in the Korean stock market. However, it is not clear whether the January effect is statistically significant in the KOSDAQ market.

---

[1] Sonu and Choi (2011) provide a comprehensive survey of seasonal anomalies in the Korean stock market.

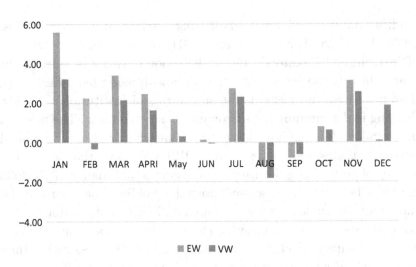

Figure 3.1.   Monthly EW and VW Returns in the KOSPI Market from 1980 to 2013

3.1.2.   *January Effect in Korean Stock Market*

According to Figure 3.1, the January effect exists in EW and VW monthly returns in the KOSPI market from 1980 to 2013. Both EW and VW returns are highest in January, but the EW January return is much higher than the VW January return. EW and VW returns are very low or negative in August and September. Historically, in the US market, September and October have low stock market returns and November has high returns. The Korean stock market shows a seasonal pattern similar to the US market. The EW return in December is close to 0, but the VW December return is 1.85%. Thus, the seasonal patterns of EW and VW returns are similar in January but different in December.

The EW monthly return in the KOSDAQ stock market shows a similar seasonal pattern for the period 1996–2013 as in the KOSPI stock market. However, the EW January return in the KOSDAQ market is much higher than in the KOSPI market. The VW January return is only 1.56%, which is only the fifth highest return among the 12 calendar months in the KOSDAQ market. EW and VW monthly

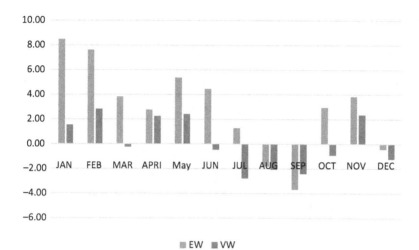

Figure 3.2. Monthly EW and VW Returns in the KOSDAQ Market from 1996 to 2013

returns in August and September are lower than in any other months. Both the VW and EW December return are negative in the KOSDAQ market (see Figure 3.2).

In summary, we find the January effect in the Korean stock markets. Both the KOSPI and KOSDAQ markets show typical seasonal patterns, especially in the case of EW monthly returns. First, the January effect is more prominent in terms of EW monthly returns. In the case of VW monthly returns, however, the January return is not the highest among the 12 calendar months in the KOSDAQ market. Second, the EW and VW monthly returns are negative in August and September in both the KOSPI and KOSDAQ markets.

Figure 3.3 presents EW returns in January from 1980 to 2013 for the KOSPI market. The highest January return is 45.3% in 1998 during the Asian financial crisis. When we divide the entire sample period into periods before and after 1998, the average January return before 1998 is 4.60% and 4.13% after 1998. The January return does not seem to be significantly weaker after 1998. However, the January effect has recently been weaker since the average January return is −0.77% from 2006 to 2013.

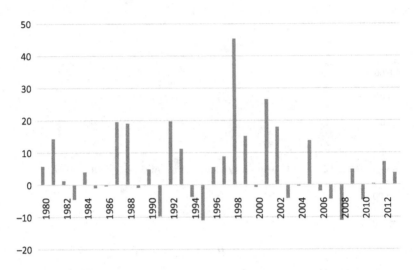

Figure 3.3. EW January Returns (%) in the KOSPI Market for 1980–2013

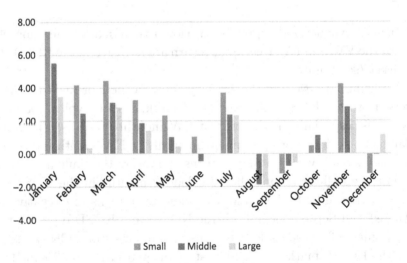

Figure 3.4. Monthly EW Returns on Size Portfolio in the KOSPI Market from 1981 to 2013

3.1.3. *Relation between January Return and Size*

Figure 3.4 presents seasonal returns based on the size portfolios in the KOSPI market from 1981 to 2013. Size portfolios are formed based on market capitalization of a firm in December of the previous year.

Small, middle, and large portfolios are formed based on the 30th and 70th percentiles. For example, the small portfolio in 2000 consists of all stocks with market capitalization less than the 30th percentile of market capitalization in December 1999. The large portfolio in 2000 consists of all stocks whose market capitalization is larger than the 70th percentile in December 1999.

Consistent with the empirical results from other countries' stock markets, January returns appear to be negatively related to size. The small portfolio has the highest January return, while the large portfolio has the lowest January return. Regardless of size, however, the January return is highest among 12 calendar months according to Figure 3.4. The small portfolio has a negative average return in December, while the large portfolio has a positive average return in December. Thus, since individual investors are more likely to hold small stocks, the negative December return and positive January return of the small portfolio appear to be consistent with the tax-loss selling hypothesis. However, since there is no capital gains tax in Korea, the tax-loss selling hypothesis cannot explain the seasonal behavior of the small portfolio.

3.1.4. *Effect of Aggregate M/B Ratios on January Return*

Since aggregate M/B ratios have predictive power for subsequent returns, we examine seasonal monthly patterns following high and low M/B months. If the aggregate M/B ratio in December of year $t-1$ is higher than the median, year t is classified as the year following the high M/B month. Since the rank of an aggregate M/B ratio in month t is determined by sorting all available aggregate M/B ratios up to month t, this sorting process yields a different number for high and low M/B months. Out of 33 years of the testing period, years following high (low) M/B months number 21 (11).

Figure 3.5 shows EW January returns following low and high M/B months by using all KOSPI and KOSDAQ stocks. The average January return is 11.07% following low M/B months and 3.39% following high M/B months. Thus, the January effect is much

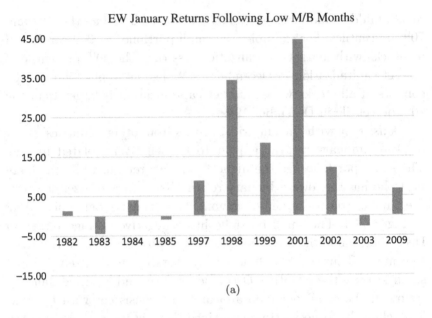

(a)

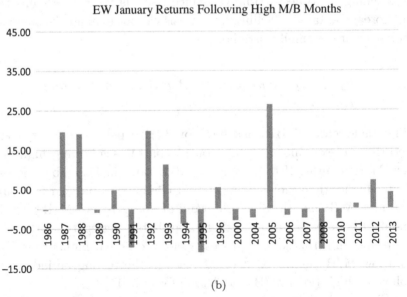

(b)

Figure 3.5.   January Returns Following Low and High M/B Months for all
KOSPI and KOSDAQ Stocks: 1981–2013

stronger following low M/B months than following high M/B months. EW January returns are 34.25% in 1998 and 44.5% in 2001 following low M/B months. These 2 years' extremely high January returns contribute a substantial portion of high January returns following low M/B months. However, the average January return excluding these 2 years is 4.78% following low M/B months, which is still higher than 3.39% for January returns following high M/B months. The relative frequency of negative January returns is also low following low M/B months. For example, negative EW January returns appear only three times, in 1983, 1985, and 2003, out of 11 years following low M/B months, but are seen 11 times out of 22 years following high M/B months. Furthermore, the average negative January return is −2.73% following low M/B months, which is higher than −4.32% following high M/B months.

3.1.5. *Trading Behavior of Investor Types*

The trading behavior of investor types may be related to the January effect. If investor types show a systematic seasonal trading pattern and can influence stock prices, the January effect can be attributed to the trade imbalance of a specific investor type. Figure 3.6 presents EW monthly returns and the trade imbalance of investor types among stocks in the KOSPI market (with *Forp* $\geq$ 5%), of which foreign investors account for at least 5% of trading value each year. The proportion of foreign investors' trading value is measured annually by foreign investors' annual trading value divided by total annual trading value. *ForIMB* (*InsIMB*) indicates the monthly trade imbalance of foreign investors (domestic institutional investors), as defined in Section 2.1.4 of Chapter 2. The right-hand number in Figure 3.6 indicates the trade imbalance (%) of investor types.

The seasonal trading pattern of *ForIMB* is consistent with seasonal monthly returns. *ForIMB* is highest in January and lowest in August, which coincides with the seasonal pattern of EW monthly return shown in Figure 3.6. *ForIMB* tends to decrease from January to December. In contrast, the trade imbalance of *IndIMB*, defined as the trade imbalance of individual investors, shows the opposite

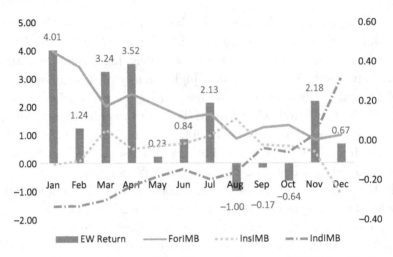

Figure 3.6.　Trade Imbalance (%) of Investor Types and EW Monthly Returns (%) for Stocks with $Forp \geq 5\%$ in the KOSPI Market from 1995 to 2013

trade imbalance of *ForIMB*. Individual investors tend to sell stocks in January and buy stocks in December, thereby providing liquidity to foreign investors. *InsIMB*, defined as the trade imbalance of domestic institutional investors, also shows a similar pattern in trade imbalance as *IndIMB* except for December. Domestic institutional investors are also liquidity providers rather than price takers. However, the trade imbalance of domestic institutional investors appears to be weaker than that of individual investors as shown in Figure 3.6. *ForIMB* is positive in all months. Thus, the buying pressure for foreign investors is stronger among stocks that foreign investors actively trade. On the other hand, *IndIMB* is negative before September but turns positive beginning in September.

Table 3.1 presents the average monthly trade imbalance of investor types from 1995 to 2013. In the case of stocks with $Forp \geq 5\%$, the average monthly *ForIMB* is 0.15%. Thus, foreign investors tend to be net buyers of stocks with $Forp \geq 5\%$ from 1995 to 2013. This is why foreign investors' net buying value is, on average, positive in Figure 3.6. However, *ForIMB* is −0.03% for stocks with $Forp < 5\%$. On the other hand, *IndIMB* is, on average, 0.14% per month for total stocks from 1995 to 2013. Individual investors, however,

Table 3.1. Average Monthly Trade Imbalance of Investor Types from 1995 to 2013

	Total Stocks	$Forp \geq 5\%$	$Forp < 5\%$
IndIMB (%)	0.138	−0.136	0.2180
ForIMB (%)	0.006	0.154	−0.0298
InsIMB (%)	−0.107	−0.042	−0.1658

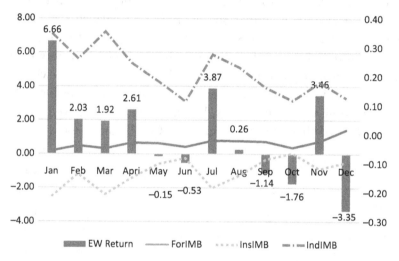

Figure 3.7. Trade Imbalance (%) of Investor Types and EW Monthly Returns (%) for Stocks with *Forp* < 5% in the KOSPI Market from 1995 to 2013

tend to sell more stocks than they buy for stocks with *Forp* ≥ 5%. Institutional investors tend to sell more stocks with both *Forp* < 5% and *Forp* ≥ 5%.

The trading patterns of investor types for stocks with *Forp* < 5% differ from those for stocks with *Forp* ≥ 5%. First, Figure 3.7 shows that the January effect is more prominent for stocks with *Forp* < 5%. Second, *IndIMB* tends to be high from January to March and low in June, October, and December, although *IndIMB* is positive across all calendar months. Third, both *InsIMB* and *ForIMB* are negative in most calendar months. However, it is difficult to argue that both domestic institutional investors and foreign investors are liquidity providers among stocks with *Forp* < 5% because the trade proportion of foreign and domestic institutional investors is usually lower than 1% and 5%, respectively. Since individual investors predominantly buy and sell those stocks, the interaction of investor types is not important in determining the prices of stocks with *Forp* < 5%. Figure 3.7 suggests that the trade imbalance of individual investors is strongly positive in January for stocks that individual investors dominantly trade.

It is interesting to examine whether domestic institutional investors also have a similar seasonal trading pattern for stocks of which institutional investors account for high proportion of trading value. Figure 3.8 shows that domestic institutional investors exhibit different seasonal patterns of trade imbalance for stocks (with *Insp* ≥ 30%) of which domestic institutional investors account for at least 30% of trading value.[2] First, *InsIMB* in January is positive but not as high as *InsIMB* from February to June. On the other hand, *ForIMB*

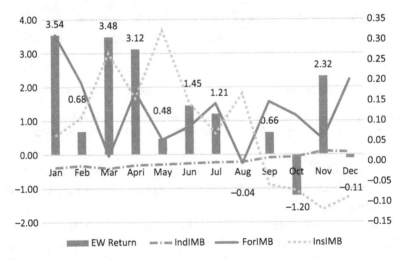

Figure 3.8.   Trade Imbalance of Investor Types and EW Monthly Returns for Stocks with *Insp* ≥ 30% in the KOSPI Market from 1995 to 2013

---

[2] According to Figure 2.1 and Table 2.4 of Chapter 2, foreign investors tend to own only limited firms' stocks, characterized as large, high M/B, and profitable stocks. On the other hand, domestic institutional investors tend to own much broader listed firms' stocks.

in January is highest among all calendar months and is even higher than *InsIMB* in January. Thus, the high January return in Figure 3.8 is more likely to be attributed to the net buying of foreign investors. Second, the January effect in stocks with *Insp* $\geq$ 30% is not as strong as in stocks with both *Forp* $\geq$ 5% and Forp $<$ 5%.

In summary, we find seasonal trading patterns of foreign investors and individual investors related to the January effect. Who causes the January effect? For the stocks with *Forp* $\geq$ 5% that three investor types interactively trade, foreign investors are net buyers in January while individual investors are net sellers. In the case of stocks with *Forp* $<$ 5% that individual investors predominantly trade, individual investors tend to be net buyers in January while the other two investor types tend to sell those stocks in January. Since the January effect is stronger for stocks with *Forp* $<$ 5%, the trading behavior of individual investors may be responsible for the January effect. However, stocks with *Forp* $<$ 5% are those that foreign investors are not willing to trade since both *ForIMB* and *InsIMB* are negative in most calendar months, as shown in Figure 3.7. Furthermore, since stocks with *Forp* $<$ 5% are more likely to be small and less profitable (see Table 2.4 of Chapter 2), they may face shallow market depths. Therefore, our empirical results are not sufficient to argue who mainly causes the January effect, although domestic institutional investors are least likely to cause high January returns.

3.1.6.   *Trading Behavior Following High/Low M/B Months*

In this section, we will study whether investor types' trading behavior following low M/B months differs from that following high M/B months. Figure 3.9 shows that the January effect occurs only following low M/B months from 1995 to 2013. The EW January return is 16.69% following low M/B months but -0.36% following high M/B years. Thus, the January effect is found in the KOSPI market only following low M/B months, which are 7 out of 19 years.

The trade imbalance of individual investors in January is 0.61% following low M/B months. Thus, the trading behavior of individual investors appears to influence January returns if their positive trade

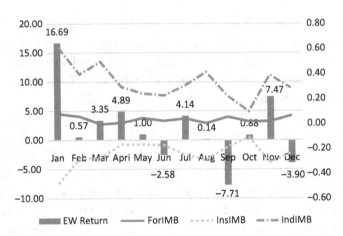

Figure 3.9. Trade Imbalance of Investor Types and EW Monthly Returns Following Low M/B Months in the KOSPI Market from 1995 to 2013

imbalance affects stock prices. In contrast, domestic institutional investors exhibit trading behavior that is opposite of individual investors. Domestic institutional investors are net sellers in January following low M/B months. On the other hand, the trade imbalance of foreign investors is positive in January but much lower than that of individual investors; 0.07% of *ForIMB* in January following low M/B months indicates that foreign investors are net buyers in January, which is almost the same as the 0.06% of *ForIMB* in December. Thus, weak net buying pressure by foreign investors does not seem to explain the January effect in the KOSPI market. In general, the trading behavior of individual investors is more likely to explain high January returns following low M/B months.

According to Figure 3.10, *IndIMB* is −0.03% in January and the January return is −0.36% following high M/B months. There is neither a January effect nor net buying pressure of individual investors following high M/B months. A low aggregate M/B month may be coincidental with the stock market decline. If so, individual investors, as contrarian investors, are more likely to be net buyers in January following low M/B months. In contrast, individual investors will not be net buyers of stocks following high M/B months. Nevertheless, it is puzzling why the January return is higher than in any other month.

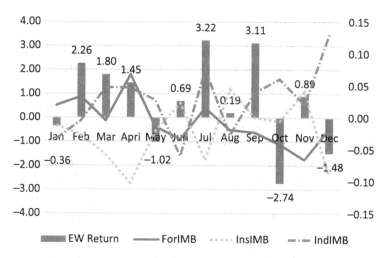

Figure 3.10. Trade Imbalance of Investor Types and EW Monthly Returns Following High M/B Months in the KOSPI Market from 1995 to 2013

Since Korea does not have a capital gains tax, the tax-loss selling hypothesis fails to explain this phenomenon. Individual investors tend to maintain strong buying pressure in all calendar months except for October following low M/B months. For example, the average trade imbalance of individual investors is 0.33% following low M/B months, while it is only 0.03% following high M/B months.

In addition, the trade imbalance of all investor types is low following high M/B months. The highest trade imbalance of individual investors is only 0.13% in December when the EW monthly return is lowest. The highest monthly return following high M/B months is 3.22% in July, which is lower than the 4.14% July return following low M/B months.

In short, the January return is, on average, 16.69% following low M/B months and −0.36% following high M/B months. As a result, the January effect exists only following low M/B months when individual investors exhibit strong buying pressure. However, there is no strong buying pressure of individual investors following high M/B months. In addition, the January effect appears to be stronger in the case of stocks with *Forp* < 5%, which individual investors predominantly trade.

3.2. January Barometer

Cooper *et al.* (2006) document that the January return is a predictor of market returns for the subsequent 11 months of the year after controlling for macroeconomic and political variables, and investor sentiment. They find that when the Center for Research in Security Prices (CRSP) equally weighted return is positive, the average EW return for the following 11 months is 14.17% for 1940–2003. The EW return for the next 11 months averages −3.87% following negative EW January return. According to them, the published street lore regarding the January barometer can be found as early as 1973. Dzhabarov and Ziemba (2015) also confirm the January barometer effect by using the longer period of 1940–2010.

We examine the existence of the January barometer effect in the Korean stock market by using equally weighted average returns of all KOSPI and KOSDAQ stocks from 1980 to 2013. According to Figure 3.11, when January returns are positive, the average 11-month return is 22.4%, which is much higher than the 8.5% 11-month return when January returns are negative. Thus, the January barometer effect is also found in the Korean stock market. Figure 3.11(a) shows the 11-month returns following positive January returns. We can obtain more than 90% for the 11-month returns in 1987, 1999, and 2005 if we invest stocks in February following positive January returns. However, there is also a serious decline in 11-month returns in 1990, 1997, and 2002. Returns are negative four times in the 11-month holding period for the 20 years of positive January returns.

Figure 3.11(b) shows the 11-month returns following negative January returns. In general, the 11-month holding period returns are not as high as those following positive January return years. Eleven-month returns are higher than 10% in 5 out of 14 years with negative January returns. In contrast, 12 out of the 20 years with positive January returns show returns higher than 10% for the remaining 11 months. When we eliminate years following low M/B months, the average 11-month return is 22.2% following positive January returns and 7.9% following negative January returns. As a result, the January return appears to predict the subsequent 11-month returns regardless of low or high M/B months.

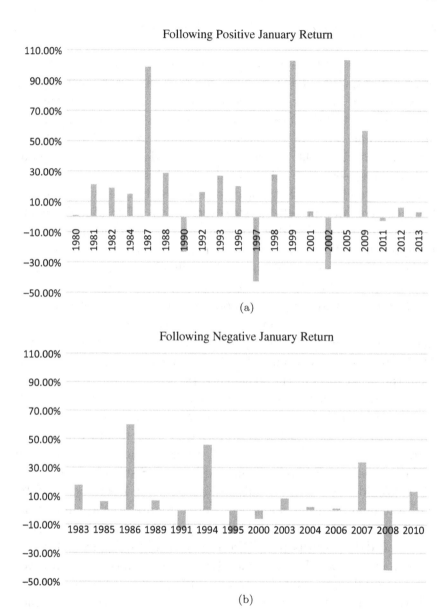

Figure 3.11.   11-Month Holding Period Return in Non-January Months for All KOSPI and KOSDAQ Stocks: 1980–2013

3.3.   Weekend Effect

French (1980) finds that the average daily return on Monday is unusually negative. Laknonishok and Maberly (1990) argue that investors tend to place heavy sell orders on Monday, resulting in negative returns. Kamara (1995) shows that individual trading is an important cause of the negative Monday returns. In contrast, Sias and Starks (1995) suggest that the Monday effect is more prominent in securities where institutional investors more actively participate and argue that delays in reporting bad news might cause the negative Monday effect. However, a few other studies report negative returns on Tuesday. For example, Ho (1990) documents that the stock markets of Australia, Hong Kong, Japan, Korea, Singapore, Malaysia, Philippines, Taiwan, and Thailand have negative returns on Tuesdays. This Tuesday effect may be related to time zone differences. However, Schwert (2003) examines the weekend effect for a more extended period and argues that the weekend effect disappeared after 1978. He reports a negative Monday return over 1885–1977, but the weekend effect has not been significantly different from the other days of the week since 1978.

Yun *et al.* (1994) find the weekend effect in the Korean stock market for 1980–1992. Kim and Chung (2004) find the lowest return on Monday for 1995–2002. However, they also report the highest return on Wednesday in the KOSPI market, which differs from the highest return on Friday documented in the US stock market.

We divide data into two sub-periods based on December 5, 1998, with the final Saturday trading in Korea. Figure 3.12(a) shows that the Tuesday daily return is negative and the Monday return is lower than the daily returns from Wednesday to Saturday from 1980 to December 5, 1998. However, the Monday return has not been lower since December 5, 1998, as shown in Figure 3.12(b). The Monday return is 0.09% from December 7, 1998 to 2013, which is higher than the 0.05% Wednesday return. For both sub-periods, the Tuesday return is negative but not statistically significant in the Korean stock market. As a result, the weekend effect is not as prominent as the January effect in the Korean stock market.

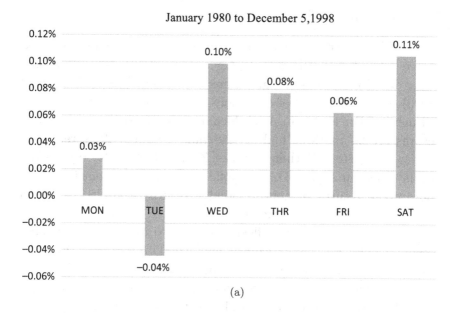

(a)

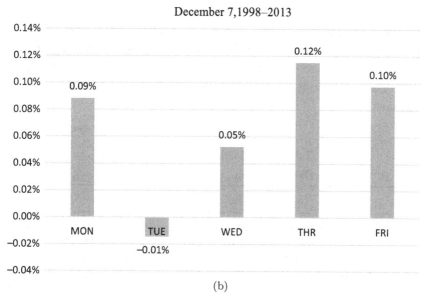

(b)

Figure 3.12.   Weekend Effect and EW Returns in the KOSPI and KOSDAQ Markets

3.4. Holiday Effect

The holiday effect is an anomaly showing that the trading day just before a holiday has a much higher average daily return than any other day. Zweig (1986), Lakonishok and Smidt (1988), and Ariel (1990) provide evidence of extremely high pre-holiday returns in the US market. For example, Ariel documents that average pre-holiday returns are 24 times as high as the value-weighted daily return of all New York Stock Exchange stocks. Ziemba (1994) also reports the holiday effect in Japan. The pre-holiday returns are about five times the average returns of non-pre-holiday returns from 1949 to 1988 based on Nikkei stock average returns.

We examine the holiday effect from 1981 to 2013 by using equally weighted daily returns of KOSPI and KOSDAQ stocks. Table 3.2 demonstrates the holiday effect by separately measuring daily returns on 5 trading days around holidays with dummy variables. For example, Day_{-1} is a dummy variable equal to 1 when the day is the last trading day before a holiday. The average pre-holiday return is 3.6 times the average return on the days excluding the 5 trading days around holidays. The pre-holiday return is about 0.143% higher than the 0.054% average daily return, which is statistically significant at 10%. There are no extreme daily returns on the other 4 days around holidays.

Table 3.2.　Holiday Effect: 1981–2013

$$R(\%) = \alpha + \beta_1 Day_{-3} + \beta_2 Day_{-2} + \beta_3 Day_{-1} + \beta_4 Day_{+1} + \beta_5 Day_{+2}$$

	α	β_1	β_2	β_3	β_4	β_5
Total	0.0548***	0.0027	−0.0716	0.1430*	0.0636	−0.0423
	(3.57)	(0.04)	(−0.57)	(1.94)	(1.08)	(−0.57)
Following Low	0.0829***	−0.0311	−0.2700*	0.0654	0.1520	0.0685
M/B Months	(2.99)	(−0.22)	(−1.92)	(0.48)	(1.15)	(0.50)
Following High	0.0394**	0.0218	0.0276	0.1830**	0.0416	−0.0989
M/B Months	(2.15)	(0.24)	(0.31)	(2.12)	(0.72)	(−1.14)

Notes: ( ) indicates t value. *, **, and *** indicate the 10%, 5%, and 1% statistical significance level, respectively.

When high and low M/B months are defined as the aggregate M/B ratio of the previous month, the holiday effect is only found in the month following a high M/B month. The pre-holiday return is 0.183% following high M/B months, which is 5.6 times as high as the average daily returns excluding the 5 days around holidays. The average daily return excluding the 5 trading days around holidays is 0.0829% following low M/B months, which is also higher than the 0.0394% average daily return following high M/B months. In summary, the holiday effect exists in the Korean stock market, but the pre-holiday return is significantly positive only following high M/B months.

References

Ackert, L. F. and G. Athanassakos, 2000, Institutional Investors, Analyst Following, and the January Anomaly, *Journal of Business Finance & Accounting* 27, 469–485.

Berges, A., J. McConnell, and G. Schlarbaum, 1984, The Turn of the Year in Canada, *Journal of Finance* 39(1), 195–192.

Booth, D. G. and D. Keim, 2000, Is There Still a January Effect? In D. B. Keim and W. T. Ziemba (eds.), *Security Market Imperfection in World Wide Equity Markets*, Cambridge University Press, pp. 169–178.

Choi, H. S. and S. H. Kim, 1994, Regularities in Monthly Stock Returns in Korea, In S. H. Sonu, Y. S. Yun *et al.* (eds.), *Stock Price Volatility and Anomaly*, Hakhyungsa, Seoul, Korea, pp. 33–51 (in Korean).

D'Mello, R., S. P. Ferris, and C. Y. Hwang, 2003, The Tax-Loss Selling Hypothesis, Market Liquidity, and Price Pressure around the Turn-of-the Year, *Journal of Financial Markets* 6(1), 73–98.

Dyl, E. and E. D. Maberly, 1992, Odd-Lot Transactions around the Turn of the Year and the January Effect, *Journal of Financial and Quantitative Analysis* 27(4), 591–604.

Dzhabarov, C. and W. T. Ziemba, 2015, Seasonal Anomalies, in L. Zacks (eds.), *The Handbook of Equity Market Anomalies: Translating Market Inefficiencies into Effective Investment Strategies*, John Wiley & Sons, Hoboken, New Jersey.

Easterday, K., P. Sen, and J. Stephan, 2009, The Persistence of the Small Firm/January Effect: Is it Consistent with Investor's Learning and Arbitrage Efforts? *The Quarterly Review of Economics and Finance* 49, 1172–1193.

Fountas, S. and K. N. Segredakis, 2002, Emerging Stock Markets Return Seasonality: The January Effect and the Tax-Loss Selling Hypothesis, *Applied Financial Economics* 12, 291–299.

Gu, A. Y., 2003, The Declining January Effect: Evidences from the US Equity Markets, *The Quarterly Review of Economics and Finance* 43, 395–404.

Gultekin, M. N. and N. B. Gultekin, 1983, Stock Market Seasonality and the Turn of the Tax-Year Effect: Information Evidence, *Journal of Financial Economics* 12, 469–481.

Haugen, R. and J. Lakonishok, 1988, *The Incredible January Effect: The Stock Market's Unsolved Mystery*, Dow Jones Irwin Publishers.

Kim, D. H. and C. H. Chung, 2003, The Day of the Week Effect on Stock Market Volatility: Evidence from the Korean Stock Market, *Journal of Financial Engineering* 3, 43–60 (in Korean)

Kato, K. and J. Schallheim, 1985, Seasonal and Size Anomalies in the Japanese Stock Market, *Journal of Financial and Quantitative Analysis* 20(02), 243–260.

Keim, D., 1983, Size Related Anomalies and Stock Return Seasonality: Further Empirical Evidence, *Journal of Financial Economics* 12, 3–12.

Keim, D., 1989, Trading Patterns, Bid-Ask Spreads, and Estimated Security Returns: The Case of Common Stock Returns at the Turn of the Year, *Journal of Financial Economics* 25, 75–98.

Keim, D. and W. T. Ziemba, 2000, *Security Market Imperfection in World Wide Equity Markets*, Cambridge University Press.

Mehdian, S. and M. J. Perry, 2002, Anomalies in US Equity Markets: A Re-examination of the January Effect, *Applied Financial Economics* 12, 141–145.

Ng, L. and Q. Wang, 2004, Institutional Trading and the Turn-of-the Year Effect, *Journal of Financial Economics* 74, 343–366.

O'Neal, E. S., 2001, *Window Dressing and Equity Fund*, Babcock Graduate School of Management, Wake Forest University.

Oritiz, C., J. Sarto, and L. Vincente, 2012, Portfolio in Disguise? Window Dressing in Bond Fund Holdings, *Journal of Banking and Finance* 36(2), 418–427.

Poterba, J. and S. J. Weisbenner, 2001, Capital Gains Tax Rules, Tax-Loss Trading, and Turn-of-the-Year Returns, *Journal of Finance* 56(1), 353–368.

Reinganum, M. R., 1983. The Anomalous Stock Market Behavior of Small Firms in January: Empirical Test for Tax-loss Selling Effect, *Journal of Financial Economics* 12, 89–104.

Ritter, J., 1988, The Buying and Selling Behavior of Individual Investors at the Turn of the Year, *Journal of Finance* 43, 701–707.

Roll, R., 1983, Vas Ist Dat: The Turn of the Year Effect and the Return Premia of Small Firms, *Journal of Portfolio Management* 9(winter), 18–28.

Rozeff, M. and W. Kinney, 1976, Capital Market Seasonality: The Case of Stock Returns, *Journal of Financial Economics* 3, 379–402.

Schwert, G. W., 2003, Anomalies and Market Efficiency, In G. Constantinides, M. Harris, and R. Stulz (eds.), *Handbook of the Economics of Finance*, Elservier/North-Holland, Amsterdam, Boston.

Sonu, S. and H. Choi, 2011, Capital Market Anomalies in Korea, *Asian Review of Financial Research* 24, 1231–1284.

Yoon, H. G. and Y. H. Lee, 2009, A Revisit on the Monthly Effect in Korean Stock Market, *Korean Association of Logos Management Symposium*, pp. 271–294 (in Korean).

Chapter 4

Cross-Sectional Anomalies

Asset pricing models suggest that a stock's performance should not ultimately depend on the stock's characteristics but on its risk. Academicians, however, have documented several anomalies related to size, book-to-market (B/M) ratio, past returns and so on which cannot be explained by asset pricing models. Several hypotheses and empirical results in the academic literature have been provided to explain the source of these anomalies. On the other hand, practitioners of the asset management industry have paid attention to these anomalies since the anomalies imply that, based on their characteristics, certain categories of stocks can consistently outperform others. According to Bernstein (1995), the investment world developed investment products to take advantage of anomalies long before the academic world agreed that anomalies even exist. However, styling investments based on size and B/M ratio began to spread rapidly within the institutional investor community during the 1980s when academic research confirmed the persistence and robustness of the anomalies.

Academic research of anomalies has sometimes inspired the investment business world with the insightful intuition of investment management. For example, Dimensional Fund Advisors, which is recognized as a successful investment company, developed its investment strategy based on academic research. Dimensional Fund Advisors' strategy is to achieve high expected returns by taking advantage of the size effect and the B/M effect. The firm created international small-stock and value-stock investment funds based on academic findings that both small stocks and value stocks outperform the market in the global stock markets. Since the Dimensional Fund Advisors believes that the stock market is efficient, it does not make efforts toward stock-picking. The company continues to apply new academic findings and insights to the development of investment strategies and the improvement of its portfolio management. This case indicates that understanding anomalies is important to the investment business world.

This chapter will comprehensively examine several anomalies, including size, B/M ratio effect, long-term reversal, short-term momentum, and turnover ratio effect. We also examine whether these anomalies are related to the time series aggregate market-to-book (M/B) ratios and the trading behavior of investor types.

4.1. Size Effect

4.1.1. *Literature Review*

Banz (1981) finds that stocks with lower market capitalization tend to have higher average returns. After Banz's finding of the size effect in 1981, several studies have documented that the size effect became weaker or disappeared after 1980 in the US (Fama and French 1992; Eleswarapu and Reinganum, 1993; Dichev, 1998; Chan et al., 2000; Amihud, 2002; Roll, 2003) and in the UK (Dimson and Marsh, 1999; Michou et al., 2010). Similar results have been found in global stock markets as well. Barry et al. (2002) do not find the size effect in 35 emerging markets and Fama and French (2012) find no size effect in four regions after observing stocks in 23 countries from November 1990 to September 2010: North America, Europe, Japan, and Asia Pacific excluding Japan.

Contrary to these findings, Hou and Dijk (2010) argue that the size effect still exists. They use a complex econometric model to assess the cause of the size effect and claim that US stocks of smaller firms have not had higher returns since the early 1980s because of profitability "shocks": Smaller firms had negative earnings surprises and larger firms had positive earnings surprises during this time. Hou and Dijk argue that had it not been for these inverse earnings surprises of smaller and larger firms, shareholders in smaller firms would have had higher returns than those of larger firms since the early 1980s. Based on this argument, they claim that the size effect still exists. The disappearance of the size effect is due to the sample's specific period when small firms' earnings happened to be unexpectedly poor.

On the other hand, by using the Fama and MacBeth (1973) regression, earlier studies such as Kim (1994) and Kam (1997) find that size does not have predictive power in explaining cross-sectional differences in stock returns in the Korean stock market. However, Song and Lee (1997) document that differences in monthly returns between small stocks and large stocks have significant power to explain time series differences in returns that are not explained by market risk during 1980–1995. Kim and Yun (1999) confirm that size and B/M are important variables in explaining cross-sectional differences in stock returns listed on the Korean Stock Exchange (KRX) from January 1980 to March 1997. Kim and Kim (2000) confirm the usefulness of the Fama–French three-factor model over the sample period 1990–1997 but show that the size anomaly is subject to new listing bias. However, they provide evidence that the B/M effect is still strong and robust after controlling for new listing bias and survivorship bias. On the other hand, Yun *et al.* (2009) find that the size effect has statistical power to explain the cross-sectional stock returns in Korea while the B/M effect is not statistically significant during 1991–2007. Instead of the B/M effect, liquidity proxy measured by a turnover ratio, is powerful in explaining stock returns. However, Kim (2009) provides evidence that the B/M effect is statistically significant from 1988 to 2007. He documents that small and value stocks have positive abnormal returns after controlling for risk factors by using the Fama–French three factor model.

4.1.2. *Size Effect in Korean Stock Market*

We examine the size effect in Korea by constructing size portfolios. All stocks in the KOSPI and KOSDAQ markets are classified annually into small, middle, and large portfolios based on the 30th

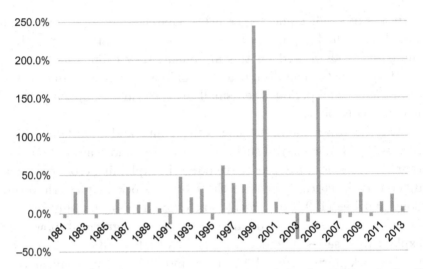

Figure 4.1.   Annual Returns on the S–L Strategy, Defined as Buying the Small Portfolio and Shorting the Large Portfolio in the KOSPI and KOSDAQ Markets: 1981–2013

Notes: All stocks in the Korea Exchange (KOSPI and KOSDAQ) markets are classified annually into small, middle, and large portfolios based on the 30th and 70th percentiles of market capitalization of all KOSPI stocks in December of the previous year. The annual holding period returns from January 1981 to December 2013 are calculated by using the monthly EW returns of size portfolios. The annual holding period return of the strategy is defined as buying the small portfolio and shorting the large portfolio from 1981 to 2013.

and 70th percentiles of market capitalization of all KOSPI stocks in December of year $t - 1$. For example, if the market capitalization of a stock is smaller than or equal to the 30th percentile, it belongs to the small portfolio. The annual returns from January to December of year t are calculated by using the monthly equally weighted (EW) returns of size portfolios. The annual holding period return of the strategy is defined as buying the small portfolio and shorting the large portfolio (S–L strategy) from 1981 to 2013. Figure 4.1 shows that the size effect is observed in the Korean stock markets for the entire sample period. First, the annual return of the small portfolio, on average, exceeds that of the large portfolio by 28.0%. Second, The S–L strategy yields positive annual returns more frequently than negative returns. Positive annual returns of the S–L strategy

Table 4.1. Average Monthly Returns of Size Portfolios in the KOSPI and KOSDAQ Markets

Portfolio	Jan. 1980– Dec. 2013	Jan. 1980– April 1991	May 1991– Aug. 2002	Sep. 2002– Dec. 2013
Small Portfolio	2.65	2.52	3.90	1.50
	(10.74)	(7.71)	(14.75)	(7.91)
Middle Portfolio	1.28	2.02	1.13	0.77
	(9.08)	(6.73)	(11.90)	(7.59)
Large Portfolio	0.92	1.60	0.18	1.05*
	(8.60)	(6.99)	(10.95)	(7.15)
S–L Strategy	1.72***	0.92**	3.72***	0.46
	(8.38)	(4.87)	(12.37)	(4.94)

Note: Parentheses indicate the standard deviation of monthly returns *, **, and *** indicate 10%, 5%, and 1% significance levels for the S–L strategy, respectively.

have been obtained in 22 of the 33 years of the sample period. Furthermore, the magnitude of the strategy's positive annual returns is much larger than that of its negative annual returns. However, Figure 4.1 shows that the size effect tends to diminish after 2000, except for 2005 showing a 149.7% annual return of the S–L strategy.

The sample period is divided into three sub-periods to examine whether the size effect gradually decreases as most academic papers have documented. As shown in Table 4.1, the small portfolio has 2.65% of average EW monthly return and the large portfolio has 0.92% for the entire period. The difference is 1.72%, which is statistically significant at the 1% level. The size effect is also statistically significant for the first and second sub-periods. The second sub-period covers the Asian financial crisis in 1997–1998. The average monthly return of the S–L strategy increased from 1.99% in 1997 to 11.1% in 1999 when the Korean economy recovered sharply after the Asian financial crisis. The average monthly return of the S–L strategy, however, is only 0.46% for the third sub-period of September 2002 to December 2013. The monthly return of the middle portfolio is lower than that of the large portfolio for the third sub-period. As a result, the size effect has been weaker since September 2002, which is consistent with earlier literature that examines the size effect in the US and other markets.

4.1.3. Relation between Size Effect and Aggregate M/B Ratios

To examine the effect of time series aggregate M/B ratios on the size effect, we semiannually classify the holding period of size portfolios into two periods based on the aggregate M/B ratios discussed in Chapter 2. If the aggregate M/B ratio in July of year t is lower (higher) than the median of all aggregate M/B ratios, the subsequent 6 months from August of year t to January of year $t+1$ are classified as the period following the low (high) M/B month. Similarly, if the aggregate M/B ratio in January of the current year is lower (higher) than the median, the following 6 months from February to July are classified as the period following the low (high) M/B month.

Table 4.2 shows that the size effect exists following both low M/B months and high M/B months for the entire sample period. The S–L strategy yields 1.66% of monthly return following low M/B months, while it yields 1.31% following high M/B months. In general, the average monthly returns on size portfolios tend to be higher following low M/B months than following high M/B months, which confirms that stock returns tend to be higher following low M/B months, as discussed in Chapter 2. However, the size effect is not persistent for the sub-periods. The monthly return of the S–L strategy is not statistically significant for the first sub-period and even yields a negative monthly return following low M/B months for the third sub-period.

Although the monthly return of the S–L strategy is statistically significant following high M/B months for the third sub-period, it is smaller for the third sub-period than for the other two sub-periods. The average return of the S–L strategy is much higher for the second sub-period covering May 1991–August 2002, which includes the Asian financial crisis and information technology (IT) bubble. The standard deviations of monthly returns for the size portfolios as well as the standard deviation of the S–L strategy are much higher for the second sub-period as well. In short, the size effect exists in the KRX market but has been weaker since 2000, which is consistent with the empirical results of other countries' stock exchange markets.

Table 4.2. Average Monthly Return of Size Portfolios Following High or Low M/B Months from August 1981 to December 2013

Classification	Aug. 1981– Dec. 2013		Aug. 1981– April. 1991		May 1991– Aug. 2002		Sep. 2002– Dec. 2013	
M/B ratio	Low M/B months	High M/B months	Low M/B months	High M/B months	Low M/B months	High M/B months	Low M/B months	High M/B months
Observation	149	240	42	75	63	69	44	96
Small	3.25	1.90	1.41	2.75	5.79	1.87	1.37	1.25
Portfolio	(12.22)	(9.42)	(3.99)	(9.13)	(16.91)	(11.90)	(8.35)	(7.48)
Middle	1.88	0.91	1.45	1.98	2.39	0.41	1.56	0.45
Portfolio	(10.97)	(7.90)	(3.92)	(7.77)	(14.95)	(8.79)	(8.76)	(7.29)
Large	1.59	0.58	0.62	1.73	2.10	−0.73	1.78	0.63
Portfolio	(11.29)	(7.47)	(4.17)	(8.11)	(15.93)	(7.21)	(7.39)	(7.03)
S–L	1.66**	1.31***	0.79	1.02	3.69*	2.60**	−0.41	0.62*
Strategy	(10.95)	(7.25)	(3.61)	(5.85)	(15.86)	(10.95)	(5.15)	(4.26)

Notes: The holding period of size portfolios is semiannually classified into two periods based on the aggregate M/B ratios discussed in Chapter 2. If the aggregate M/B ratio in July of year t is lower (higher) than the median of all aggregate M/B ratios, the subsequent 6 months from August of year t to January of year $t+1$ are classified as the period following the low (high) M/B month. Similarly, if the aggregate M/B ratio in January of the current year is lower (higher) than the median, the following 6 months from February to July are classified as the period following the low (high) M/B month.

Parentheses indicate the standard deviation of monthly returns *, **, and *** indicate 10%, 5%, and 1% significance levels for the S–L strategy, respectively.

In addition, the size effect becomes more stable following high M/B months than low M/B months, although the S–L strategy tends to yield higher returns following low M/B months.

4.1.4. *Relation between Size and January Effects*

Figure 4.2 shows seasonal EW monthly returns on small, middle, and large portfolios in the KOSPI and KOSDAQ markets whose criteria are the 30th percentile and 70th percentile of capitalization of the KOSPI stocks in December of the previous year. According to Figure 4.2, January returns on small, middle, and large portfolios are 7.7%, 5.6%, and 3.1%, respectively, which are the highest monthly returns on size portfolios. Figure 4.2 confirms the earlier finding that the January effect is prominent among small stocks. In addition, the

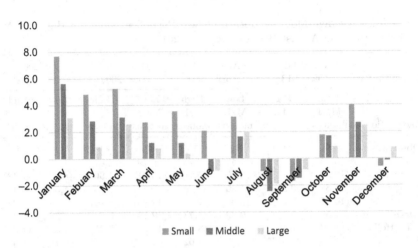

Figure 4.2. Monthly EW Returns of Size Portfolios in the KOSPI and KOSDAQ Market from 1981 to 2013

January return is negatively related to the market capitalization of the stocks. The negative relation is also consistent with the result of Figure 3.4 of Chapter 3 which examines only KOSPI stocks. For the small and middle portfolios, February and March have high monthly returns as well. Thus, including the KOSDAQ stocks does not change the major results of Chapter 3.

The size portfolios have negative or extremely low monthly returns in June to September, which is consistent with the Halloween effect, the tendency of stock market returns to be higher in the November–April period than in May–October across many stock exchange markets (Bouman and Jacobsen, 2001). The 6-month returns on the small, middle, and large portfolios are 23.9%, 15.2%, and 10.6%, respectively, from November to April. However, the 6-month returns on the same size portfolios from May to October are 7.8%, −0.4%, and −0.4%, respectively. Thus, positive annual returns are mainly obtained from November to April regardless of market capitalization, while all size portfolios have negative returns in August and September.

The average December return on the small portfolio is negative, which is consistent with the stylized fact of earlier literature. The low December returns on small stocks are often interpreted as a result of

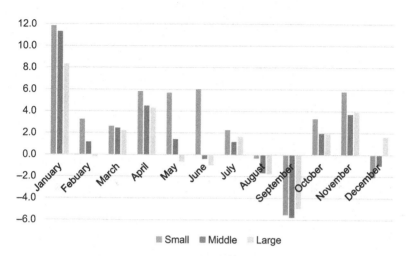

Figure 4.3. Monthly EW Returns of Size Portfolios Following Low M/B Months in the KOSPI and KOSDAQ Markets from 1981 to 2013

individual investors' selling pressure on stocks with negative returns in December to realize losses from the stock investment for tax reduction. However, there is no tax-selling incentive in Korea because there is no capital gains tax. Therefore, the tax-loss selling hypothesis cannot account for the empirical results shown in Figure 4.2.

Figure 4.3 exhibits the calendar effect of size portfolios following low M/B months in December of the previous year. The January returns on the small and middle portfolios are 11.8% and 11.3%, respectively, following low M/B months. The large portfolio also has the highest January return following low M/B months. The January returns following low M/B months are even higher than the January returns in Figure 4.2. All size portfolios have negative returns in August and September. In particular, September negative returns on size portfolios are statistically significant at least at 5%. In short, January returns are prominent following low M/B months.

In contrast, Figure 4.4 shows that the January effect does not appear to be prominent following high M/B months. First, January returns are even lower following high M/B months than low M/B months. For example, the middle portfolio has a 2.7% January return following high M/B months, while it has an 11.3% January return

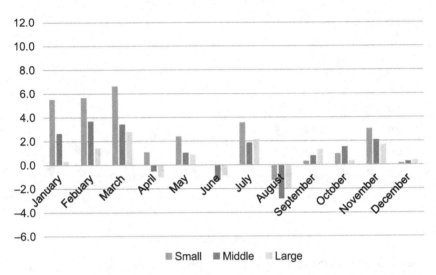

Figure 4.4.   Monthly EW Returns of Size Portfolios Following High M/B Months in KOSPI and KOSDAQ Stocks from 1981 to 2013

following low M/B months. Second, the January return is not the highest across calendar months following high M/B months. For example, the March return on the small portfolio is 6.6%, which is higher than the 5.5% January return. The January return on the large portfolio is only 0.3% following high M/B months.

The Halloween effect holds following both low M/B months and high M/B months. For example, the small portfolio yields 27.2% of 6-month returns from November to April following low M/B months, while it yields only 11.4% from May to October. The middle and large portfolios yield higher than 20% of 6-month returns from November to April following low M/B months and negative 6-month returns from May to October following low M/B months. On the other hand, the small portfolio obtains 22.1% of 6-month returns from November to April following high M/B months, while it yields 5.9% from May to October. Regardless of the size of portfolio, the 6-month returns from November to April of the following year are higher than those from May to October following high M/B months.

4.2. Book-to-Market Effect

4.2.1. *Literature Review*

It is widely acknowledged that value stocks outperform growth stocks. The value strategies call for buying value stocks with low prices relative to dividends, earnings, historical prices, and book value of equity and selling growth stocks with high prices relative to these values. Although most academicians agree on the high returns of the value strategies, they have different opinions about the source of the high returns. The source of the B/M effect is especially controversial.

Rosenberg *et al.* (1984) argue that stocks with a high book value relative to the market value of equity outperform stocks with a low book value relative to the market value of equity. Further work, such as Chan *et al.* (1991), Fama and French (1992), and Lakonishok *et al.* (1994), has confirmed the B/M effect. This value premium is not limited to only a few countries. Fama and French (1998) find a value premium for the US and 12 major Europe, Australia, and Far East (EAFA) countries. The difference between average returns on global portfolios of high and low B/M stocks is 7.6% per year ($t = 3.39$). Fama and French (2012) confirm that the value premium tends to decrease with size in the three regions (North America, Europe, and Asia Pacific). Davis (1994) shows that the B/M effect is also found in the US for the earlier period of 1929–1963. Substantial out-of-sample tests provide clear evidence to refute the argument that the effect may be due to the outcome of the specific sample.

However, controversy exists regarding what causes the B/M effect. Fama and French (1993, 1996) argue that the value premium is compensation for the relative distress risk missed by the capital asset pricing model. They claim that the B/M effect is a proxy for such a risk factor.

An alternative explanation of value premium is that the premium is due to undervaluing distressed stocks such as high B/M stocks and overvaluing growth stocks such as low B/M stocks by extrapolating past earnings growth too far into the future. For example, naive investors simply equate a good investment with a well-run company regardless of price or overreact to good news about such companies. As these pricing errors are corrected, low (high) B/M stocks earn poor (good) performance [Lakonishok *et al.*, 1994; Haugen, 1995].

In the same overreaction camp, Daniel and Titman (1997) and Daniel *et al.* (2001) suggest that the value premium results from the characteristics of the B/M ratio in the US and Japanese markets, respectively, rather than the risk factors captured by B/M ratios. Their research shows a clever way to distinguish the characteristics story from the risk-based argument. According to the risk-based argument, expected returns compensate risk loadings regardless of the B/M ratio. On the other hand, the characteristics story says that the characteristics of a B/M ratio determine the expected return of a stock regardless of factor loadings. Suppose that certain stocks' returns covary with common risk factors, such as the same industry factor and which industry becomes relatively distressed in a specific time, but their performance appears to be less financially distressed than other stocks in the same industry. As a result, these stocks may have high risk loadings on the relative distress risk factor, but their B/M ratio may be substantially less than that of others in the same industry. The risk-based story predicts that these stocks have similarly high expected returns because of high risk loadings. On the other hand, the characteristics story predicts that the stocks with high risk loadings but low B/M ratios will have lower expected returns than stocks with a similarly high loading and high B/M ratio. Daniel and Titman (1997) and Daniel *et al.* (2001) provide empirical evidence supporting the characteristics story in the US and Japanese markets. However, Davis *et al.* (2000) document that the three-factor risk model explains the value premium better than the characteristics model.

Daniel and Titman (2006) provide a different view of overreaction related to the B/M effect. They decompose the current B/M ratio into tangible information and intangible information and provide empirical evidence that the predictability of the B/M ratio results from overreaction to intangible information rather than tangible information. The tangible information is the accounting measures of past performance, while the intangible information is the component of news about future performance, which is orthogonal to the measures of past fundamental performance. Daniel and Titman (2006) provide an example of overreaction to intangible information as follows. Many high-tech firms in the late 1990s looked financially distressed in terms of accounting performance like earnings or book value growth. However, since information about these firms' future growth opportunities was viewed very favorably, their market values were high, resulting in extremely low B/M ratios. The subsequent low returns of the high-tech stocks can be interpreted as a result of overreaction to the intangible information rather than the tangible accounting information. This argument differs from the previous overreaction argument of Lakonishok *et al.* (1994) suggesting that investors tend to overreact to past fundamental performance by extrapolating past sales or earnings growth.

In general, earlier studies find that the B/M effect exists in the Korean stock market (Kim and Yun 1999; Kim and Kim, 2000; Kim and Kim, 2007). However, Yun *et al.* (2009) provide evidence that HML strategy, defined as the High B/M portfolio Minus the Low B/M portfolio, does not yield statistically significant positive returns from 1990 to 2007. On the other hand, Kim (2009) presents different empirical results showing that HML is statistically significant from 1988 to 2007. Yun *et al.* employ 624 non-financial stocks listed on the KOSPI market, while Kim's (2009) sample includes non-financial stocks listed on the KOSPI market but eliminates delisted stocks for 1 year before the delisted date because of extreme price volatility in those stocks.

4.2.2. *B/M Effect in Korean Stock Markets*

We break KOSPI and KOSDAQ stocks into three B/M groups based on the 30th and 70th percentiles of B/M ratios among KOSPI stocks. The book value of equity in year $t - 1$ is defined as the total assets book value minus the total liabilities when the fiscal year ends in calendar year $t - 1$, divided by the market value of equity at the end of December of year $t - 1$. We eliminate the stocks with negative book value of equity and the stocks of financial firms. EW monthly

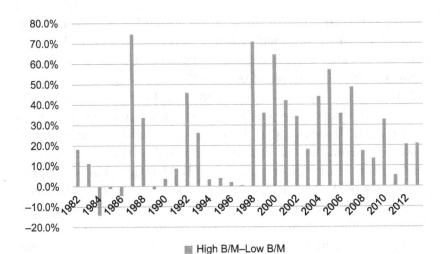

Figure 4.5. Annual Returns of the Strategy of Buying the High B/M Portfolio and Shorting the Low B/M Portfolio: 1982–2013

Notes: KOSPI and KOSDAQ stocks are classified into three B/M groups based on the 30th and 70th percentiles of B/M ratios among KOSPI stocks. The book value of equity is the book common equity for the fiscal year ending in calendar year $t-1$ divided by the market value of equity at the end of December of year $t-1$. We eliminate stocks with negative book value of equity and stocks of financial firms. EW monthly returns on three B/M portfolios are calculated from May of year t to April of year $t+1$. The high B/M portfolio is composed of stocks with higher B/M ratios than the 70th percentile, while the low book-to-market portfolio is composed of stocks with lower B/M ratios than the 30th percentile.

returns on three B/M portfolios are calculated from May of year t to April of year $t+1$.[1] The high B/M portfolio is composed of stocks with higher B/M ratios than the 70th percentile, while the low B/M portfolio is composed of stocks with lower B/M ratios than the 30th percentile.

Figure 4.5 presents the annual return of the value strategy, which buys the high B/M portfolio and shorts the low B/M portfolio. The value strategy yields 24.1% of annual returns between 1982 and 2013.

---

[1]Since information from financial statements in fiscal year $t-1$ is usually available at most by the end of April in year t, investors can employ the value strategy using B/M portfolios in May of year t.

Thus, the B/M effect is strong from 1982 to 2013.[2] The B/M effect has not been weakened at all since 2000. For the entire period, the value strategy of buying the high B/M portfolio and shorting the low B/M portfolio provides negative annual returns only in 1984, 1986, and 1989. The annual returns of the value strategy have exceeded 20% for 10 of 14 years since 2000. Therefore, in contrast to the size effect, the B/M effect is still a noteworthy anomaly in the Korean stock market, which is consistent with Kim (2009).[3]

Table 4.3 shows monthly returns on B/M portfolios. The high B/M portfolio earns 2.58% for the entire period, while the middle and low B/M portfolios earn 1.81% and 0.90%, respectively. When the entire period is divided into three sub-periods, the B/M effect is statistically significant for all sub-periods. The value strategy earns

Table 4.3. Monthly Returns on B/M Portfolios and the Strategy of Buying High B/M Portfolios and Shorting Low B/M Portfolios in the KOSPI and KOSDAQ Markets

Portfolio	Aug. 1981– Dec. 2013	Aug. 1981– April. 1991	May 1991– Aug. 2002	Sep. 2002– Dec. 2013
High B/M Portfolio	2.58	2.28	3.11	2.28
	(9.38)	(7.30)	(14.11)	(7.38)
Middle B/M Portfolio	1.81	1.81	1.89	1.72
	(9.00)	(6.82)	(11.72)	(7.28)
Low B/M Portfolio	0.90	1.58	0.99	0.28
	(9.38)	(6.59)	(12.29)	(7.81)
High–Low B/M Strategy	1.68***	0.71**	2.12***	2.00***
	(6.02)	(3.70)	(8.61)	(3.98)

Note: Parentheses indicate the standard deviation of monthly returns *, **, and *** indicate the 10%, 5%, and 1% significance levels for monthly return of the value strategy, respectively.

---

[2]When we exclude KOSDAQ stocks, the average annual return of the value strategy is 17.5%. The value premium appears to be stronger among small stocks given that KOSDAQ stocks tend to be much smaller than KOSPI stocks.

[3]Yun *et al.* (2009) report that HML (high B/M stocks minus low B/M stocks) does not yield statistically positive monthly returns for the KOSPI stocks and the B/M ratio is not statistically significant in explaining cross-sectional stock returns. On the contrary, Kim (2009) provides evidence that the monthly return of HML is statistically significant although the sample period is similar.

at least 2% for the second and third sub-periods, while it earns only 0.71% for the first sub-period of May 1982–April 1991.

4.2.3. *Cross-sectional B/M Effect and Time Series Aggregate M/B Ratio*[4]

The relation between the B/M effect and the time series aggregate M/B months is shown in Table 4.4. We semiannually classify 6 months based on the aggregate M/B ratios as explained in Table 4.2. If the aggregate M/B ratio in July of year t is lower (higher) than the median of all available aggregate M/B ratios, the following 6 months from August of year t to January of year $t+1$ are classified as the period following the low (high) M/B month. If the aggregate M/B ratio in January of year t is lower (higher) than the median,

Table 4.4.   Average Monthly Return of B/M Portfolios Following High or Low M/B Months in the KOSPI and KOSDAQ Markets

Classification M/B ratio	May 1982–Dec. 2013		May 1982–April. 1991		May 1991–April. 2002		Sep. 2002–Dec. 2013	
	Low M/B months	High M/B months	Low M/B months	High M/B months	Low M/B months	High M/B months	Low M/B months	High M/B months
Observation	146	234	39	69	67	69	40	96
High B/M	3.39	2.07	1.71	2.61	4.90	1.37	2.50	2.18
Portfolio	(12.60)	(8.50)	(4.37)	(8.53)	(17.49)	(9.18)	(6.80)	(7.65)
Middle B/M	2.51	1.37	1.41	2.04	3.18	0.63	2.45	1.42
Portfolio	(10.57)	(7.85)	(4.22)	(7.94)	(14.14)	(8.69)	(7.58)	(7.17)
Low B/M	1.51	0.52	1.38	1.68	1.67	0.33	1.37	-0.18
Portfolio	(11.34)	(7.93)	(4.45)	(7.57)	(14.87)	(9.18)	(9.18)	(7.17)
High-Low B/M Strategy	1.88*** (7.66)	1.55*** (4.74)	0.33 (2.81)	0.93* (4.12)	3.24* (10.41)	1.04 (6.29)	1.13 (4.56)	2.36*** (3.67)

Note: Parentheses indicate the standard deviation of monthly returns. *, **, and *** indicate 10%, 5%, and 1% significance levels for monthly return of value strategy, respectively.

---

[4]The M/B ratio is an inverse of the B/M ratio. Since the B/M ratio is mostly commonly used in the cross-sectional analysis, I employ a B/M ratio regarding cross-sectional analysis. With regard to predictability of its ratio, I use the M/B ratio. The M/B ratio shows more straight forward relation with the profitability growth and risk as discussed in Chapter 2.

the following 6 months from February to July are classified as the period following the low (high) M/B month.

The average monthly returns on B/M portfolios are higher following low M/B months than high M/B months for the entire period of January 1982–December 2013, while their standard deviations are also higher following low M/B months. The high standard deviation of each portfolio following low M/B months may indicate relatively high risk. In other words, the subsequent 6 months following the low M/B months may capture a relatively risky period, while those following the high M/B months capture a less risky period.

The empirical results of sub-periods, however, show that the monthly returns on B/M portfolios following low M/B months have higher standard deviations only for the second sub-period of May 1991–April 2002. For the second sub-period, the average monthly return of the high B/M portfolio is 4.90% and its standard deviation is 17.49% following low M/B months, which is 1.9 times the standard deviation of the same portfolio following high M/B months. Furthermore, the strategy of buying the high B/M portfolio and shorting the low B/M portfolio yields 3.24% of monthly returns following low M/B months, which is even higher than the three times returns following high M/B months for the second sub-period. However, the value strategy does not yield higher returns following low M/B months than following high M/B months except for the second sub-period. As a result, the time series aggregate M/B ratio does not appear to strongly influence the cross-sectional B/M effect. In addition, the value strategy's monthly returns are positive for all sub-periods but not statistically significant following low M/B months for the first and third sub-periods and following high M/B months for the second sub-period.

Stambaugh *et al.* (2012) argue that overvaluation is more prevalent under high investor sentiment but undervaluation is not more prevalent during low investor sentiment. Rational investors will easily remove undervaluation of stocks by purchasing undervalued stocks. Thus, undervaluation during low investment sentiment is easily corrected. In contrast, the increased prevalence of overvaluation is due to the limits of short sales. Since rational investors who recognize overvalued stocks have the limitation of shorting these stocks, their prices will not be corrected immediately. The returns on these overvalued stocks will become lower for at least several months in the process of gradually correcting their overvaluation following high investor sentiment.

In the same context, low B/M stocks are expected to have lower returns following high M/B months since these stocks are more likely to be overvalued during high M/B months if a high M/B ratio indicates the degree of market overvaluation. Table 4.4 reports that the low B/M portfolio tends to have lower returns following high M/B months, which is consistent with Stambaugh *et al.* (2012). However, it is difficult to explain why the high B/M portfolio has higher monthly returns following low M/B months than following high M/B months. Since undervaluation is not prevalent, there is no reason to believe that the high B/M portfolio yields higher returns especially following low M/B months than following high M/B months.

4.2.4. *B/M Effect for Stocks with Dominance of Individual Investors' Trading*

As explained in Chapter 2, individual investors are more likely to dominantly trade small stocks with low profitability and high leverage. The dominance of their trading may influence the valuation of these stocks as well. To examine the possibility that valuation of stocks with dominance of individual investors' trading differs from that of other stocks, stocks are separated based on the proportion of individual investors' trading value in total trading value. Panel A of Table 4.5 displays the financial ratios of B/M portfolios in the case of stocks for which the proportion of individual investors' trading value is less than or equal to 90% (*Indp* ≤90%) and Panel B does so for stocks with the proportion of individual investors' trading value is higher than 90% (*Indp* >90%).

All financial variables in Table 4.5 are calculated by summing these variables across listed firms in a given year. For example, in year *t*, the sales (operating income) of the high B/M portfolio is calculated by summing all sales (operating income) across all KOSPI firms that belong to the high B/M portfolio. The operating margin

Table 4.5. Characteristics of B/M Portfolios for *Indp* >90% and *Indp* ≤90% in the KOSPI Market

Panel A: *Indp* ≤90%

Year	B/M Portfolios	N	B/M	Margin (%)	ROE (%)	D/A	TIE
1995–2003	Equity <0	7.0	−8.81	−22.57	N.A.	1.34	−2.87
	Low B/M Portfolio	90.4	0.61	10.40	10.17	0.60	4.43
	Middle B/M Portfolio	118.3	1.80	5.90	3.89	0.63	1.92
	High B/M Portfolio	81.1	4.09	4.98	0.55	0.63	1.30
2004–2013	Equity <0	1.5	−2.58	−15.58	N.A.	1.26	−9.82
	Low B/M Portfolio	113.0	0.52	8.76	14.20	0.45	12.18
	Middle B/M Portfolio	142.8	1.20	5.74	6.81	0.47	4.72
	High B/M Portfolio	94.9	2.37	1.79	1.26	0.48	2.00
Total	Equity <0	5.2	−6.73	−20.24	N.A.	1.31	−5.19
	Low B/M Portfolio	102.3	0.56	9.54	12.29	0.52	8.51
	Middle B/M Portfolio	131.2	1.49	5.81	5.43	0.55	3.39
	High B/M Portfolio	88.4	3.18	3.30	0.92	0.55	1.67

Panel B: *Indp* >90%

Year	B/M Ranking	N	B/M	Margin (%)	ROE (%)	D/A	TIE
1995–2003	Equity <0	39.8	−13.4	−5.39	N.A.	1.61	−1.11
	Low B/M Portfolio	76.6	0.69	4.66	−3.20	0.72	1.06
	Middle B/M Portfolio	104.8	1.91	4.43	−0.26	0.64	1.25
	High B/M Portfolio	86.2	4.61	4.15	−1.08	0.70	1.15
2004–2013	Equity <0	5.2	−3.01	−35.75	N.A.	1.54	−13.63
	Low B/M Portfolio	76.3	0.48	2.27	−5.01	0.64	0.62
	Middle B/M Portfolio	110.1	1.24	3.41	2.08	0.52	2.08
	High B/M Portfolio	94.1	2.67	2.20	0.17	0.52	1.45
Total	Equity <0	22.5	−8.20	−20.57	N.A.	1.57	−7.37
	Low B/M Portfolio	76.4	0.58	3.40	−4.16	0.68	0.83
	Middle B/M Portfolio	107.6	1.56	3.89	1.0	0.58	1.69
	High B/M Portfolio	90.4	3.59	3.12	−0.42	0.61	1.31

Notes: All financial variables are calculated by summing these variables across all KOSPI firms in a given year. For example, in year t, the sales (operating income) of the high B/M portfolio is calculated by summing all sales (operating income) across all listed firms that belong to the high B/M portfolio. The operating margin of the high B/M portfolio is the percentage of its total operating income divided by its total sales. *Indp* ≤90% in Panel A indicates stocks for which the proportion of individual investors' trading value in total trading value is less than or equal to 90%. *Indp* >90% in Panel B shows stocks for which individual investors trade higher than 90% of the total value.

of the high B/M portfolio is the percentage of its total operating income divided by its total sales.

Since the proportion of foreign or institutional investors' trading value is higher for stocks with *Indp* ≤90%, the valuation of those stocks in Panel A is more likely to be influenced by interaction of individual, foreign, and institutional investors' trading. Panel A of Table 4.5 indicates that the B/M ratio is negatively related to the operating margin rate and return on equity (ROE). The high B/M portfolio tends to have a low operating margin rate and low ROE, while the low B/M portfolio tends to have a high margin rate and high ROE. The negative relation between the B/M ratio and the profitability ratios confirms the stylized facts documented in earlier literature. Stocks with past good fundamental performance tend to be highly valued because high profitability growth of these stocks is expected in the future based on their past good performance. In addition, the high B/M portfolio tends to have a lower times interest earned ratio (or interest coverage ratio), which suggests that they may have difficulty in paying interest expenses out of their earnings. However, the B/M ratio does not appear to have any relation to the debt ratio except for stocks with negative equity. In general, Panel A confirms the B/M effect of earlier academic literature regarding the negative relation between the B/M ratio and the profitability ratio.

Indp >90% in Panel B of Table 4.5 means that individual investors trade more than 90% of the total trading value. The average B/M ratios of the B/M portfolios in the case of *Indp* >90% are similar to those of *Indp* ≤90%. For example, the average B/M ratio of the low B/M portfolio is 0.56 in Panel A and 0.58 in Panel B for the entire period. However, the profitability ratios, such as ROE and the margin rate, are much lower for *Indp* >90% than *Indp* ≤90%, which is consistent with the preference of investor types shown in Table 2.4 of Chapter 2. The most important difference in stocks between *Indp* >90% and *Indp* ≤90% is the relation between the B/M portfolios and profitability ratios. Although the low B/M portfolios have similar B/M ratios in both *Indp* >90% and *Indp* ≤90%, their profitability ratios and sales growth rates for *Indp* ≤90% are much higher than for *Indp* >90%.

The low B/M portfolio does not appear to be more profitable than the high B/M portfolio for *Indp* >90%. For example, the average operating margin rate of the low B/M portfolio is 3.40% for the entire period, while that of the high B/M portfolio is 3.12%. The ROE of the low B/M portfolio is −4.16%, which is worse than the −0.42% ROE for the high B/M portfolio. Thus, no clear relation exists between the B/M portfolios and the profitability ratios for stocks with the dominance of individual investors' trading. The empirical results of the sub-periods even suggest that the low B/M stocks tend to have worse ROE. Moreover, the low B/M portfolio appears to suffer from making interest payments as well. Its time interest earned ratio, which measures the ability to pay interest costs from earnings before interest and taxes (EBIT), is 0.83 for the entire period. Such a low time interest earned ratio suggests that some companies of the low B/M portfolio do not make enough earnings to pay interest expenses. The low B/M portfolio has a high debt ratio compared to the middle and high B/M portfolios.

The poor profitability of the low B/M portfolio in the case of *Indp* >90% can be explained by Daniel and Titman's (2006) overreaction argument with respect to intangible information. Despite the current and past poor profitability of the stocks, investors highly value stocks with favorable intangible information about future profitability. If this valuation is due to overreaction to the favorable intangible information, the valuation of the low B/M portfolio in the case of *Indp* >90% will be reversed, resulting in low returns. Another possible explanation is that these stocks may have extremely low risk. However, they appear to have severe financial risk since their debt ratio is high and time interest earned ratio is less than the 1 for the entire sample period.

Table 4.6 provides the average monthly return of B/M portfolios for both *Indp* >90% and *Indp* ≤90% from 1995 to 2013. The low B/M portfolio of *Indp* >90% has 0.55% of the monthly average return, which is lower than the 0.83% return of the low B/M portfolio in the case of *Indp* ≤90%. The high valuation of the low B/M portfolio for *Indp* >90% appears to be adjusted for the following 6 months. On the other hand, the high B/M portfolio for *Indp* >90% has 2.37% of

Table 4.6. Monthly Return of B/M Portfolios, Their Margin and Sales Growth Before and After Portfolio Formation in the KOSPI Market in the Case of Both *Indp* >90% and *Indp* ≤90% from 1995 to 2013

		Indp >90%			*Indp* ≤90%		
		Low B/M	Middle B/M	High B/M	Low B/M	Middle B/M	High B/M
Monthly Return (%)		0.55	1.74	2.37	0.83	1.4	1.65
		(11.04)	(11.29)	(11.51)	(9.28)	(9.47)	(10.61)
Margin (%)	$t-3$	2.50	4.17	4.21	9.61	6.92	5.21
	$t-2$	1.82	4.01	3.41	9.60	6.94	4.69
	$t-1$	2.07	3.80	3.10	9.38	6.63	4.02
	$t+1$	3.69	3.40	2.67	9.09	5.47	2.53
	$t+2$	3.36	3.94	2.42	9.19	5.45	2.68
	$t+3$	3.30	3.74	2.44	9.18	5.39	3.38
Sales	$t-3$	−11.97	4.12	5.98	13.04	11.48	9.29
Growth (%)	$t-2$	3.40	8..39	7.40	17.41	11.38	10.42
	$t-1$	7.05	11.02	4.50	16.66	12.21	8.62
	$t+1$	5.69	1.45	1.15	10.01	6.36	2.49
	$t+2$	−0.48	−2.56	3.37	7.86	4.80	4.91
	$t+3$	6.71	0.61	−1.49	7.42	4.43	4.37

monthly return, which is higher than the 1.65% return of the high B/M portfolio in the case of *Indp* ≤90%. Since the value strategy has a higher return for *Indp* >90% than *Indp* ≤90%, the B/M effect is stronger in stocks with dominance of individual investors' trading.

Table 4.6 also displays future and past profitability of B/M portfolios. For example, $Margin_{t-3}$ is the operating margin in year $t-3$ when B/M portfolios are determined in year t. Earlier financial literature documents that the fundamental performance of low B/M stocks tends to be excellent in the past as well as in the future because low B/M stocks are characterized by rapid growth in sales and earnings. The operating margin rates of B/M portfolios are distinctively negatively related to the B/M ratio in the case of *Indp* ≤90%. For example, the low B/M portfolio of *Indp* ≤90% has a higher operating margin rate 3 years before and after the B/M portfolios are formed. Likewise, the low B/M portfolio of *Indp* ≤90% appears to be composed of rapid growth stocks in terms of sales growth. The sales growth rates of the low B/M portfolio are consistently higher than those of both high and middle B/M portfolios in the case of *Indp* ≤90% 3 years before and after the B/M portfolios are formed.

In contrast, the low B/M portfolio for *Indp* >90% does not appear to be profitable compared to the high B/M portfolio. The operating margin rates of the low B/M portfolio before portfolio formation are not higher than either the high or middle B/M portfolios. Although the operating margin rates of the low B/M portfolio tend to improve after portfolio formation, they are not higher than the middle B/M portfolio. In addition, the low B/M portfolio does not seem to consist of rapidly growing stocks. The sales growth rates of the low B/M portfolio in the case of *Indp* >90% tend to be higher in year $t + 1$ and year $t + 3$ after portfolio formation year t than both the middle and high B/M portfolios. However, the sales growth rates of the low B/M portfolio are much lower for *Indp* >90% than for *Indp* ≤90%. Thus, the B/M effect for *Indp* >90% is not consistent with earlier literature such as Lakonishok *et al.* (1994) and Fama and French (1995), who argue that low B/M stocks are more likely to exhibit high profitability in the future as well as in the past.[5]

The valuation of stocks with *Indp* >90% may be understood with Daniel and Titman's (2006) overreaction argument with respect to intangible information. Individual investors may put more weight on intangible information than on tangible information such as information about earnings and book value. Therefore, individual investors highly value stocks with favorable intangible information, resulting in low B/M ratios for these stocks although their past fundamental performance is not attractive. According to Table 4.6, favorable intangible information, however, does not appear to be

---

[5]Lankonishok *et al.* (1994) provide empirical evidence showing that the low B/M portfolio exhibits temporary good financial performance in the future, suggesting that the market incorrectly extrapolates past performance. However, Fama and French (1995) show that good financial performance of the low B/M portfolio persists at least for 5 years after the B/M portfolio is determined. Although they do not agree on the persistence of financial performance, both document that past financial performance continues in the future at least over the short term.

valid within 3 years after portfolio formation. Thus, investors may overreact to intangible information.

4.2.5. *B/M Effect and January Effect*

The B/M effect is known to be related to the January effect. It is well known that high B/M stocks tend to have much higher January returns than low B/M stocks. However, no prominent relation exists between the January effect and the B/M effect in the Korean stock markets. Figure 4.6 presents the seasonal monthly returns of high and low B/M portfolios and HML in the KOSPI market in the case of *Indp* >90%. Both high B/M and low B/M portfolios have high monthly average returns in January. However, HML, which is defined as the monthly return difference between a high B/M portfolio and low B/M portfolio, is not positive. HML is −1.20% in January, which is the lowest among the 12 calendar months. It is noteworthy that HML is positive except for January and June. The highest and second highest HMLs are 3.47% in March and 3.11% in November.

Figure 4.7 shows that the January return is higher for *Indp* >90% than for *Indp* ≤90%, which is shown in Figure 4.6. This result confirms that the January effect is more prominent in stocks

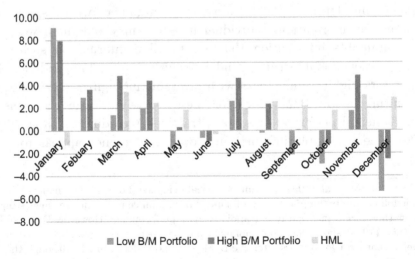

Figure 4.6. Seasonal Returns (%) of B/M Portfolios in the KOSPI Market in the Case of *Indp* >90% from 1982 to 2013

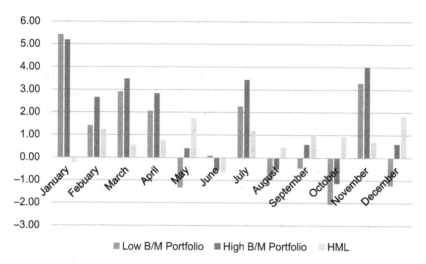

Figure 4.7. Seasonal Returns (%) of B/M Portfolios in the KOSPI Market in the Case of *Indp* ≤90% from 1982 to 2013

with dominance of individual investors' trading in the Korean stock market. In addition, the seasonal returns of B/M portfolios for *Indp* ≤90% are similar to those for *Indp* >90%. The low B/M portfolio has a little higher January return than the high B/M portfolio in the case of *Indp* ≤90% as well. However, their difference in January returns is negligibly small.

In summary, the B/M effect is strong in the Korean stock markets. However, the low B/M portfolio does not have a higher January return than the high B/M portfolio, which is inconsistent with earlier studies on other countries' stock markets. The B/M effect is not related to the January effect in the Korean stock markets.

4.3. Long-term Reversal

DeBondt and Thaler (1985) initially document empirical evidence about the profitability of the original contrarian strategy, that is, of buying long-term past losers and selling long-term past winners. The long-term past losers are referred to as stocks with extremely poor return performance over 3–5 years, while the long-term past winners as stocks with extremely good return performance over 3–5 years.

They argue that since investors tend to overreact to a long series of good news (associated with long-term past winners) and a long series of bad news (associated with long-term past losers), stocks exhibiting the former (latter) become overvalued (undervalued). As a result, a contrarian strategy of buying long-term losers and shorting long-term winners can obtain positive abnormal returns as the prices of both types of stocks eventually return to equilibrium values.

The profitability of the contrarian strategy attracts many practitioners and academicians because the contrarian strategy is constructed with easily accessible information, such as past returns. Many hypotheses attempt to explain the abnormal returns of this strategy, such as the measurement error hypothesis, survivorship hypothesis, overreaction hypothesis, and risk-based hypothesis. Along with the intermediate momentum phenomenon, the evidence of long-term reversal has motivated rigorous behavioral models to account simultaneously for both long-term reversal and intermediate momentum. Since long-term losers (winners) usually experience substantial decreases (increases) in their prices over several years, they tend to be high (low) B/M stocks. After Fama and French (1992, 1993) documented that three factors (beta, B/M, and size) successfully account for long-term reversal and other anomalies except price momentum, interest in the long-term reversal has gradually decreased.

For every stock that has 36 consecutive monthly returns without any missing data, we construct quintile portfolios by year in ascending order of 36-month cumulative returns from $t-36$ to $t-1$ where t is January of each year covering 1983–2013.[6] The first quintile portfolio is called a loser portfolio and the last a winner portfolio. The EW average monthly return is calculated for all stocks that belong to the same quintile portfolio. The portfolio is assumed to hold for 36 months. The 36-month holding period and annual portfolio formation result in three same-ranking quintile portfolios constructed

---

[6]The 36-, 48-, and 60-month past returns are employed as a sorting criterion for the long-term reversal test. The contrarian strategy of buying long-term losers and shorting long-term winners provides 0.64%, 0.42%, and 0.60% for the 36-, 48-, and 60-month past returns' sorting, respectively.

in different years in a calendar month, each of which has its own monthly returns in the calendar month. For example, each of the three loser portfolios constructed at the end of December 1982, 1983, and 1984 has a monthly return in January 1985.[7] Average monthly returns are calculated for every month covering January 1983 to December 2013.

Figure 4.8 shows that the long-term loser tends to have higher monthly returns for the 3-year holding period. However, the

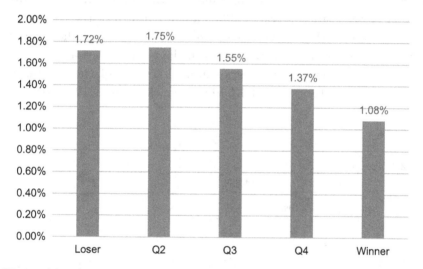

Figure 4.8. Average Monthly Return on Quintile Portfolios Sorting with 36-month Past Returns in the KOSPI and KOSDAQ Markets January 1983–December 2013

Notes: For every stock with 36 consecutive monthly returns without any missing data, quintile portfolios are constructed by year in ascending order of 36-month cumulative returns from $t - 36$ to $t - 1$ where t is January of each year covering 1983–2013. The first quintile portfolio is called a loser portfolio and the last a winner portfolio. The EW average monthly return is calculated for each quintile portfolio. The holding period is 36 months.

---

[7]There are two exceptions for 24 monthly returns from January 1983 to December 1984. Twelve monthly returns from January to December in 1983 are held only by the first portfolios constructed at the end of 1982 based on 36-month past returns from January 1980 to December 1982. Another 12 monthly returns from January to December 1984 are held by two portfolios: the first portfolios and the second portfolios constructed at the end of 1983 by using 36-month past returns from January 1981 to December 1983.

contrarian strategy of buying the long-term loser and shorting the long-term winner yields only 0.64% of monthly return, which is much lower than the 1.68% of alternative contrarian strategy of buying a high B/M portfolio and shorting a low B/M portfolio, discussed in Section 4.2 of this chapter.

Although the empirical results of DeBondt and Thaler (1985, 1986) show a positive relation between the January effect and monthly returns of the contrarian strategy, Figure 4.9 suggests that the January effect does not contribute to abnormal returns of the contrarian strategy in Korean stock markets. The January return of the contrarian strategy is only 0.01%, while its July return is 2.1%. Thus, the January effect does not seem to be related to the long-term reversal.

Figure 4.10 shows time series annual returns of the contrarian strategy in the KOSPI and KOSDAQ markets from 1983 to 2013.

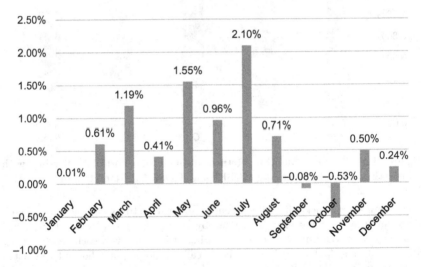

Figure 4.9.   January Effect and Monthly Returns on the Contrarian Strategy in the KOSPI and KOSDAQ Markets January 1983 through December 2013

Notes: For every stock with 36 consecutive monthly returns without any missing data, quintile portfolios are constructed by year in ascending order of 36-month cumulative returns from $t − 36$ to $t − 1$ where t is January of each year covering 1983–2013. The first quintile portfolio is called a loser portfolio and the last a winner portfolio. The EW average monthly return is calculated for each quintile portfolio. The holding period is 36 months. The contrarian strategy is to buy the long-term loser and short the long-term winner.

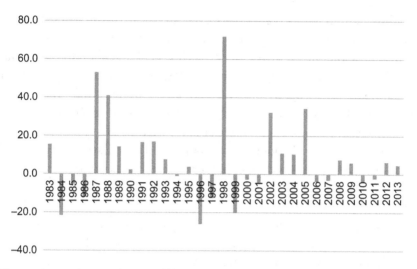

Figure 4.10. Annual Return (%) of Contrarian Strategy in the KOSPI and KOSDAQ Markets 1983 to 2013

Notes: For every stock with 36 consecutive monthly returns without any missing data, quintile portfolios are constructed by year in ascending order of 36-month cumulative returns from $t - 36$ to $t - 1$ where t is January of each year covering 1983–2013. The first quintile portfolio is called a loser portfolio and the last a winner portfolio. The EW average monthly return is calculated for each quintile portfolio. The holding period is 36 months. The contrarian strategy is to buy the long-term loser and short the long-term winner.

The contrarian strategy does not provide consistent positive returns for the holding period. The contrarian strategy yields 13 negative annual returns out of a total of 31 years, which accounts for 41.9%. After 2005, there are no significant positive annual returns for the contrarian strategy. Thus, the long-term reversal does not appear to yield stable annual returns. Although the contrarian strategy yields a positive average return, its return does not appear to be consistent and its magnitude is also small compared to the B/M effect.

4.4. Price Momentum

4.4.1. *Literature Review*

A substantial amount of literature has documented that US stocks with the best returns over 3–12 months continue to perform better over the subsequent 3–12 months than stocks with the worst returns over the same periods. This phenomenon is known as price momentum. The momentum strategy of buying past winners and shorting past losers appears to be a profitable strategy. The price momentum phenomenon is recognized as an anomaly differentiated from other anomalies. For example, the B/M effect, long-term reversal, and size effect are correlated with each other since high B/M stocks tend to be long-term losers with poor performance and small stocks. However, short-term winners that yield higher returns than short-term losers are not positively correlated with high B/M stocks, small stocks, or long-term losers.

Price momentum does not seem to be the result of data snooping. Price momentum is also found from outside the US sample and in most regions, including Europe, the US, and Asia Pacific (Rouwenhorst, 1998; Griffin et al., 2003, 2005; Fama and French, 2012). It also exists in different types of assets, such as currency (Shleifer and Summers, 1990), commodities (Erb and Harvey, 2006; Gorton et al., 2013), and global bond futures (Asness et al., 2010).

The risk-based explanations and the behavioral hypotheses[8] attempt to explain price momentum. Neither explanation, however, successfully accounts for why there is no price momentum in the Japanese stock market. Fama and French (2012) argue that the non-existence of price momentum in the Japanese stock market may be due to a chance result. Hameed and Kusnadi (2002) and Chui et al. (2010) also report that there is no price momentum in Korea, Hong Kong, Singapore, and Thailand.

Chui et al. (2010) argue that cultural difference across countries can explain why several Asian stock markets do not have weak

---

[8]The risk-based explanations argue that price momentum is due to risk differences between winners and losers (Conrad and Kaul, 1998; Berk et al., 1999; Chordia and Shivakumar, 2002; Bansal et al., 2002). For example, Conrad and Kaul argue that price momentum can be explained by higher expected returns on winners. However, the risk-based explanations are not likely to explain the high magnitude of momentum profits, about 12% per year in the US and Europe. On the other hand, the behavioral explanations suggest that investors suffering from cognitive biases may cause price momentum (Grinblatt and Han, 2005; Hong and Stein, 1999; Barberis et al., 1998; Daniel et al., 1998).

or negative profits of momentum strategies. When investors live in a culture of strong individualism, they are more vulnerable to overconfidence and self-attribution bias, which can cause price momentum in Daniel *et al.*'s (1998) model. Chui *et al.* document that individualism is positively related to price momentum across countries. Thus, their finding indicates that the less individualistic cultures in Asian countries result in weak or negative momentum in Asian stock markets.

Recent papers by Kim (2012) and Eom (2013) show that price momentum appears in Korean stock markets after the Asian financial crisis. They conjecture that since foreign investors' trading gradually increases after the Asian financial crisis, price momentum may be caused by these foreign investors, who are mostly institutional investors from Western countries exhibiting strong momentum trading behavior in their stock markets. Because of the existence of price momentum in Korea after the Asian financial crisis, it is interesting to examine the trading behavior of different investor groups in the Korean stock markets and whether any specific trading interactions or systematic patterns of different investor groups may generate price momentum.[9]

4.4.2. *Price Momentum*

We employ Jegadeesh and Titman's (1993) methodology to form momentum portfolios. Each month, stocks in the KRX market are sorted into quintiles in ascending order based on 9-month past compounded returns. The first (last) quintile consists of the lowest (highest) 9-month past returns. The first (last) quintile is referred to as a loser (winner) portfolio. The momentum strategy is to buy the winner portfolio and short the loser portfolio. One month is skipped between a formation period and a portfolio holding period

---

[9]The financial literature documents systematic trading behavior among various investor groups. For example, individual investors tend to be short-term contrarians and hate selling past losers, while institutional investors tend to be momentum traders, buying past winners and selling losers (Grinblatt *et al.*, 1995; Nofsinger and Sias, 1999; Grinblatt and Keloharju, 2001; Hvidkjaer, 2006; Kaniel *et al.*, 2008).

to reduce market microstructure biases such as non-synchronous bias and bid-ask spread. The holding period is 6 months. The first monthly return of the momentum strategy begins with November 1980. In any month t of the holding period from April 1981, average monthly return is calculated from monthly returns of six momentum strategies constructed from month $t - 7$ to month $t - 2$.

Figure 4.11 displays annual returns of the momentum strategy in the KOSPI and KOSDAQ markets. Before 2000, the returns are frequently negative. However, the strategy tends to yield positive annual returns beginning with 2002. It is noteworthy that the annual

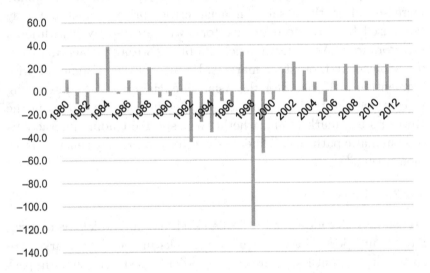

Figure 4.11. Annual Returns of Momentum Strategy

Notes: Stocks in the KOSPI and KOSDAQ markets are formed each month into quintiles in ascending order based on 9-month past (compounded) returns. The first (last) quintile, referred to as the loser (winner) portfolio, consists of the lowest (highest) 9-month past returns. The EW monthly returns are calculated as monthly raw returns on each portfolio. The momentum strategy is defined as longing winner portfolios and shorting loser portfolios. The holding period of the momentum strategy is 6 months and begins 1 month after portfolio formation. In holding month t, there are six winner (loser) portfolios formed from month $t - 2$ to month $t - 7$. The average monthly return of six portfolios is calculated from November 1980 to December 2013. The monthly returns are annualized for every year.

return of the momentum strategy is −117.3% in 1998 when the Asian financial crisis severely hurt Korean economy. In particular, the monthly return of the momentum strategy is −110.9% in November 1998 when average monthly returns on winner and loser portfolios are 9.3% and 120.2%, respectively. Such an extreme negative return is consistent with the phenomenon of momentum crashes examined by Daniel and Moskowitz (2016). They argue that momentum crashes occur with a market rebound in panic states when market volatility is high in bear markets. The source of this negative return is high returns of losers whose valuation is like a call option at the money in panic states. The option-like payoffs of equity may account for momentum crashes. However, the authors argue that the existence of the same phenomena in futures, bonds, currencies, and commodities is difficult to reconcile with the story of the option-like payoff since these securities do not have an option's features. Thus, the source of momentum crashes has not yet been clearly explained.

The Korean economy has been stable since September 1999 when Korea made advanced redemption of USD 19.5 billion SRF (Supplement Reserve Facility), which is short-term high interest credit of the International Monetary Fund (IMF). Thus, we divide the entire period of 1980–2013 into two sub-periods to examine whether the momentum strategy is stronger after the Asian financial crisis when foreign investors were allowed to invest in the Korean stock market without any ownership limit.

Table 4.7 presents average monthly returns of the momentum strategy and the relative frequencies of positive and negative monthly returns in the KOSPI and KOSDAQ markets. The average monthly return of the momentum strategy from November 1980 to December 2013 is −0.11% which implies no price momentum for the entire sample period. However, the average monthly return of the momentum strategy is 1.13% after the Asian financial crisis which is statistically significant at 1%. Thus, price momentum exists after the Asian financial crisis which confirms earlier studies on the Korean stock market. For the earlier period including the financial crisis, the number of months with a positive return from the momentum

Table 4.7. Average Monthly Return of Momentum Strategy: Two Sub-periods

	November 1980–September 1999		October 1999–December 2013	
	N (%)	Average Return	N (%)	Average Return
Return ≥ 0	116 (51.1%)	4.55	106 (62.0%)	4.20
Return < 0	111 (48.9%)	−6.87	65 (38.0%)	−3.90
Total	227	−1.03	171	1.13***
		(−1.44)		(2.64)

Note: Stocks in the KRX markets are formed each month into quintiles in ascending order based on 9-month past (compounded) returns. The first (last) quintile, referred to as the loser (winner) portfolio, consists of the lowest (highest) 9-month past returns. The momentum strategy is defined as longing winner portfolios and shorting loser portfolios. The holding period of the momentum strategy is 6 months and begins 1 month after portfolio formation. N indicates the number of months that have either positive or negative returns from the momentum strategy out of the total months for each sub-period.

Parentheses indicate *t*-value. *,**, and *** indicate 10%, 5%, and 1% significance levels for the monthly return of value strategy, respectively.

strategy is 116 out of 227 months which is about 51%. However, the percentage of months with positive monthly returns increases to 62% after the financial crisis. Furthermore, the average negative return of the momentum strategy increases from −6.87% to −3.90% which is larger than the 0.35% point decrease in the average positive return between the first sub-period and the second sub-period. Thus, price momentum appears in the Korean stock market after the financial crisis.

Price momentum, however, seems to result from low returns on short-term losers rather than high returns on winners. Table 4.8 shows that returns on the losers are extremely low compared to other portfolios. The momentum strategy yields positive returns at least at the 5% significance level for 3, 6, and 9-month holding period but not for the 12-month holding period. The strategy, however, that is to long any quintile portfolio except the loser and short the loser portfolio also has statistically significant positive returns. For example, the strategy of longing Q4 and shorting the loser consistently earns higher returns than the momentum strategy does.

Table 4.8. Monthly Returns of Quintile Portfolios after the Asian Financial Crisis (October 1999–December 2013)

Holding Period	3-month	6-month	9-month	12-month
Loser	0.24	0.30	0.46	0.63
Q2	1.18	1.26	1.34	1.43
Q3	1.42	1.46	1.53	1.54
Q4	1.80	1.72	1.62	1.56
Winner	1.53	1.42	1.23	1.04
Q2-Loser	0.94*** (2.88)	0.96*** (3.57)	0.88*** (3.39)	0.80*** (3.10)
Q3-Loser	1.18*** (2.83)	1.17*** (3.31)	1.07*** (3.20)	0.91*** (2.76)
Q4-Loser	1.56*** (3.37)	1.43*** (2.64)	1.16*** (3.24)	0.93*** (2.70)
Winner–Loser	1.29*** (2.43)	1.13*** (2.64)	0.77** (2.08)	0.41 (1.16)

Notes: Stocks in the KRX markets are formed each month into quintiles in ascending order based on 9-month past (compounded) returns. The first (last) quintile, referred to as the loser (winner) portfolio, consists of the lowest (highest) 9-month past returns. The holding periods vary from 3 months to 12 months.

Parentheses indicate t-value. *, **, and *** indicate 10%, 5%, and 1% significance levels for the monthly return of value strategy, respectively.

4.4.3. *Trading Behavior of Investor Types and Price Momentum*

Ownership by foreign investors sharply increases after the financial crisis. Their ownership is 13.73% in 1997 but increases to 26.69% in 2000. Except for 2008, foreign investors' ownership is above 30%, which is higher than for individual investors and domestic institutional investors. Thus, foreign investors may play a critical role in generating price momentum after the financial crisis.

If the momentum phenomenon in the Korea stock market is driven by foreign investors, the trade behavior of foreign investors will influence the returns of winner and loser portfolios. Table 4.9 presents average monthly returns on portfolios based on the trade imbalance of foreign investors within momentum portfolios. Stocks are sorted into three groups based on 9-month past returns for a 6-month holding period. The criteria for loser, middle, and winner portfolios are the 30th and 70th percentiles of 9-month past returns. For each group, stocks are again sorted into quintiles based on the trade imbalance

Table 4.9. Average Monthly Returns of Foreign Investors' Trade-Imbalance Portfolio within Momentum Portfolios from October 1999 to December 2013

| | Momentum Portfolio | | | | | |
| | Loser | | Middle | | Winner | |
Trade-Imbalance of Foreign Investors	Raw Returns	B/M and Size-adjusted Returns	Raw Returns	B/M and Size-adjusted Returns	Raw Returns	B/M and Size-adjusted Returns
Low	0.33	−0.55**	1.17**	0.09	0.96	−0.01
Q2	1.06	−0.02	1.43**	0.00	1.29**	−0.10
Q3	1.60**	0.00	1.98***	0.18	1.69**	0.04
Q4	1.12*	−0.24	1.51***	0.05	1.51**	0.22
High	0.53	−0.47**	1.14**	0.11	1.60***	0.72***
High–Low	0.20	0.08	−0.03	0.02	0.64***	0.73***
	(0.80)	(0.37)	(−0.21)	(0.14)	(2.68)	(3.51)

Notes: Stocks in the KOSPI market are sorted each month into three portfolios based on 9-month past returns. The criteria for loser, middle, and winner portfolios are the 30th and 70th percentiles of 9-month past returns, respectively. The stocks are then again sorted into quintiles based on trade imbalance of foreign investors. The portfolios are held for 6 months. One month is skipped between the formation period and the holding period. The EW monthly returns are presented as monthly raw returns on each portfolios. The size and B/M adjusted returns are also calculated by using 5 (size) × 5 (B/M) benchmark portfolios which are independently sorted into quintiles by size and B/M of stocks. The parentheses contain the t value.

Parentheses indicate t-value. *, **, and *** indicate 10%, 5%, and 1% significance levels for monthly returns of the value strategy, respectively.

of foreign investors during the 9-month sorting period.[10] The first (last) quintile, referred to as a low (high) trade imbalance portfolio,

---

[10]As explained in Chapter 2, the trade imbalance (*IMB*) of foreign investors for stock i is defined as:

$$ForIMB_{it} = 100 \times \frac{(ForB_{it} - ForS_{it})}{MV_{it-1}} \qquad (1)$$

where *ForB* (*ForS*) is (KRW) buying (selling) volume of foreign investors and *MV* is the market value defined as the number of outstanding shares multiplied by the close price of stock i at $t - 1$.

consists of the lowest (highest) trade imbalance of foreign investors, which measures selling (buying) pressure of foreign investors. It is interesting to examine the subsequent monthly returns of the loser (winner) portfolio when the selling (buying) pressure of foreign investors is high during the 9-month sorting period.

According to Table 4.9, the winner portfolio with the high trade imbalance of foreign investors has 1.60% in monthly returns, which is the second highest return within the winner portfolio. However, after controlling B/M and size by using 5 (size) × 5 (B/M) benchmark portfolios, the winner portfolio with the high trade imbalance has 0.72% of the B/M and size-adjusted return, which is the highest within all portfolios. Although the middle portfolio has high monthly raw returns, its B/M and size-adjusted return does not seem to be statistically significant. On the other hand, both low and high trade imbalance portfolios of foreign investors within the loser portfolio have statistically significant negative B/M and size-adjusted returns. Thus, the trade imbalance of foreign investors appears to influence future returns of momentum portfolios.

Table 4.9 shows that the winner portfolio with the high trade imbalance of foreign investors has the highest B/M and size-adjusted return, while the loser portfolio with the low trade imbalance of foreign investors has the lowest B/M and size-adjusted return. Figures 4.12 and 4.13 display the trade imbalance of major investor types during the 9-month sorting period as well as the 6-month holding period for these winner and loser portfolios.

According to Figure 4.12, the winner portfolio with the high trade imbalance of foreign investors by definition shows strong net buying of foreign investors, which is between 0.60% and 0.85% during the portfolio formation period. The positive trade imbalance of foreign investors continues after the formation period, although it gradually decreases to zero. As a result, the winner portfolio tends to have high returns when foreign investors exhibit momentum trading. In contrast, individual investors show the opposite trading behavior. Individual investors continue to sell winners during and after the formation period. Since the domestic institutional investors do not show any significant buying or selling pressure, the foreign investors appear to be main drivers of price momentum.

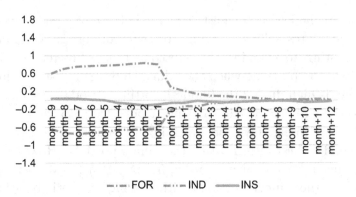

Figure 4.12.   Winner Portfolio with High Trade Imbalance of Foreign Investors
from October 1999 to December 2013

Notes: Stocks in the KOSPI market are sorted each month into three portfolios
based on 9-month past returns. The criteria for loser, middle, and winner
portfolios are the 30th and 70th percentiles, respectively. The winner stocks are
then again sorted into quintiles based on the trade imbalance of foreign investors.
The winner portfolio with the high trade imbalance consists of winner stocks with
the highest net buying of foreign investors. The portfolios are held for 6 months.
One month is skipped between the formation period and the holding period.

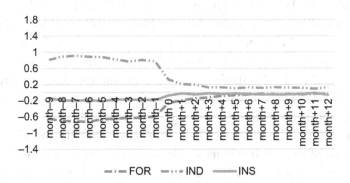

Figure 4.13.   Loser Portfolio with Low Trade Imbalance of Foreign Investors from
October 1999 to December 2013

Notes: Stocks in the KOSPI market are sorted each month into three portfolios
based on 9-month past returns. The criteria for loser, middle, and winner
portfolios are the 30th and 70th percentiles, respectively. The loser stocks are
then again sorted into quintiles based on the trade imbalance of foreign investors.
The loser portfolio with the low trade imbalance consists of loser stocks with the
highest net selling of foreign investors. The portfolios are held for 6 months. One
month is skipped between the formation period and the holding period.

The momentum trading of foreign investors may be interpreted as trade behavior in the process of overreacting to good or bad information about stocks. Daniel *et al.* (1998) suggest that overconfidence and the subsequent biased selfattribution of informed investors may result in momentum trading of informed investors who cause price momentum. However, momentum trading of informed investors can occur in the process of correcting undervaluation. For example, strong selling pressure of individual investors can delay the price reaction to good information. Thus, the buying pressure of foreign investors may continue in the process of correcting a delayed price reaction to good information.

Figure 4.13 displays the trade imbalance of major investor types for the loser portfolio with the low trade imbalance of foreign investors. Foreign investors show a negative trade imbalance during and after the formation period, exhibiting momentum trading. In contrast, individual investors show the opposite trading pattern. However, domestic institutional investors have a weakly negative trade imbalance during and after the formation period. Thus, both domestic institutional investors and foreign investors are momentum traders for the loser portfolio with a low trade imbalance of foreign investors, although domestic institutional investors are not momentum traders for the winner portfolio with a high trade imbalance of foreign investors. In short, price momentum appears strongly when foreign investors exhibit momentum trading behavior during both sorting and holding periods.

Table 4.10 shows empirical results regarding the relation between the trade imbalance of domestic institutional investors and price momentum. According to Table 4.10, the momentum portfolios combined with the trade imbalance of domestic institutional investors do not provide any statistically significant B/M and size-adjusted return, unlike the momentum portfolios with the trade imbalance of foreign investors. Thus, domestic institutional investors do not seem to be major investors in generating price momentum. However, the loser portfolio with the low trade imbalance of domestic institutional investors has a negative B/M and size-adjusted return that is statistically significant at 5%.

Table 4.10.   Average Monthly Returns of Domestic Institutional Investors' Trade Imbalance Portfolio within Momentum Portfolios from October 1999 to December 2013

Trade-Imbalance of Domestic Institutional Investors	Momentum Portfolio					
	Loser		Middle		Winner	
	Raw Returns	B/M and Size-adjusted Returns	Raw Returns	B/M and Size-adjusted Returns	Raw Returns	B/M and Size-adjusted Returns
Low	0.24	−0.63**	1.36**	0.16	1.35**	0.25
Q2	0.94	−0.18	1.55***	0.12	1.20*	−0.23
Q3	1.17*	−0.15	1.69***	0.12	1.66**	0.14
Q4	1.34*	−0.09	1.52***	0.02	1.30**	0.17
High	0.94	−0.24	1.13**	0.03	1.57**	0.57
High–Low	0.70**	0.39*	−0.23	−0.13	0.22	0.32
	(2.44)	(1.71)	(−1.27)	(−0.73)	(0.86)	(1.40)

Notes: Stocks in the KOSPI market are sorted each month into three portfolios based on 9-month past returns. The criteria for loser, middle, and winner portfolios are the 30th and 70th percentiles, respectively. The stocks are then again sorted into quintiles based on the trade imbalance of domestic institutional investors. The portfolios are held for 6 months. One month is skipped between the formation period and the holding period. The EW monthly returns are presented as monthly raw returns on each portfolio. The B/m and size-adjusted returns are also calculated by using 5 (size) × 5 (B/M) benchmark portfolios which are independently sorted into quintiles by size and B/M of stocks. The parentheses indicate the t value.

Parentheses indicate the t-value. *, **, and *** indicate 10%, 5%, and 1% significance levels for monthly return of value strategy, respectively.

Figure 4.14 shows the trade imbalances of investor types for the winner portfolio with the high trade imbalance portfolio of domestic institutional investors, as defined in Table 4.10. By definition of the portfolio, domestic institutional investors strongly buy stocks during the formation period. However, after the formation period, they turn into net sellers although their trade imbalance is negligibly small, above −0.2%. Thus, they are not momentum traders for winners. Individual investors are strong buyers during the formation period

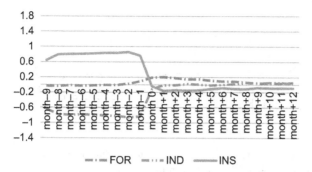

Figure 4.14. Winner Portfolio with High Trade Imbalance of Domestic Institutional Investors from October 1999 to December 2013

Notes: Stocks in the KOSPI market are sorted each month into three portfolios based on 9-month past returns. The criteria for loser, middle, and winner portfolios are the 30th and 70th percentiles, respectively. The winner stocks are then again sorted into quintiles based on the trade imbalance of domestic institutional investors. The winner portfolio with the high trade imbalance consists of stocks with highest net buying of domestic institutional investors. The portfolios are held for 6 months. One month is skipped between the formation period and the holding period.

and turn into net sellers afterward. Thus, it is interesting to note that domestic institutional investors do not show any momentum trading for winners with the high trade imbalance of domestic institutional investors. Foreign investors do not show any specific trading pattern but turn into net buyers for stocks after the formation period.

Figure 4.15 shows the trade imbalance of investor groups for the loser portfolio with the low trade imbalance of domestic institutional investors, as defined in Table 4.10. Domestic institutional investors continue to be net sellers during and after the formation period, while individual investors are net buyers. Foreign investors are also net sellers but their selling pressure appears to be negligibly small. Table 4.10 shows that the loser portfolio with a low trade imbalance of domestic institutional investors has a -0.63% B/M and size-adjusted return, which is statistically significant at 5%. Given the aforementioned four cases, the trade imbalance of investor types appears to significantly influence the returns of both winners and losers when they exhibit momentum trading during and after the formation period. On the other hand, the momentum portfolios of

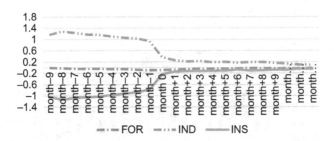

Figure 4.15.   Loser Portfolio with Low Trade Imbalance of Domestic Institutional Investors from October 1999 to December 2013

Notes: Stocks in the KOSPI market are sorted each month into three portfolios based on 9-month past returns. The criteria for loser, middle, and winner portfolios are the 30th and 70th percentiles, respectively. The stocks are then again sorted into quintiles based on the trade imbalance of domestic institutional investors within loser stocks. The loser portfolio with the low trade imbalance consists of stocks with highest net selling of domestic institutional investors. The portfolios are held for 6 months. One month is skipped between the formation period and the holding period.

winners do not have statistically significant positive B/M and size-adjusted returns in Table 4.10 when domestic institutional investors do not show momentum trading for winners as shown in Figure 4.14.

Table 4.11 presents average monthly returns on momentum portfolios with individual investors' trade imbalance. The trade imbalance of individual investors also appears to influence future returns on momentum portfolios. However, their trade behavior seems to negatively influence returns on momentum portfolios. As they sell winners during the formation period, returns on the winners are high during the holding period. As they strongly buy losers during the formation period, the returns on the losers are significantly negative. If we implement a strategy to buy winners with a low trade imbalance of individual investors and sell losers with a high trade imbalance, Table 4.11 suggests that the strategy would yield a 1.88% raw monthly return and 1.73% B/M and size-adjusted return.

Figure 4.16 shows the trade imbalance of major investor types for the winner portfolio with a low trade imbalance of individual investors. The trade imbalance of individual investors is lower than −1% during the formation period except for the first month, which

Table 4.11.   Average Monthly Returns of Individual Investors' Trade Imbalance Portfolio within Momentum Portfolios from October 1999 to December 2013

			Momentum Portfolio			
	Loser		Middle		Winner	
Trade-Imbalance Portfolio	Raw Returns	B/M and Size-adjusted Returns	Raw Returns	B/M and Size-adjusted Returns	Raw Returns	B/M and Size-adjusted Returns
Low	1.12*	−0.11	1.25**	0.06	1.72***	0.75***
Q2	1.35**	−0.13	1.45***	0.10	1.57***	0.39*
Q3	1.37**	0.05	1.54***	0.03	1.76***	0.29
Q4	0.92	−0.14	1.68***	0.22	1.09*	−0.32
High	−0.16	−0.98***	1.31**	0.04	0.93	−0.23
High–Low	0.23	−0.87***	0.06	−0.02	−0.79**	−0.98***
	(1.01)	(−2.71)	(0.27)	(−0.08)	(−2.32)	(−3.40)

Notes: Stocks in the KOSPI market are sorted each month into three portfolios based on 9-month past returns. The criteria for loser, middle, and winner portfolios are the 30th and 70th percentiles, respectively. The stocks are then again sorted into quintiles based on the trade imbalance of individual investors. The portfolios are held for 6 months. One month is skipped between the formation period and the holding period. The EW monthly returns are presented as monthly raw returns on each portfolio. The B/M and size-adjusted returns are also calculated by using 5 (size) × 5 (B/M) benchmark portfolios that are independently sorted into quintiles by size and B/M of stocks.

Parentheses indicate the *t*-value.

*, **, and *** indicate 10%, 5%, and 1% significance levels for monthly return of value strategy, respectively.

indicates strong selling pressure of individual investors. In the case of the winner portfolio with the high trade imbalance of foreign investors as shown in Figure 4.12, the trade imbalance of individual investors is between −0.6% and −0.7%. Thus, Figure 4.16 shows stronger selling pressure of individual investors.

Since both foreign and domestic institutional investors strongly buy winners with a low trade imbalance of individual investors, individual investors appear to sell those as the counter trader. Figure 4.16 presents the different trading patterns of foreign investors

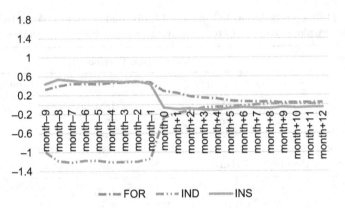

Figure 4.16. Winner Portfolio with a Low Trade Imbalance of Individual Investors from October 1999 to December 2013

Notes: Stocks in the KOSPI market are sorted each month into three portfolios based on 9-month past returns. The criteria for loser, middle, and winner portfolios are the 30th and 70th percentiles, respectively. The winner stocks are then again sorted into quintiles based on the trade imbalance of individual investors. The winner portfolio with the high trade imbalance consists of stocks with the highest net buying of individual investors. The portfolios are held for 6 months. One month is skipped between the formation period and the holding period.

and domestic institutional investors. Foreign investors continue to buy the winners after the formation period. However, although domestic institutional investors buy those stocks during the formation period, they begin to sell them after the formation period. Since domestic institutional investors are not momentum traders, their trading pattern does not seem to be related to price momentum.

Domestic institutional investors, however, are momentum traders for losers with a high trade imbalance of individual investors. As shown in Figure 4.17, domestic institutional investors continue to sell the losers during and after the formation period, while individual investors continue to buy them. Such a trading pattern of domestic institutional investors is similar to that of the loser portfolio with a low trade imbalance of domestic institutional investors shown in Figure 4.15. Foreign investors are also momentum traders although their negative trade imbalance is smaller than that of domestic

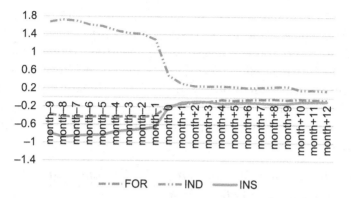

Figure 4.17. Loser Portfolio with High Trade Imbalance of Individual Investors from October 1999 to December 2013

Notes: Stocks in the KOSPI market are sorted each month into three portfolios based on 9-month past returns. The criteria for loser, middle, and winner portfolios are the 30th and 70th percentiles, respectively. The loser stocks are then again sorted into quintiles based on the trade imbalance of individual investors. The loser portfolio with the low trade imbalance consists of stocks with highest net selling of individual investors. The portfolios are held for 6 months. One month is skipped between the formation period and the holding period.

institutional investors, likely because foreign investors do not own many losers to sell.

Our results suggest that price momentum is strongly related to the trade behaviors of both foreign investors and individual investors. Price momentum appears to be positively related to the direction of foreign investors' trade imbalance but negatively related to that of individual investors. With respect to winners, domestic institutional investors do not show any momentum trading behavior. However, they exhibit momentum trading behavior in the loser portfolios with either the low trade imbalance of foreign investors or the high trade imbalance of individual investors. It is noteworthy that price momentum strongly occurs only when major investor types exhibit momentum trading behavior. Such momentum trading behavior is consistent with both the overreaction and the underreaction hypotheses. If price momentum is caused by overreaction of foreign investors, individual investors are more likely to be rational traders to prevent overreaction. On the other hand, if price momentum is caused by underreaction of individual investors, their trading is interpreted as trading forces to delay price reaction to new information and foreign investors' momentum trading is seen as trading forces that reflect new information to the stock price. Since domestic institutional investors do not exhibit momentum trading behavior, price momentum in the Korean stock market appears to be attributed to trading interaction of both foreign and individual investors.

4.4.4.   *Relation between Price Momentum and Aggregate M/B Ratios*

Figure 4.18 presents the relation between price momentum and time series aggregate M/B ratios. The 6 months from August of year t to January of year $t+1$ are divided into a period following either high or low M/B months based on the aggregate M/B ratio in July of year t. The 6 months from February to July are divided into a period following either high or low M/B months based on the aggregate M/B ratio in January of year t. For example, if the aggregate M/B ratio in January is less than the median, the subsequent 6 months from February to July are classified as a period following a low M/B month.

Figure 4.18 shows monthly returns of momentum portfolios and strategy from October 1999 to December 2013 when price momentum exists. Following high M/B months, monthly returns on momentum portfolios are low, while their monthly returns are high following low M/B months. This result is consistent with earlier findings related to the aggregate M/B ratio. However, average monthly returns of the momentum strategy appear to be higher following high M/B months than following low M/B months. The higher returns of the momentum strategy following high M/B months are due to low returns on the loser portfolio following high M/B months. The monthly return on the loser portfolio is only 0.27% following high M/B months, while it is 1.38% following low M/B months.

Stambaugh *et al.* (2012) argue that anomalies are stronger following high investor sentiment when overvaluation is more prominent. Stronger anomalies result from low returns of overvalued stocks after

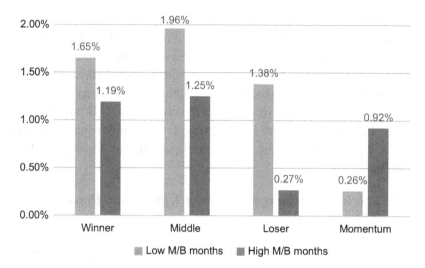

Figure 4.18.   Monthly Returns of Momentum Portfolios with High and Low M/B Ratios: October 1999–December 2013

Notes: Stocks in the KOSPI market are sorted each month into three portfolios based on 9-month past returns. The criteria for loser, middle, and winner portfolios are the 30th and 70th percentiles, respectively. The holding period is 6 months. The 6 months are classified into a period following either a high or low M/B ratio month based on the aggregate M/B ratio of KOSPI stocks. The holding period covers October 1999–December 2013.

high investor sentiment. When we try to interpret our results in the context of Stambaugh *et al.* (2012), the high M/B month is consistent with the high investor sentiment period and overvalued stocks are short-term losers. Short-term losers can be overvalued because the strong buying pressure of individual investors may delay price adjustment of short-term losers to bad information. However, this requires more explanation of why short-term losers are more overvalued than short-term winners during high investor sentiment since investors may be more likely to be excited to buy short-term winners with good news than short-term losers with bad news.

In summary, price momentum has appeared since the Asian financial crisis; it is related to the trading interaction of both foreign investors and individual investors. Price momentum is stronger when foreign investors exhibit momentum trading behavior during the portfolio formation period and holding period. At the same time, individual investors become counter traders with momentum trading of foreign investors. According to Figure 4.18, monthly returns on the winner and loser portfolios are higher following low M/B months than following high M/B months, but the momentum strategy appears to obtain more stable positive returns following high M/B months. The average high return of the momentum strategy following high M/B months appears to be due to low returns on the short-term loser portfolio.

4.4.5. *Relation between January Effect and Price Momentum*

Jegadeesh and Titman (1993) report that the monthly return of the momentum strategy is lower in January. In US stock market, the momentum strategy loses about 7% on average in January while it earns positive returns in the other months. Figure 4.19 shows

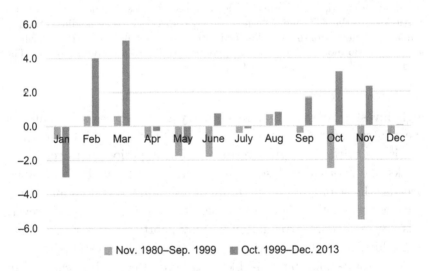

Figure 4.19.   January Effect and Momentum Strategy

Notes: Stocks in the KOSPI and KOSDAQ markets are sorted each month into quintile portfolios based on 9-month past returns. The momentum strategy is defined as buying short-term winners and shorting short-term losers. The holding period is 6 months. The entire period is divided into two sub-periods: November 1980–September 1999 and October 1999–December 2013.

that the momentum strategy yields negative returns in January in the Korean stock market although its loss is not as high as in the US. For the period of October 1999–December 2013, the momentum strategy yields positive returns in 7 out of 12 months. In contrast, the momentum strategy yields negative returns in most of the calendar months before October 1999.

4.5. Trading Volume

4.5.1. *Literature Review*

Trading volume has been used as a proxy of liquidity. Chordia *et al.* (2001) and Datar *et al.* (1998) find that stocks with lower trading volume have higher returns in the future and regard their higher returns as a liquidity premium. Since illiquidity is costly when investors immediately want to convert stocks into cash, investors may require higher returns to compensate for holding illiquid stocks. However, trading volume or liquidity can also be a proxy of investor sentiment. Baker and Stein (2004) provide a model in which high liquidity is a symptom of an overvalued market dominated by irrational investors. In their model, irrational investors overreact to private signals and actively buy stocks in the case of good signals. Conversely, irrational investors may go out of the market in the presence of short-sales constraints when they receive bad signals. Thus, high liquidity of securities implies overvalued securities, followed by low subsequent abnormal returns on the securities, while low liquidity is followed by high abnormal returns. As a result, trading volume can be a proxy for either liquidity risk or investor sentiment.

Yang and Choe (2009) find a liquidity premium in the Korean stock market. The inter-market comparison between the Korean and US markets suggests that the liquidity premium in the Korean stock market is higher than in the US and this premium cannot be fully explained by information asymmetry risk. They argue that a substantial portion of the liquidity premium is more likely attributable to investor sentiment. Yun *et al.* (2009) find that the Fama–French three-factor model does not have strong power to explain portfolio returns in the Korean stock market because of the weak B/M effect.

Instead of High Minus Low B/M Portfolios' Returns (HML), Low Minus High Turnover Portfolios' Returns (LMH) has stronger power to explain returns on portfolios sorted by size, B/M, or turnover ratio.

4.5.2.   *Trading Volume Effect*

We measure a stock's monthly turnover ratio as monthly trading value divided by market capitalization at the end of month. At the beginning of year t, we sort all stocks into quintiles based on the average monthly turnover ratio of year $t-1$; the holding period is 1 year from January to December in year t. Table 4.12 presents average monthly returns on turnover quintile portfolios. The low turnover portfolio, which consists of stocks with the lowest turnover ratios, consistently have higher returns than the high turnover portfolio. Thus, the turnover ratio is negatively related to subsequent returns. The strategy that longs the low turnover portfolio and shorts the high turnover portfolio yields 1.53% per month for the entire sample period, which is also statistically significant at 1%. The trading volume effect is one of the stronger anomalies in the Korean stock market. However, the B/M effect seems to be a little stronger than the trading volume effect. As shown in Table 4.3, when all stocks are classified into low, middle, and high B/M portfolio based on the 30th and 70th percentiles of B/M ratios, the high–low B/M strategy yields 1.68% per month.

The analysis of two sub-periods also provides similar results. The trading volume negatively affects subsequent returns, which is consistent with earlier literature. According to Table 4.12, the strategy of longing the low turnover portfolio and shorting the high turnover portfolio earns 0.67% of monthly return for January 1981–September 1999 and 2.66% for October 1990–December 2013. The trading volume effect is more prominent for the second sub-period.

4.5.3.   *Relation between January Effect and Trading Volume Effect*

As shown in Figure 4.20, the high turnover portfolio tends to have much higher returns in January than the low turnover portfolio,

Table 4.12. Average Monthly Returns on Portfolios Sorted by Turnover Ratio in the KOSPI and KOSDAQ Markets

	January 1981–December 2013	January 1981–September 1999	October 1999–December 2013
Low	2.32 (10.12)	2.25 (3.21)	2.41 (9.61)
Q2	2.07 (8.94)	2.09 (3.29)	2.06 (8.15)
Q3	1.56 (9.33)	1.79 (2.74)	1.26 (8.64)
Q4	1.40 (10.15)	1.89 (2.70)	0.75 (9.65)
High	0.79 (11.90)	1.58 (1.90)	−0.25 (11.08)
Low–High	1.53*** (11.42)	0.67 (12.69)	2.66*** (9.41)

Notes: Stocks are sorted into quintiles based on average monthly turnover ratios over the previous year. The monthly turnover ratio is defined as monthly trading value divided by market capitalization. The low (high) turnover portfolio consists of stocks with the lowest (highest) turnover ratio in the previous year. The holding period is 1 year from January to December. The test period covers January 1981 to December 2013.

Parentheses indicate the standard deviation of monthly returns.

*, **, and *** indicate 10%, 5%, and 1% significance levels for monthly return of value strategy, respectively.

while the latter continues to have higher returns in the other months. The positive relation between January returns and trading volume is contrary to the stylized empirical results. It is well known that the January effect is stronger for small stocks than large stocks in most countries. The tax-loss selling hypothesis implies that selling pressure on stocks with past poor performance is more likely to result in the price closing at the bid price in late December and the buying pressure of these stocks with their prices closing at the ask price in early January. Thus, the January effect is more likely to be prominent for the least liquid stocks, which makes it difficult to exploit the January effect for any significant profit because of high transaction costs of illiquid stocks.

The January effect in the Korean stock market, however, is different. First, the tax-loss hypothesis cannot be applied to the Korean stock market due to the lack of capital gains tax in Korea. Second, although the January effect is stronger for small stocks,

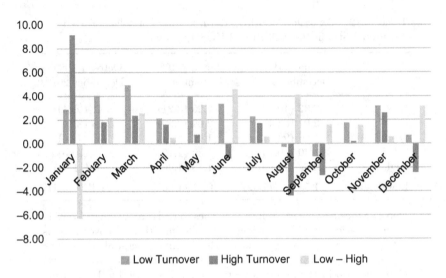

■ Low Turnover   ■ High Turnover   ▨ Low – High

Figure 4.20.   Relation between Trading Volume and Seasonality of Monthly Returns in the KOSPI and KOSDAQ Markets 1981 to 2013

Notes: Stocks are sorted into quintiles based on average monthly turnover ratios over the previous year. The monthly turnover ratio is defined as monthly trading value divided by market capitalization. The low (high) turnover portfolio consists of stocks with the lowest (highest) turnover ratio in the previous year. Low–high is referred to as a strategy that longs low turnover portfolios and shorts high turnover portfolios. The holding period is 1 year from January to December.

actively traded stocks have high January returns. The high turnover stocks capture more than 9% of the January return. Since stocks with highly active trading usually have low transaction costs, the strategy of buying actively traded stocks in December and selling them in January seems to be attractive in the Korean stock markets. It is an interesting question why high turnover stocks in the Korean stock markets have higher returns only in January.

4.5.4.   *Relation between Trading Volume Effect and Aggregate M/B Ratios*

We also examine whether the effect of trading volume on returns is influenced by the time series aggregate M/B ratios. As discussed earlier, the 6 months from January to June are classified into a period following either the high or low M/B month based on the aggregate

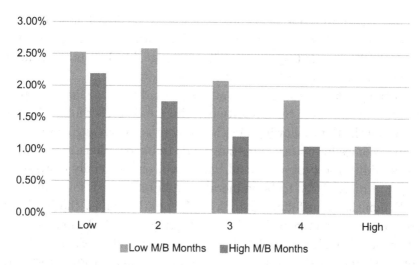

Figure 4.21. Average Monthly Returns of Turnover Ratio Portfolios Following Low and High M/B Months in the KOSPI and KOSDAQ Markets 1982 to 2013

Notes: Stocks are sorted into quintiles based on average monthly turnover ratios over the previous year. The monthly turnover ratio is defined as monthly trading value divided by market capitalization. The low (high) turnover portfolio consists of stocks with the lowest (highest) turnover ratio in the previous year. Low–high is referred to as a strategy that longs low turnover portfolios and shorts high turnover portfolios. The holding period is 1 year from January to December. The 6 months from January to June are classified into a period following either the high or low M/B month based on the aggregate M/B ratio in December of the previous year. The 6 months from July to December are defined as a period following either high or low M/B months based on the aggregate M/B ratio in June of the same year.

M/B ratio in December of the previous year. The 6 months from July to December are defined as a period following either high or low M/B months based on the aggregate M/B ratio in June of the same year. For example, if the aggregate M/B ratio in June is higher than or equal to the median, the subsequent 6 months from July to December are classified into the period following the high M/B month.

According to Figure 4.21, average returns following low M/B months are consistently higher than average returns of the same level's portfolio following high M/B months. However, the L–H strategy, defined as buying the low turnover portfolio and shorting the high turnover portfolio, provides higher returns following high M/B months than following low M/B months. The L–H strategy yields 1.73% in monthly return following high M/B months, while it yields 1.46% following low M/B months.

If the positive returns of this strategy are due to the liquidity premium, we can expect the liquidity premium to be higher following low M/B months than following high M/B months. As an aggregate M/B ratio becomes low, stock valuation tends to be low. Since stocks with low liquidity are typically small, neglected, or financially distressed, they are more likely to be vulnerable to liquidity risk following low M/B months than following high M/B months. Thus, the liquidity premium is expected to be higher following low M/B months than following high M/B months. Therefore, the result of Figure 4.21 is not consistent with the liquidity premium's expectation. However, a distinctively low monthly return on the high turnover portfolio following high M/B months appears to be more consistent with the investor sentiment hypothesis with a limit on short sales, as Stambaugh *et al.* (2012) suggest.

References

Amihud, Y., 2002, Illiquidity and Stock Returns: Cross-Section and Time-Series Effects, *Journal of Financial Markets* 5, 31–56.

Asness, C. S., T. J. Moskowitz, and L. H. Pedersen, 2013, Value and Momentum Everywhere, *Journal of Finance* 58, 929–895.

Asness, C. S., A. Frazzini, R. Israel, and T. J. Moskowitz, 2014, Fact, Fiction, and Momentum Investing, *Journal of Portfolio Management* 40, 75–92.

Baker, M. and J. C. Stein, 2004, Market Liquidity as a Sentiment Indicator, *Journal of Financial Markets* 7, 271–299.

Bansal, R., R. F. Dittmar, and C. T. Lundblad, 2005, Consumption, Dividends, and the Cross-Section of Equity Returns, *Journal of Finance* 60, 1639–1672.

Banz, R.W., 1981, The Relationship between Return and Market Value of Common Stocks, *Journal of Financial Economics* 9, 3–18.

Barberis, N., A. Shleifer, and R. Vishny, 1998, A model of investor sentiment, *Journal of Financial Economics* 49, 307–343.

Barry, C. B., E. Goldreyer, L. Lockwood, and M. Rodriguez, 1981, Robustness of Size and Value Effects in Emerging Equity Markets, 1985–2000, *Emerging Markets Review* 3, 1–30.

Berk, J., R. Green, and V. Naik, 1999, Optimal Investment, Growth Options, and Security Returns, *Journal of Finance* 54, 1553–1607.

Bernstein, R., 1995, *Style Investing*, Hoboken, NJ: John Wiley & Sons, Inc.

Chan, L. K., Y. Hamao, and J. Lakonishok, 1991, Fundamentals and Stock Returns in Japan, *Journal of Finance* 46, 1739–1764.

Chan, L. K., J Jarceski, and J. Lakonishok, 2000, New Paradigm or Same Old Hype in Equity Investing? *Financial Analysts Journal* 56, 23–36.

Chordia, T., A. Subrahmanyam, and V. R. Anshuaman, 2001, Trading Activity and Expected Stock Returns, *Journal of Financial Economics* 59, 3–32.

Chordia, T. and L. Shivakumar, 2002, Momentum, Business Cycles, and Time-Varying Expected Returns, *Journal of Finance* 57, 989–1019.

Chui, A. C. W., S. Titman, and K. C. J, Wei, 2010, Individualism and Momentum around the World, *Journal of Finance* 65, 361–392.

Conrad, J. S. and G. Kaul, 1998, An Anatomy of Trading Strategies, *Review of Financial Studies*, 11(4), 489–519.

Daniel, K. and T. J. Moskowitz, 2016, Momentum Crashes, *Journal of Financial Economics* 122, 221–247.

Daniel, K. and S. Titman, 1997, Evidence on the Characteristics of Cross-Sectional Variation in Common Stock Returns, *Journal of Finance* 52, 1–33.

Daniel, K, S. Titman, and K. C. J. Wei, 2001, Explaining the Cross-Section of Stock Returns in Japan: Factors or Characteristics? *Journal of Finance* 56, 743–766.

Daniel, K. D., D. Hirshleifer, and A. Subrahmanyam, 1998, Investor Psychology and Security Market Under- and Overreactions, *Journal of Finance* 53, 1839–1886.

Daniel, K. and S. Titman, 2006, Market Reactions to Tangible and Intangible Information, *Journal of Finance* 61, 1605–1643.

Datar, V.T., N. Y. Naik, and R. Radeliffe, 1998, Liquidity and Stock Returns: An Alternative Test, *Journal of Financial Markets* 1, 205–219.

Davis, J, 1994, The Cross-section of Realized Stock Returns: The pre-COMPUSTAT Evidence, *Journal of Finance* 49, 1579–1593.

Davis, J, E. F. Fama, and K. French, 2000, Characteristics, Covariances, and Average Returns: 1929 to 1997, *Journal of Finance* 55, 389–406.

DeBondt, W. F. M. and R. Thaler, 1985, Does the Stock Market Overreact? *Journal of Finance* 40, 793–805.

Dichev, I. D., 1998, Is the Risk of Bankruptcy A Systematic Risk? *Journal of Finance* 53, 1131–1147.

Dimson, E. and P. Marsh, 1999, Murphy's Law and Market Anomalies, *Journal of Portfolio Management* 25, 53–69.

Elsewarapu, V. R. and M. R. Reinganum, 1993, The Persistence of the Small Firm/January Effect: Is It Consistent with Investors' Learning and Arbitrage Efforts? *Quarterly Review of Economics and Finance* 49, 1172–1193.

Eom, Y., 2013, Momentum Profits and Firm Size, *Korean Journal of Financial Studies* 42, 901–927 (in Korean).

Erb, C. B. and C. R. Harvey, 2006, The Strategic and Tactical Value of Commodity Futures, *Financial Analysts Journal* 62, 69–97.

Fama, E. F. and K. R. French, 1992, The Cross-Section of Expected Stock Returns, *Journal of Finance* 47, 427–465.

Fama, E. F. and K. R. French, 1993, Common Risk Factors in the Returns on Stocks and Bonds, *Journal of Financial Economics* 33, 3–56.

Fama, E. F. and K. R. French, 1995, Size and Book-to-Market Factors in Earnings and Returns, *Journal of Finance* 50, 131–155.

Fama, E. F. and K. R. French, 1996, Multifactor Explanations of Asset Pricing Anomalies, *Journal of Finance* 51, 55–84.

Fama, E. F. and K. R. French, 1998, Value versus Growth: The International Evidence, *Journal of Finance* 53, 1975–1999.

Fama, E. F. and K. R. French, 2012, Size, Value, and Momentum in International Stock Returns, *Journal of Financial Economics* 105, 457–472.

Fama, E. F. and J. D. MacBeth, 1973, Risk, Return, and Equilibrium: Empirical Tests, *Journal of Political Economy* 81, 607–636.

Gorton, G., F. Hayashi, and G. Rouwenhorst, 2013, The Fundamentals of Commodity Futures Returns, *Review of Finance* 17, 35–105.

Griffin J. M., S. Ji, and J. S. Martin, 2005, Global Momentum Strategies, *Journal of Portfolio Management* 31, 23–39.

Griffin, J. M., S. Ji, and J. S. Martin, 2003. Momentum Investing and Business Cycle Risk: Evidence from Pole to Pole, *Journal of Finance* 58, 2515–2548.

Grinblatt, M. and B. Han, 2005, Prospect Theory, Mental Accounting and Momentum, *Journal of Financial Economics* 78, 311–339.

Grinblatt, M. and M. Keloharju, 2001, What Makes Investors Trade? *Journal of Finance* 56, 589–616.

Grinblatt, M., S. Titman, and R. Wermers, 1995, Momentum Investment Strategies, Portfolio Performance, and Herding: A Study of Mutual Fund Behavior, *American Economic Review* 85, 1088–1105.

Hameed, A. and Y. Kusnadi, 2002, Momentum Strategies: Evidence from Pacific Basin Stock Markets, *Journal of Financial Research* 25, 383–397.

Haugen, R, 1995, The New Finance: The Case against Efficient Markets, Prentice Hall: Englewood Cliffs, New Jersey.

Hong, H. and J. C. Stein, 1999, A Unified Theory of Underreaction, Momentum Trading and Overreaction in Asset Markets, *Journal of Finance* 54, 2143–2184.

Hou, K. and M. V. Dijk, 2014, Resurrecting the Size Effect: Firm Size, Profitability Shocks, and Expected Stock Returns, Dice Center Working Paper No. 2010-1.

Hvidkjaer S., 2006, A Trade-Based Analysis of Momentum, *Review of Financial Studies* 19, 457–491.

Jegadeesh, N, and S. Titman, 1993, Returns to Buying Winners and Selling Losers: Implication for Stock Market Efficiency, *Journal of Finance* 48, 65–91.

Jegadeesh, N, and S. Titman, 2001, Profitability of Momentum Strategies: An Evaluation of Alternative Explanations, *Journal of Finance* 56, 699–720.

Kam, H. K., 1997, An Empirical Study of the Relationship between Fundamental Variables and the Korean Stock Market, *Korean Journal of Financial Management* 14, 21–55 (in Korean).

Kaniel, R., G. Saar, and S. Titman, 2008, Individual Investor Trading and Stock Returns, *Journal of Finance* 63, 273–310.

Kim, K. Y. and Y. B. Kim, 2007, Does the CAPM Explain the Value Premiums in the Korean Stock Market? *DAEHAN Journal of Business* 20, 667–689 (in Korean).

Kim, S. C. and J. Y. Kim, 2000, Firm Size and Book-to-Market Factors in Korean Stock Returns, *Korean Journal of Finance* 13, 21–47 (in Korean).

Kim, S. P. and Y. S. Yun, 1999, Fundamental Variables, Macroeconomic Factors, Risk Characteristics and Equity Returns, *Korean Journal of Financial Management* 5, 179–213 (in Korean).

Kim, S. U., 1994, Analysis of Size Effect in Korean Stock Market Returns, In Sukho Sonu and Y. S. Yun *et al.*, Sock Price Volatility, Hakhyunsa, Seoul, Korea, pp. 131–140 (in Korean).

Kim, S., 2009, Explaining the Cross-section of Stock Returns: Characteristics or Risk Factors, *Korean Journal of Financial Studies* 38, 289–323 (in Korean).

Kim, S., 2012, A Study on the Profitability of the Trading Strategies Using Past Returns, *Asian Review of Financial Research* 25, 203–246 (in Korean).

Laknonishok, J., Shleifer A., and R. W. Vishny, 1994, Contrarian Investment, Extrapolation, and Risk, *Journal of Finance* 49, 1541–1578.

Michou, M., S. Mouselli, and A. Stark, 2010, Fundamental Analysis and the Modelling of Normal Returns in the UK, Working Paper. Retrieved from https://papers.ssrn.com/sol3/papers.cfm?abstract_id=1607759.

Nofsinger, J. R. and R. W. Sias, 1999, Herding and Feedback Trading by Institutional and Individual Investors, *Journal of Finance* 54, 2263–2295.

Roll, R., 2003, Style Return Differentials: Illusions, Risk Premium, or Investment Opportunities, In T. D. Coggin and F. J. Fabozzi, (eds.), *Handbook of Equity Style Management*, 3rd edn., John Willey: Hoboken.

Rosenberg, B., K. Reid, and R. Lanstein, 1984, Persuasive Evidence of Market Inefficiency, *Journal of Portfolio Management* 11, 9–17.

Rouwenhorst, K. G., 1998, International Momentum Strategies, *Journal of Finance* 53, 267–284.

Song, Y. C. and J. K. Lee, 1997, A Study for Estimation of Cost of Equity, *Korean Journal of Financial Management* 14, 157–181 (in Korean).

Stambaugh, R. F., J. Yu, and Y. Yuan, 2012, Short of It: Investor Sentiment and Anomalies, *Journal of Financial Economics* 104, 288–302.

Yang, C. W. and H. Choe, 2009, Liquidity Risk and Asset Returns: The Case of the Korean Stock Market, *Korean Journal of Financial Management* 26, 103–140.

Yun, S. Y., B. I. Ku, Y. H. Eom, and J. H. Han, 2009, The Cross-section of Stock Returns in Korea, An Empirical Investigation, *Korean Journal of Finance* 22, 1–44 (in Korean).

Chapter 5

Corporate Event

We examine stock-price movements around the announcement of corporate events such as IPOs, SEOs, stock splits, share repurchases, and dividend payments. According to the efficient market hypothesis (EMH), stock price reacts to new information fully and instantaneously. Thus, it is difficult to earn abnormal returns using an investment strategy based on corporate events. However, many researchers claim that the markets under- or overrespond to the information from a behavioral perspective. Thus, we summarize market behavior related to the announcement of corporate events in Korea.

Researchers have used event studies to produce useful knowledge about how stock prices respond to new information. Event studies can be performed to find out how quickly security prices react to the release of new information and have been used to analyze many corporate events. Do stock prices react to the announcement of corporate events rapidly or slowly? Are the returns following the announcement date abnormally high or low, or are they simply normal? Here, "normal returns" are defined as the expected returns provided by an equilibrium asset-pricing model such as CAPM, or multi-factor models. Thus, an event study is a so-called joint test, which involves testing the asset-pricing model's validity and market efficiency. Abnormal returns after the announcement of corporate events might be due to an inefficient market, use of an improper testing model, or both.

Figure 5.1 shows what happens when favorable information about a firm's value arrives in the market at time 0. The horizontal axis

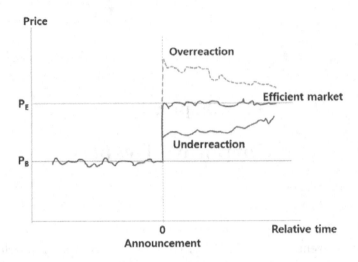

Figure 5.1.   Possible Effects of Information on a Firm's Stock Price

indicates the timeline and the vertical axis shows the stock price. Figure 5.1 shows the stock price over time. At time 0 ($t = 0$), information about a corporate event is released. The timeline has a positive sign at $t = 0$. Observe that shortly before the news arrives, the stock price moves randomly around the base price (P_B). With the arrival of the information the price immediately moves to its new equilibrium price (P_E), where it stays until additional information arrives. This is consistent with the semi-strong form of market efficiency.

However, Figure 5.1 shows two alternative situations that cannot occur in an efficient market when good news arrives. In the lower upward-sloping line, the stock price reacts slowly to the information and does not reach an P_E at $t = 0$, the event date. Consequently, the stock reaches its P_E long after the information is released. We call this type of price pattern "underreaction." Conversely, in the higher downward-sloping line, the security's price overreacts to the information and then slowly settles to its equilibrium value.

Earlier studies have examined stock returns following important corporate announcements. Event studies, introduced by Fama *et al.* (1969), produce useful evidence on how stock prices respond to

Table 5.1. Event Studies Evidence

Event	Announcement Return	Long-term Post-event Return	Initial Market Reaction
Earnings announcement	+	+	Underreaction
Dividend initiations	+	+	Underreaction
Dividend omissions	−	−	Underreaction
IPOs	+	−	Overreaction
Mergers (acquiring firm)	0	−	Underreaction
New exchange listing	+	−	Overreaction
Proxy fights	+	− (0)	Overreaction (No)
SEOs	−	−	Underreaction
Share repurchase (open market)	+	+	Underreaction
Share repurchase (tender offer)	+	+	Underreaction
Stock spin-off	+	+ (0)	Underreaction (No)
Stock splits	+	+	Underreaction

Source: Fama (1998).

information. According to traditional finance theory, the stock price instantaneously adjusts to and fully reflects new information. However, many studies on long-term performance after corporate events indicate that the initial market response may be an overreaction or underreaction to corporate events, as Figure 5.1 describes. Table 5.1 summarizes some results of corporate event studies in the US market that have examined the reaction of security prices to the release of information, such as earnings and dividends, share repurchases, stock splits, stock listings, mergers, acquisitions, and stock sales (IPOs and SEOs).

The semi-strong form of the EMH is supported by studies that document the absence of abnormal returns after public announcements of important new information. As shown in Table 5.1, the result of a semi-strong form EMH test is somewhat mixed. Apparent underreaction seems to be about as frequent as apparent overreaction, which may be consistent with the EMH as Fama (1988) claims. However, when analyzed one by one, the results are inconsistent with the EMH. Long-lived price responses may give investors the opportunity to profit from such information and thus are inconsistent with the EMH.

It is important to determine whether the stock market is efficient or not because we may make abnormal returns by using patterns in stock price after the announcement. In this section, we analyze corporate events, such as IPOs, SEOs, stock splits, share repurchases, and dividends in the Korean stock market. We also analyze the trading patterns of investor types around and after the events.

5.1.   IPOs

The Korean IPO market can be divided into two markets: the KOSPI (main board) and the KOSDAQ market. The number of IPOs on the Korea Exchange (KRX) by year and industry are summarized in Table 5.2. In 2010 and 2011, the number of IPOs on the market is fairly high due to the recovery of IT companies, although most Korean IPO firms are in manufacturing. In 2012, the number of IPOs decreases sharply because of the European debt crisis and global economic recession, but it gradually recovers. After 2012, IPO activities recover to the previous level but are still lower than in 2010 and 2011. It is well known that IPOs have hot and cold markets; however, IPOs do not appear to be related to the overall KOSPI and KOSDAQ index performance, likely because of the short sample period.

The returns of the first-trading day after IPOs are often extremely high, which is called the IPO puzzle. The most dominant hypothesis regarding the IPO puzzle is that stocks tend to be underpriced when they are issued to the public for the first time. High returns on the first trading day of IPO stocks may be obtained as their prices increase to the fundamental price. The 1-day average return for IPOs has historically been very large around the world. On average, the first day's return was 18.3% in the US market between 1960 and 2003. First-day high returns exist in other stock exchange markets around the world. On the other hand, Ritter (1991) find that newly listed firms appear to perform relatively poorly over the 3–5 years after their IPOs. This long-term underperformance is also associated with subsequent issuance of equities (i.e., SEOs).

Table 5.2. Number of IPOs on KRX: 2010–2016

Year	Manufacturing	Services	Financial Services	Wholesale & Retail	Others	Total IPOs	KOSPI Return	KOSDAQ Return
2010	50	18	23	4	1	96	21.9	−0.6
2011	54	12	1	4	2	73	−11.0	−2.1
2012	22	2	1	0	3	28	9.4	−0.8
2013	33	3	2	1	1	40	0.7	0.7
2014	35	7	26	2	2	72	−4.8	8.6
2015	31	5	7	3	1	47	2.4	25.6
2016	22	9	4	2	3	41	3.3	−7.5

Source: Korea Exchange, FnGuide.

IPOs in the Korean market also show strong first-day returns. The average first-day returns on IPO stocks in Korea is large compared to those in other developed countries, but there is a substantial decrease in the first-day returns over time. This decreasing trend can be attributed to a learning process for each of the major parties involved: issuers, underwriters, and investors. However, it is more likely that this trend is strongly associated with changes in regulations covering the mechanics and the valuation process of IPOs.

A long list of studies has been conducted on long-term performance of IPOs in Korea. Among them, Kim and Jung (2010) explore if the higher initial returns and the poorer long-run performance observed in the IPO markets are associated with a firm's IPO into hot markets; they then empirically examine the effect of investor optimism on this phenomenon using 432 IPO firms from 2001 to 2005. They find that the initial returns and long-run underperformance of IPOs in a hot market are significantly higher than those of IPOs in a cold market. They provide evidence that investor optimism has a positive effect on the initial return and a negative effect on the long-run performance.

Large initial returns together with poor long-term performance, as shown in Table 5.3, lead to IPO puzzles in Korea. Some researchers suggest a behavioral explanation for the puzzles. Behavioral theories assume that the favorable market conditions that prevail at the time of the IPO generate overoptimism among some investors. Such

Table 5.3.   Empirical Results of Korean IPOs

Study	Sample Periods: Numbers	Initial Return	Long-term Return
Kim and Jung (2010)	2001–2005: 432	+	−
Lee and Kim (2009)	2000–2007: 569	+	not test
Park and Shin (2007)	1999–2006: 819	+	not test
Kim and Kim (2000)	1988–1994: 267	not test	+(0)
Choi and Huh (2000)	1992–1996: 107	+	−
Lim (1997)	1988–1994: 342	+	−
Lim and Lee (1995)	1980–1990: 331	not test	−

Table 5.4.   First-day Return and Post-IPO Return

Market	High/Low M/B Months		First-Day Return	One-Month Return
KOSPI	High M/B	82	32.8%	−3.33%
	Low M/B	13	30.6%	−6.12%
	Total	95	32.5%	−4.59%
KOSDAQ	High M/B	711	37.4%	−0.05%
	Low M/B	317	65.7%	0.00%
	Total	1,028	46.2%	−0.05%

Note: High and low M/B months are classified by the aggregate M/B ratio of the previous month.

investors bid up the offer price beyond the intrinsic value, and the aftermarket share price eventually falls in subsequent months.

As a separate empirical test, we analyze 1,123 IPOs between 2000 and 2013: 95 KOSPI firms and 1,028 KOSDAQ firms. High and low M/B months are classified by the aggregate M/B ratio of the previous month. The months following the high (low) aggregate M/B ratio are referred to as periods following high (low) M/B months.[1] Because of the IT bubble in the early 2000s, most IPOs occurred in the KOSDAQ market. Abnormally high first-day returns are also found in our sample. The average first-day return is 44.96%, and the KOSPI has more moderate first-day returns (32.5%) than the KOSDAQ (46.2%). The 1-month returns in the KOSPI and KOSDAQ markets after the IPOs are −4.59% and −0.05%, respectively.

The majority of IPOs occur in periods following high M/B months: 86.3% of KOSPI IPOs and 69.1% of KOSDAQ IPOs occur following high M/B months, showing a similar result. IPOs are known to concentrate in hot markets or in periods when the valuation of equities is high. High frequencies of IPOs following high M/B months are consistent with earlier findings. On the other hand, the first-day returns following the low M/B months are not higher than those in the high M/B months in the KOSPI market. However, the first-day

---

[1]For details, please refer to "iterative sorting of M/B ratios to avoid look ahead bias" in Chapter 2.

Table 5.5.   12- or 24-Month Buy-and-Hold Abnormal Returns (BHAR) of IPO Stocks

	KOSPI		KOSDAQ		Total	
Year	BHAR12 (%)	BHAR24 (%)	BHAR12 (%)	BHAR24 (%)	BHAR12 (%)	BHAR24 (%)
2000	NA	NA	38.94	28.60	38.94	28.60
2001	NA	NA	−11.98	−6.24	−11.98	−6.24
2002	4.45	−15.92	7.22	−2.59	7.13	−3.02
2003	−69.65	−81.98	−2.53	2.64	−8.63	16.53
2004	4.39	−15.04	11.86	34.80	10.78	27.55
2005	−21.99	−27.10	−40.78	−60.22	−38.4	−56.03
2006	−50.24	−31.51	14.41	11.69	5.93	6.03
2007	3.58	−9.49	−9.33	11.62	−7.83	9.17
2008	16.94	20.93	26.10	26.24	25.01	25.61
2009	8.34	16.91	−13.32	−8.18	−9.58	−3.85
2010	−10.39	−20.38	−13.70	−9.72	−12.98	−12.04
2011	−2.46	1.56	−7.12	−9.09	−6.13	−6.84
2012	31.75	25.27	−6.52	−35.98	3.05	−20.66
2013	NA	NA	13.25	7.92	13.25	7.92
Total	−6.24	−10.57	3.02	3.22	2.19	1.99

Notes: BHAR is defined as the difference between the realized buy-and-hold return and the value-weighted buy-and-hold return. BHAR12 and BHAR24 are the 12-month and 24-month buy-and-hold abnormal returns, respectively.

returns in the KOSDAQ market following the low M/B months are much higher than those following the high M/B months. Thus, the first-day returns do not appear to have any consistent relation to high or low M/B months.

Table 5.5 shows the long-term performance of IPO stocks. We report the 12-month and 24-month buy-and-hold abnormal returns (BHAR12 and BHAR24) after the IPOs. BHAR is defined here as the difference between the realized buy-and-hold return and the value-weighted buy-and-hold return. Although the first-day returns are largely positive and statistically significant, BHAR12 and BHAR24 are small positive returns of about 2.19% (12 months) and 1.99% (24 months), respectively, which is not statistically significant. In the KOSPI market, the average long-term abnormal returns are negative. We also can see negative returns in many years, as shown in Table 5.5.

In some cases, the 24-month BHARs are less than −60% in KOSDAQ and less than –80% in KOSPI. Highly volatile markets are a typical aspect of high risks in IPOs.

However, the BHAR12 and BHAR24 of KOSDAQ IPO stocks do not show any negative returns, which is not consistent with earlier studies in Korea. The non-negative long-term performance may result from either our new sample of IPOs or an inappropriate benchmark. Because IPO stocks tend to face severely uncertain future prospects, they are recognized as highly risky stocks. If the expected returns of IPO stocks are much higher than market returns, our BHAR should be much lower than Table 5.5 reports. Nevertheless, Table 5.5 suggests that the long-term return performance of IPO stocks, on average, does not underperform the market return.

5.2. Seasoned Equity Offering

It is well known that, on average, the market reacts negatively to news of seasoned equity offerings (SEOs), thus decreasing stock price. In addition, Loughran and Ritter (1995) find that the average return of shares over 5 years after the issuance of SEOs is below the average return of non-issuing firms between 1970 and 1990 in the US. This long-term underperformance may suggest that the initial stock-price decrease is not large enough. The most promising hypothesis regarding negative market reaction to SEO announcements is the overvaluation hypothesis. When a firm believes that its shares are overvalued, the firm may issue SEOs to sell additional shares at the overvalued price. In this case, the market will negatively react to the announcement of SEOs because the market interprets SEO announcements as indicating overvaluation of stocks. However, if the negative reaction of the market is not sufficient, the firm's managers can transfer the wealth of investors to that of existing shareholders by issuing SEOs.

Unlike US market-based studies, most Korean market-based studies show that stock price increases around the SEO announcement date but decreases after the announcement in the long run. Table 5.6 summarizes the test results of SEOs in Korea. Using Korean data, Kim and Byun (1998) find that the long-run performance of stocks

Table 5.6.   Empirical Results of Korean SEOs

Study	Sample Periods: Numbers	Announcement Return	Long-term Return
Chung and Jeong (2008)	2000–2005: 122	− (KOSPI 200), + (etc)	not test
Shim and Ahn (2005)	1990–1997: 315	+	−
Kim and Kong (2000)	1987–1997: 147	+	−
Kho and Park (2000)	1981–1995: 1222	+	− (mixed)
Kim and Byun (1998)	1982–1993: 102	not test	−

with SEOs is significantly lower than that of non-issuing firms, a result that is consistent with that of Loughran and Ritter. The size-adjusted and the market-adjusted cumulative abnormal returns (CARs) for 36 months after an SEO are −18.10% and −6.31%, respectively. More recently, Chung and Jeong (2008) divide SEO firms into two sub-groups, one with firms from the KOSPI 200 and the other including firms from the rest of KOSPI, assuming the former is more informationally efficient than the latter. They find that the market reacts negatively to the announcement of SEOs on the KOSPI 200, which is similar to results in the US market. They argue that differences in market reaction between Korean and US SEOs may partially result from the degree of informational efficiency in the market.

It is important to note that direct rights offering is much more popular than cash offering in Korea. The direct rights offerings of SEOs may explain the positive market reactions to SEOs in Korea. A direct rights offering is an offer made by an issuer directly to the existing shareholders. In rights offering in which shares are offered to existing shareholders, there is no incentive for a firm to issue SEOs at an overvalued price because existing shareholders do not receive any benefits from SEOs.

As a new empirical test, we analyze 2,405 SEOs from 1995 to 2013, in which 1,002 KOSPI and 1,403 KOSDAQ SEOs are selected. The CAR is cumulative realized returns minus cumulative market returns. CAR (−3,0) is measured from 3 days before a corporate event's announcement date to the announcement date.

Table 5.7.   CARs Around the SEO Announcement

Market	High/Low M/B	Months	CARs (−3, 0)	CARs(−1,+1)
KOSPI	High M/B	637	1.02%**	−0.67%*
	Low M/B	365	0.19%	−0.62%
	Total	1,002	0.72%*	−0.65%**
KOSDAQ	High M/B	1,191	2.09%**	1.56%**
	Low M/B	212	0.39%	0.29%
	Total	1,403	1.83%**	1.37%**

Notes: *, **, and *** indicate 10%, 5%, and 1% significance level, respectively. High and low M/B months are classified by the aggregate M/B ratio of the previous month. CAR (−3,0) and CAR (−1,+1) are the cumulative abnormal returns from 3 days before a corporate announcement date to the announcement date and from 1 day before the announcement date to 1 day after it, respectively.

CARs (−3,0) of SEO stocks around the announcement date using the market adjusted model are 0.72% in the KOSPI market and 1.83% in the KOSDAQ market. These positive market reactions are consistent with the earlier literature on SEOs in the Korean stock market. However, the market reaction in the KOSPI market shows a negative sign when we use a CAR (−1,+1) window. This finding is similar to that of Chung and Jeong (2008), who find a negative reaction to KOSPI 200 SEOs. However, SEO stocks in the KOSDAQ market have a significantly positive CAR (−1,+1). Differences in the market reactions to SEO announcements between the KOSPI and KOSDAQ markets may be related to the trading behaviors of individual investors, given that individual investors predominantly trade KOSDAQ stocks. We will discuss this issue in Section 6.

Although a high M/B month indicates that the aggregate M/B ratio of the previous month is high, high M/B months may coincide with a high investor sentiment period. If so, a stronger positive market reaction to SEO announcements following high M/B months may be due to high investor sentiment. However, it is difficult to understand why the first-day returns of IPO stocks in the KOSDAQ market are much higher following low M/B months if low M/B months imply low investor sentiment. In addition, the number of SEOs in both markets is much larger following high M/B months than following low M/B months. If the high aggregate M/B ratio indicates general equity overvaluation, a larger number of SEOs following high M/B months is consistent with the overvaluation hypothesis.

One interesting finding is that firms with more than 5% of foreign investor trading have a negative market reaction around the SEO announcement. In addition, foreign investors and institutional investors tend to sell their shares before the the announcement, while individual investors tend to buy stocks. We give more analyses of investor types in Section 6.

We report the long-term BHARs of SEOs in Table 5.8, which shows poorer performance in low M/B months than in high M/B months. KOSPI SEOs in particular have both negative BHAR12 and BHAR24 in low M/B months. KOSDAQ stocks with SEOs show also a negative BHAR12 of −11.64% but a positive BHAR24 of 29.89%. The total average BHAR12 and BHAR24 are 8.60%, and 13.03%, respectively. In general, the market response and long-term performance of SEO stocks are better following high M/B months than following low M/B months.

Table 5.8. 12-Month or 24-Month Buy-and-Hold Returns of SEOs

Market	High/Low M/B	Months	BHAR12 (%)	BHAR24 (%)
	High M/B	637	4.16	19.86
KOSPI	Low M/B	365	−8.62	−29.50
	Total	1,002	−4.99	−9.49
	High M/B	1,191	19.90	29.09
KOSDAQ	Low M/B	212	−11.64	29.89
	Total	1,403	15.13	29.21
Total Average		2,405	8.60	13.03

Notes: High and low M/B months are classified by the aggregate M/B ratio of the previous month.

BHAR is defined as the difference between the realized buy-and-hold return and the valueweighted buy-and-hold return. BHAR12 and BHAR24 are 12-month and 24-month buy-and-hold abnormal returns, respectively.

According to Table 5.8, positive total averages of BHAR12 and BHAR24 are obtained when investors purchase SEO stocks after the announcement date. Because the expected returns of SEO stocks are assumed to be market returns, the results of Table 5.8 may be exposed to the benchmark problem. Thus, the positive market reaction to SEO announcements and the positive long-term performance of SEO stocks do not necessarily imply a market underreaction to SEO announcements, However, Table 5.8 suggests that SEO stocks outperform the market return over at least 24 months.

Recently Kim and Byun (2016) analyzed Korean SEOs (i.e., rights-offering SEOs) and the trade behavior of the stockholder who has the largest shareholding. They classify SEO firms into two sub-samples to examine management's incentive to protect the wealth of existing shareholders: increasing the shareholding ratio of the largest shareholder and decreasing the shareholding ratio of the largest shareholder. The empirical results of the study are as follows. First, CARs around the announcement date of an SEO in the sample with an increase in the largest shareholder's shareholding ratio are higher than those in the sample with a decrease in the largest shareholder's shareholding ratio. This finding supports the idea that the information of the SEO is more favorable news to the market when SEOs are aligned with the largest shareholder's incentive. Second, the relationship between discretionary accruals during the year before an SEO and a change in largest shareholder's shareholding ratio is negative. This is consistent with the idea that there is more earnings management to increase reported earnings in an SEO with a reduction in the largest shareholder's shareholding ratio than in an SEO with an increase in the largest shareholder's shareholding ratio. Third, the relationship between the 3-month BHAR of an SEO and a change in the largest shareholder's shareholding ratio is positive, which supports the idea that post-SEO stock performance is higher when the largest shareholder's shareholding ratio increases.

Overall, Kim and Byun's findings show that, if the change in the largest shareholder's shareholding ratio is greater, the market reaction to the announcement of an SEO is more positive, earnings management is less, and post-SEO stock performance is higher. This result is explained by the positive market response to the announcement of an SEO in Korea, which differs from the negative market response to an SEO in other countries.

5.3. Stock Split

A stock split increases the number of outstanding equity shares but has no effect on either the firm's fundamental value or the shareholders' proportional ownership of shares. Thus, investors can easily gauge information implications. Two dominant hypotheses, the signaling hypothesis and the liquidity hypothesis, attempt to explain the positive market response to a split announcement. The signaling hypothesis indicates that stock split announcements convey favorable information about a firm's future cash flow prospects. Substantial empirical results are consistent with the signaling hypothesis. In contrast, the liquidity hypothesis suggests that a stock split attracts small investors by reducing stock prices and making round lots more affordable for small investors. As more small investors are willing to trade the split stock, the stock becomes more liquid. The empirical evidence surrounding marketability and liquidity, however, is not conclusive.

Regarding long-term performance, Desai and Jain (1997) and Ikenberry *et al.* (1996) find that stock splits are followed by 7% abnormal returns in the year after the split. Abnormal returns are calculated relative to benchmarks that control for size, book-to-market, and price momentum in Desai and Jain. Byun and Rozeff (2003) retest stock splits with a longer sample period using various methodologies to avoid the misspecification problem. They could not find significant 1-year abnormal returns of stock splits and suggest that the stock market is efficient with respect to stock splits.

In Korea, Nam (2000) finds a positive market reaction to stock split announcements by using 47 split stocks between 1997 and 1999. He attributes the positive market response to the stock splits to an increase in liquidity, such as trading volume, rather than a change in the future earnings of splitting firms. However, because he examines trading volume around the stock-split announcement date instead of trading volume in the post-split period, it is doubtful that it can be determined whether the positive effect of a stock split stems from a liquidity increase or from other causes, such as attention-driven buying.

In contrast, Byun (2003) shows that a split does not appear to convey favorable information about a firm's future earnings or cash flows, although the degree of the stock-split factor does have a positive effect on announcement returns. Furthermore, Byun and Jo (2007) find that the long-term performance of split stocks is negative, suggesting that poor long-term performance can result from initial market overreaction to the split announcement.

Using 182 samples from 1999 to 2008, an empirical study by Park *et al.* (2010) finds that return volatility increases after a stock split. When volatility is decomposed into noisy and permanent volatility, the volatility increase after a stock split is mainly due to the increase in noisy volatility, which is short-lived. The results suggest that positive short-term abnormal return followed by negative long-term return seems to result from the market's overreaction to the stock-split announcement. Thus, the long-term performance of splitting stocks is negative in Korea but positive in the US.

Kim and Byun (2010) create monthly investor sentiment indices for Korea and provide evidence that these indices can predict the subsequent 6-month buy-and-hold returns of stock splits. Their results indicate that investor sentiment positively affects market response to stock-split announcements. First, market response to a stock-split announcement is positively related to investor sentiment. Second, market response is more pronounced during high investor sentiment periods, particularly for small, young, highly volatile, and low-profit stocks, the valuations of which are highly subjective and difficult to arbitrage. Third, the initial effects of size, age, volatility, and profitability in times of investor optimism tend to be reversed over the 12-month post-split performance. These empirical results imply that the market tends to overreact to stock-split announcements for small, young, highly volatile, and low-profit firms in an optimistic period but thereafter corrects the overvaluation of

Table 5.9. Empirical Results of Korean Stock Splits

Study	Sample periods: number	Announcement Return	Long-term Return
Yi and Park (2012)	2000–2010: 195	+	Not test
Byun and Jo (2007)	1998–2002: 144	+	–
Park *et al.* (2010)	1997–2000: 182	+	Not test
Byun (2003)	1997–2001: 172	+	–
Nam (2000)	1997–1999: 47	+	–

Table 5.10. CARs around the Stock Split Announcements

Market	High/Low M/B	Months	CARs (−3, 0)	CARs (−1,+1)
KOSPI	High M/B	196	4.54%***	3.54%***
	Low M/B	75	2.97%**	2.77%**
	Total	271	4.11%***	3.32%***
KOSDAQ	High M/B	130	4.07%***	4.13%***
	Low M/B	30	3.23%**	1.24%
	Total	160	3.91%***	3.59%***

Notes: *, **, and *** indicate 10%, 5%, and 1% significance level, respectively. High and low M/B months are classified by the aggregate M/B ratio in the previous month. CARs (−3,0) and (−1,+1) are the cumulative abnormal returns from 3 days before a corporate announcement date to the announcement date, and from 1 day before the announcement date to 1 day after it, respectively.

those firms during the 12-month post-split performance. As such, the paper shows how investor sentiment affects the valuation of stocks at a corporate event level.

Kim *et al.* (2012) investigate whether a stock split can be used not only as a tool to reveal information, but also as a manipulation tool, by dividing sample firms into two groups: firms that split stocks with and without subsequent corporate events. They suggest that firms involved in other corporate events after a stock split are likely to use the stock split as a manipulation tool.

As a separate empirical test, we analyze 431 stock splits from 1996 to 2013 (271 KOSPI, and 160 KOSDAQ). As we can see in Table 5.10, the announcements usually occur in periods following high M/B months (72.3% for KOSPI and 81.3% for KOSDAQ). The market tends to react more positively to the stock split announcement following high M/B months. In addition, the positive market response to stock split announcement appears to be robust in both the KOSPI and KOSDAQ markets. The only exception is CAR(−1,+1) in the KOSDAQ market, but the number of stock splits is only 30.

Previous studies on the post-split performance of Korean stock splits consistently showed negative returns. However, we report positive abnormal returns at both 12 and 24 months after the split in Table 5.11. Only KOSPI splits that occur in low M/B months show a negative BHAR24 (−12.29%), whereas the BHARs are positive in high M/B months both in the KOSPI market and the KOSDAQ market. Such results are opposite to earlier findings in the Korean stock market, although the positive post-split returns are consistent with US results, such as those from Desai and Jain (1997) and Ikenberry *et al.* (1996).

The results of Table 5.11, which are opposite to the negative post-split returns documented by the Korean financial literature, may

Table 5.11.   Long-term Performance of Stock-Split Firms

Market	High/Low M/B Months	BHAR12(%)	BHAR24(%)
KOSPI	High M/B	22.55	35.04
	Low M/B	10.47	−12.29
	Total	19.11	21.58
KOSDAQ	High M/B	34.25	70.64
	Low M/B	53.32	75.68
	Total	37.78	71.57
Total Average		25.94	39.87

Notes: High and low M/B months are classified by the aggregate M/B ratio of the previous month.

BHAR is defined as the difference between the realized buy-and-hold return and the value-weighted buy-and-hold return. BHAR12 and BHAR24 are the 12-month and 24-month buy-and-hold abnormal returns, respectively.

suggest market underreaction to stock splits in the Korean stock market. However, we should interpret these results carefully. Our sample contains more recent splits for 1996–2013 compared to the previous studies, whose sample periods were before 2002. Our results may be due to the inclusion of the recent sample of stock splits. Another possible reason can be the benchmark problem. Because the benchmark buy-and-hold returns are defined as value-weighted buy-and-hold returns, positive BHARs imply that post-split buy-and-hold returns outperform market buy-and-hold returns. If split stocks have higher expected returns than market returns, the positive BHARs simply result from the underestimation of expected returns. Nevertheless, it is interesting that investors who buy stocks after a stock split announcement can obtain higher returns than market returns, at least over 24 months.

5.4. Stock Repurchase

Share repurchases and dividends may be similar to each other as they involve distributing cash to shareholders. However, several differences distinguish share repurchases and dividends. First, managers are much less committed to share repurchases than to dividend payments. The actual amount for stock repurchase may be less than for dividend payments, and it may take a very long time to complete the repurchase plan. Second, firms do not smooth repurchase activities as they do with dividends. Third, the cost of a share repurchase depends on the market price of the stock. Managers are more likely to repurchase shares if they believe the stock to be undervalued.

It has been well supported that the stock market in general responds favorably to a company's announcement of repurchases of its own shares. According to Ikenberry *et al.* (1995), the market reaction to the announcement of an open market share-repurchase program averages approximately 3.54%. Empirical studies in Korea have reported similar results of a positive reaction. For the long-term performance, Ikenberry *et al.* (1995) find that, on average, firms that repurchase shares outperform a control group matched in size and book-to-market over the 4 years following the event. We can call this

Table 5.12.   Empirical Results of Korean Share Repurchases

Study	Sample periods: number	Announcement Return	Long-term Return
Byun and Kim (2010)	1999–2007: 835	+	+
Byun (2004)	1994–2000: 758	+	+
Jung and Lee (2003)	1994–1998: 470	+	+ (0)
Shin *et al.* (2002)	1994–1999: 415	not test	+
Lee *et al.* (2000)	1994–1998: 425	+	+
Kim (1997)	1994–1995: 134	+	not test
Jung and Lee (1996)	1994–1994: 104	+	not test

pattern the "market underreaction hypothesis." We also may earn positive abnormal returns after the announcement of repurchases.

Table 5.12 summarizes the empirical results of stock repurchase in the Korean market. Shin *et al.* (2002) find significant positive long-term performance after repurchasing stocks using the Fama and French three factor model. Jung and Lee (2003) examine the long-term performance of 470 stock repurchases in Korea from 1994 to 1998. Positive long-term performance is found using BHAR and CARs. With the calendar-time approach, however, positive long-term performance is found only for firms that frequently repurchased their shares during the sample period. Their findings suggest that model specification affects long-run performance.

Byun and Kim (2010) examine the investor sentiment and market timing of stock repurchases using a sample of 835 KRX stock repurchase announcements between 1999 and 2007. They employ the framework of Baker and Wurgler (2006) to measure the investor attitude toward the stock market. Results of this event study are consistent with the previous empirical findings. The CARs using the market model between 0 and +3 of the event date are statistically significant, averaging 4.01%. Furthermore, the average of the 12-month CARs is 10.95% which is consistent with the underreaction hypothesis of Ikenberry *et al.* (1995). According to this result we may earn the highest long-term abnormal returns if we follow the market timing hypothesis, in which we buy stock of repurchase-announcing firms with higher sensitivity to market investor sentiment.

Table 5.13.　Long-term Performance of Stock Repurchases in Korea

Market	High/Low M/B Months	Observations	BHAR12 (%)	BHAR24 (%)
KOSPI	High M/B	659	14.14	22.47
	Low M/B	107	29.16	50.55
	Total	766	17.09	31.01
KOSDAQ	High M/B	556	19.76	33.51
	Low M/B	126	5.32	19.96
	Total	682	16.24	26.39
Total Average		1448	16.64	28.57

Notes: High and low M/B months are classified by the aggregate M/B ratio of the previous month.
BHAR is defined as the difference between the realized buy-and-hold return and the value-weighted buy-and-hold return. BHAR12 and BHAR24 are the 12-month and 24-month buy-and-hold abnormal returns, respectively.

For updated research, we collect a new sample that contains 1,454 share repurchase announcements from 1999 to 2013. The KOSPI and KOSDAQ markets have 685 and 769 announcements, respectively. It is commonly known that share repurchase is usually executed when the stock is underpriced; thus, shares are usually repurchased in low investor sentiment or bear markets. Surprisingly, however, in the Korean market, the buyback announcements are more popular following high M/B months (KOSPI 81.6%; KOSDAQ 86.1%). The market responds to the repurchase positively, which is consistent with the underpricing hypothesis.

Table 5.13 shows a positive market reaction to stock repurchase announcements and positive post-repurchase returns. As we can see, the KOSPI and KOSDAQ results are somewhat different. Firms with stock repurchase in the KOSPI market have larger positive returns following low M/B months after the repurchase announcement. However, those in the KOSDAQ market have only 5.32% of BHAR12 and 19.96% of BHAR24 following low M/B months, which is lower than that following high M/B months.

In summary, the short-term and long-term return performance related to stock repurchase is consistent with the underpricing hypothesis. Investors who buy stocks after stock repurchase announcements can see returns that are much higher than market returns, at least over 24 months. However, their long-term performance does not show any consistent relation with high or low M/B months when a stock repurchase announcement occurs.

5.5. Dividends

According to the dividend signaling hypothesis, a change in dividends reflects managers' views about a firm's future earnings prospects. Although an increase in a firm's dividends may signal management's optimism about its future cash flows, it might also signal a lack of investment opportunities. Thus, if a rapidly growing firm moves to initiate dividends, it might be seen as a result of its declining growth prospects as opposed to a signal about its increased future profitability.

The regulation and market practice of Korean dividend policy are much different from those of the US. Dividend decisions of Korean firms are made and revealed at annual shareholder meetings, and the day of the annual meeting contains much other information as well. Thus, the event-study method may not be accurate because of mixed information from the shareholder meeting. In addition, the dividend amount is relatively smaller than that of foreign companies in developed countries. As a result, academic studies on Korean dividend policy are not abundant. From 2011, Korea has allowed interim dividends once a year. However, firms that pay out the interim dividend are not popular (less than 40 firms out of over 1,500 listed). The list of interim dividend-paying firms is shown in Table 5.14.

Park *et al.* (2003) analyze the determinants of dividend policy of Korean firms listed on the Korean Stock Exchange. The empirical results show that firm size, debt ratio, operating profits, free cash flow and future capital-raising prospects affect the dividend policy of Korean firms. Investors react differently to the announcements of dividends depending on firm characteristics such as the amount of free cash flow: Firms with more free cash flow experience significantly more positive market reactions to the announcement of a dividend

Table 5.14. Additional Interim-dividend Paying Firms (dividend yield, %)

	KOSPI (20 firms)			KOSDAQ (13 firms)		
	Name	June 2015	June 2016	Name	June 2015	June 2016
1	SK Telecom	0.4	0.48	Leadcorp	0.3	0.6
2	Samsung Elec	0.08	0.07	DaeHwa Phama.	0.14	0.13
3	Hyundai Motors	0.8	0.7	Intops	0.8	0.5
4	POSCO	0.9	0.8	Neotis	1.5	1.8
5	Hana Financial	0.5	1.0	SeoHo Electric	—	1.7
6	KCC	0.21	0.27	WiSol	—	0.7
7	S-Oil	1.6	0.6	JVM	—	0.4
8	Shell Korea	0.4	0.4	China Crystal New	—	0.372
9	Hana Tour	0.6	0.8	SY Panel	—	0.9
10	KET	0.22	0.28	HRS	—	1.4
11	CYC	1.6	1.1	ChungDahm Learn	2.5	1.7
12	CY Holdings	0.9	1.1	HyoSung ONB	0.7	1.4
13	DaeKyo	1.3	1.1	GSE	2.6	2.3
14	ShinHung	0.75	0.86			
15	SamHwa Crown	1.01	1.14			
16	ChunIl Express	—	1.6			
17	KPX Holdings	0.8	1.0			
18	KPX Greenchem.	0.9	1.2			
19	KPX Chemical	0.8	1.0			
20	Hanon System	—	0.5			

increase than do firms with less free cash flow. Their result is more consistent with dividends playing an important role in reducing agency problems related to free cash flow (Jensen, 1984) and is less consistent with the signaling hypothesis.

Kim *et al.* (2010) examine how informational asymmetries affect a firm's dividend policy based on the dividend signaling theory. Using a sample of 1,798 corporations listed on the KRX from 2000 to 2008, they analyze the relation between a firm's dividend policy and information asymmetry, which is measured by the analyst earnings forecast dispersion. Prior research shows that forecast dispersion is positively correlated with the extent of information asymmetry between firms and investors. They conjecture that if the signaling theory of dividends is valid, then firms will actively use dividends as a tool to resolve asymmetric information. Thus, the dividend policies

Table 5.15. Sample of Dividend Announcements in 2010–2013

Announcement Type	Sample Size	Proportion
Dividend Increase (from previous year)	969	27.0%
Dividend Initiation (no dividends in previous year)	10	0.3%
Constant Dividend (same dividends as in previous year)	1,432	39.8%
Dividend Decrease (from previous year)	860	23.9%
Dividend Omission (paying dividends in previous year)	105	2.9%
No Dividend (no dividends in this and previous year)	219	6.1%
Total	3,595	100.0%

of firms should be positively associated with analyst earning forecast dispersion. They find that there is a negative relation between asymmetric information and the measure of dividend policy. Their results do not support the dividend signaling hypothesis; that is, firms that are more subject to information asymmetry are less likely to make dividend payments and tend to distribute smaller amounts.

For our own analysis, we collect a sample of dividend announcements from 2010 to 2013. Among the 3,595 announcements, the distribution of dividends is summarized in Table 5.15. Constant dividend-paying firms compose about 40% of the sample. The number of dividend increases is similar to that of dividend decreases. Non-dividend-paying (sum of omission and no dividend) firms are 9% of the sample. Surprisingly, many Korean firms decrease or miss dividends, whereas US firms are reluctant to do so because dividend decreases or omissions are believed to convey negative signals about their future cash flows to the market.

The market reaction to dividend announcements can be measured as different window periods: CAR (–3,+3) from 3 days before to 3 days after the announcements using the market model and the market-adjusted model; and CAR (−1,+1), or abnormal returns on the announcement date.[2] We use the returns of the KRX index as

---

[2]The market model controls expected returns by using CAPM risk, whereas the market-adjusted model uses market return as expected returns. For both models, abnormal returns are defined as actual returns minus expected returns.

Table 5.16.   One-Day Return to Dividend Announcements: 2010–2013

	Market Model	Market Adjusted Model
Announcement	Abnormal Return (%)	Abnormal Return (%)
Dividend Increase	0.340***	0.414***
Dividend Initiation	2.143*	1.928*
Constant Dividend	0.140*	0.142**
Dividend Decrease	0.429***	0.535***
Dividend Omission	−0.450*	−0.351
No Dividend	−0.060	−0.016

Note: *, **, and *** indicate 10%, 5%, and 1% significance level, respectively.

the market returns. Table 5.16 indicates that both dividend increase and dividend initiation announcements convey good news. The 1-day abnormal returns on these announcement dates are statistically significant for both the market model and the market-adjusted model. In addition, a constant dividend is, on average, considered good news, although the magnitude of abnormal returns tends to be much smaller. However, investors consider dividend omission bad news. In particular, the 1-day abnormal return on dividend omission announcements is –0.45% in the case of the market model, which is statistically significant at 10%. The negative market reaction is consistent with previous academic literature.

One exception is a dividend decrease announcement. Interestingly, a dividend decrease is positively welcomed by the market. Dividend payments are usually affected by investment opportunities. It is quite possible for firms with high growth options to use internally generated cash for future investments. In that case, firms may reduce dividend payments in order to take advantage of positive investment opportunities. However, it may be difficult to understand that all dividend change announcements except for dividend omission convey good news to investors. Barber and Odean (2008)'s argument may provide a possible explanation for the positive market reaction to corporate events. They hypothesize that individual investors tend to buy attention-grabbing stocks: stocks in the news, stocks experiencing high abnormal trading volume, and stocks with extreme

1-day return. Thus, any corporate events related to dividend change may attract individual investors, who buy the attention-grabbing stocks. However, a firm's dividend omission may indicate that the firm is seriously short of cash flows, which conveys bad news to the market.

We subgroup our sample into KOSDAQ (relatively small and growing firms) and KOSPI (main board) firms according to the firms' listing market. Table 5.17 provides the interesting results. Among the dividend-decreasing firms, KOSDAQ firms experience a much more significant market reaction than KOSPI firms. The differences between two groups are statistically significant except for CAR $(-3,+3)$ in the case of the market model. When firms decrease their dividend payments, markets are more favorable to KOSDAQ firms than to KOSPI firms. Investment opportunities may explain this difference: Because KOSDAQ firms need more money to invest in potential growth opportunities, a dividend decrease may convey a more favorable signal related to investment opportunities. However, a different explanation is possible for the same results: Because individual investors predominantly trade stocks in the KOSDAQ market, they tend to buy stocks that have attention-grabbing news, such as dividend change announcements. Because any dividend changes except for dividend omission are regarded as good news in the KOSDAQ market, we need more in-depth analyses of dividend announcement effects. However, our sample covers only the 4 years from 2010 to 2013, so sample bias may be another plausible explanation for positive market reaction to a dividend decrease announcement.

In Table 5.18, we report the BHAR12 and BHAR24 according to dividend announcement types (i.e., increase, initiation, constant, decrease, omission, and no dividend). Our results show that the highest returns occur in dividend increase stocks. Furthermore, negative returns of BHAR12 and BHAR24 are observed for dividend omission and no dividend in both KOSPI and KOSDAQ markets. In addition, stocks with dividend initiation have poor long-term performance in the KOSDAQ market but good performance in the KOSPI market over 12 or 24 months.

Table 5.17. Dividend Decrease in KOSDAQ and KOSPI Market: 2010–2013

Announcement	Market Model (%)			Market Adjusted Model (%)		
	CAR (−3,+3)	CAR (−1,+1)	AR (0)	CAR (−3,+3)	CAR (−1,+1)	AR (0)
Dividend Decrease	0.799***	0.606***	0.429***	1.387***	0.877***	0.535***
KOSDAQ Market	1.173**	1.058***	0.882***	2.075***	1.484***	0.997***
KOSPI Market	0.495	0.238	0.061	0.827**	0.383*	0.159
Difference b/w markets	0.678	0.820**	0.821***	1.248***	1.101***	0.838***

Note: *, **, and *** indicate 10%, 5%, and 1% significance level, respectively.

Table 5.18. Long-term BHAR and Dividend Announcement Types

	KOSDAQ		KOSPI		Total	
Announcement	BHAR12	BHAR24	BHAR12	BHAR24	BHAR12	BHAR24
Dividend Increase	31.01	46.13	33.35	61.85	32.05	53.13
Dividend Initiation	−16.05	−20.37	23.74	49.64	19.76	42.63
Constant Dividend	10.49	19.98	16.33	35.84	13.11	27.09
Dividend Decrease	1.29	9.32	1.63	9.60	1.44	9.44
Dividend Omission	−14.97	−6.12	−9.12	9.13	−11.13	3.89
No Dividend	−13.50	−8.62	3.63	3.51	−3.88	−1.81

Table 5.19. Trading Behavior of Investors around the Corporate Events

		Before Event (−3, −1)			Event Date (0)			After-Event (+1, +3)		
Events		IND	INS	FOR	IND	INS	FOR	IND	INS	FOR
IPO		—	—	—	Buy***	Sell***	Sell*	Buy***	Sell***	Sell
SEO	Q1	Buy*	Sell*	Sell	Buy*	Sell*	Sell	Buy***	Sell**	Sell*
	Q2	Buy	Sell	Buy	Buy	Sell	Buy	Buy	Sell*	Buy
Splits	Q1	Buy	Sell	Buy	Buy**	Sell	Sell	Buy**	Sell	Sell
	Q2	Buy**	Sell**	Buy	Buy***	Sell***	Sell	Buy***	Sell***	Buy
Rep.	Q1	Buy***	Sell*	Sell*	Buy*	Sell*	Sell	Buy***	Sell**	Sell*
	Q2	Buy	Sell	Buy	Buy	Sell	Buy	Buy	Sell*	Buy

Notes: Q1: Foreign investors have more than 5% of shares, and institutional investors have more than 5% of shares.
Q2: Otherwise. IND (INS) represents individual (institutional) investors, and FOR represents foreign investors.
Rep indicates stock repurchase.

Table 5.19 shows the trading behavior of each investor group — individual (IND), institutional (INS), and foreign (FOR). The corporate events are the same as previously (i.e. IPOs, SEOs, stock splits, and share repurchases). We measure the trading behavior as the dollar amount of buying minus selling. Thus, the sign of trading behavior indicates the net buy of the investor group. We also divide the sample into two sub-groups, Q1 and Q2. In the Q1 group, foreign investors and institutional investors each trade more than 5% of the total shares. The Q2 group includes the rest of the firms, in which foreign investors or institutional investors do not trade more than 5% of the total shares. Usually, foreign investors trade less than 5% of shares in the Q2 group, as discussed in Chapter 2. We analyze investor behavior for before-event, event date, and after-event periods.

The trading behavior of individual investors is opposite to that of institutional investors. Individuals buy stocks before, on, and after corporate event dates. As Barber and Odean (2008) point out, individual investors tend to buy stocks that attract investors through corporate events. In particular, the positive market reaction to corporate events, including SEO announcements, is more likely attributed to the trading behavior of individual investors because their buying behavior is statistically significant. In contrast, institutional and foreign investors tend to sell stocks as individual investors buy.

Foreign investors do not appear to be sensitive to corporate events. Although they show selling behavior on corporate events for the Q1 group, their selling behavior is not statistically significant. Because foreign investors do not usually trade the stocks of the Q2 group, they can scarcely sell those stocks.[3] Foreign investors tend to buy stocks of the Q2 group around and after SEO and stock repurchase events. However, their buying behavior is not statistically significant. In general, foreign investors do not actively trade based on information about corporate events. However, institutional investors tend to trade stocks as trade counters of individual investors. From a valuation viewpoint, institutional investors appear to undervalue information about corporate events whereas individual investors tend to overvalue the same information. As a result, institutional investors keep selling stocks before, on, and after corporate events, while individual investors keep buying those stocks.

Corporate events seem to be important sources of trading for both individual investors and institutional investors. However, their

---

[3]Investors can short-sell stocks that they do not own. However, short-selling is active only for highly liquid stocks, which belong to the Q1 group rather than the Q2 group.

interpretations of corporate events appear to be opposite to one another, while corporate events do not elicit active trading by foreign investors. Individual investors appear to buy stocks related to corporate events, as Barber and Odean (2008) argue. However, it is not conclusive whether individual investors play a role in generating price errors triggered by corporate events or quickly reflect new information from corporate events onto stock prices. It is also questionable whether individual investors overreact or institutional investors underreact to corporate events.

In summary, the long-term performance of stocks related to corporate events tends to be better than market returns over 24 months, except for IPOs in the KOSPI market and dividend initiations and omissions in the KOSDAQ market. Such long-term performance is subject to the benchmark problem. However, the market response to corporate events over a short window period is relatively invulnerable to the benchmark problem. Unlike the US stock market, the Korean stock market positively responds to SEO and dividend decrease announcements. In addition, the positive market response to SEO and dividend decrease announcements are much stronger in the KOSDAQ market than in the KOSPI market. Our results also indicate that individual investors are net buyers of stocks around all corporate events. Because individual investors predominantly trade stocks in the KOSDAQ market, the stronger positive responses to SEO and dividend decrease announcements in the KOSDAQ market seem to be related to the trading behavior of individual investors.

References

Baker, M. and J. Wurgler, 2004, A Catering Theory of Dividends, *Journal of Finance* 59, 1125–1165.

Baker, M. and J. Wurgler, 2006, Investor Sentiment and Cross-Section of Stock Returns, *Journal of Finance* 61, 1645–1680.

Baker, M. and J. Wurgler, 2007, Investor Sentiment in the Stock Market, *Journal of Economic Perspectives* 21, 129–152.

Barber, B. M. and T. Odean, 2008, All That Glitters: The Effect of Attention and News on the Buying Behavior of Individual and Institutional Investors, *Review of Financial Studies* 21(2), 785–818.

Byun, Jinho, 2004, Signaling Effects and the Long-term Performance of False Signaling Firms: Evidence from the Under-valuation Stock Repurchases, *Journal of Korea Securities Association* 33(1), 207–248 (in Korean).

Byun, Jinho, 2010, Investor Sentiment and Stock Repurchase in KOSDAQ Market, *Productivity Review* 24(2), 149–169 (in Korean).

Byun, Jinho and Keunsoo Kim, 2010, Investor Sentiment and Market Timing of Stock Repurchase, *Deahan Journal of Business* 23(4), 2271–2288 (in Korean).

Byun, Jinho and M. Rozeff, 2003, Long-run Performance after Stock Splits: 1927 to 1996, *Journal of Finance* 58, 1063–1085.

Byun, Jong-Cook, 2003, Market Response to Stock Split, *Korean Journal of Financial Studies* 9, 119–144 (in Korean).

Byun, Jong-Cook and Jeong-Il Jo, 2007, Long-Term Performance of Stock Splits, *Korean Journal of Financial Management* 24(1), 1–27 (in Korean).

Cho, Seong-Soon, Kyounghee Park, and Jinho Byun, 2017, Empirical Test on a Catering Theory of Dividends in the Korean Stock Market, *Korean Journal of Financial Studies* 46(2), 343–379 (in Korean).

Choi, Moon-Soo, 2011, Review of Empirical Studies on IPO Activity and Pricing Behavior in Korea, *Asian Review of Financial Research* 24(2), 621–663.

Choi, Moon-Soo and Hyung-Joo Huh, 2000, The Long-Run Performance of Initial Public Offerings Revisited, *Korean Journal of Finance* 13(1), 99–122 (in Korean).

Chung, Hyunchul and Youngwoo Jeong, 2008, Seasoned Equity Offering Announcement and Market Efficiency, *Korean Journal of Financial Management* 25(3), 79–109 (in Korean).

Desai, H. and P. Jain, 1997, Long-run Common Stock Returns Following Stock Splits and Reverse Splits, *Journal of Business* 70, 409–433.

Fama, E., 1998, Market Efficiency, Long-Term Returns, and Behavioral Finance, *Journal of Financial Economics* 49, 283–306.

Fama, E., L. Fisher, M. Jensen, and R. Roll, 1969, The Adjustment of Stock Prices to New Information, *International Economic Review* 10, 1–21.

Ikenberry, D., J. Lakonishok, and T. Vermaelen, 1995, Market Underreaction to Open Market Share Repurchases, *Journal of Financial Economics* 39, 181–208.

Ikenberry, D., G. Rankine, and E. Stice, 1996, What Do Stock Splits Really Signal? *Journal of Financial and Quantitative Analysis* 31, 357–375.

Jensen, M. C., 1984, Agency Costs of Free Cash Flow, Corporate Finance, and Takeovers, *American Economic Review* 76(2), 323–329.

Jung, Sung-Chang and Yong-Gyo Lee, 1996, Analysis of Share Repurchase and Repurchase Funds, *Korean Journal of Finance* 11, 241–271 (in Korean).

Jung, Sung-Chang and Yong-Gyo Lee, 2003, Long-Term Performance of Repurchased Stocks, *Korean Journal of Finance* 16(1), 129–162 (in Korean).

Kho, Bong-Chan and Rae-Soo Park, 2000, An Empirical Analysis on the Abnormal Performance of Security-Issuing Firms in Korea, *Journal of Korea Securities Association* 27, 439–476 (in Korean).

Kim, Byoung-Gon, Dong-Wook Kim, and Dong-Hoe Kim, 2010, Information Asymmetry and Dividend Policy: The Consequences of Dividend Signaling Hypothesis, *Korean Journal of Financial Engineering* 9(1), 99–124 (in Korean).

Kim, Chul-Kyo, 1997, An Empirical Analysis of Stock Market Reaction to Share Repurchases, *Korean Journal of Finance* 13, 169–195 (in Korean).

Kim, Dong-Wook, 1989, Empirical Study on Information Contents of Dividends, *Korean Journal of Financial Management* 6(2), 97–112 (in Korean).

Kim, Hyun-A and Sung-Chang Jung, 2010, The Effect of Optimistic Investors' Sentiment on Anomalous Behaviors in the Hot Market IPOs, *Korean Journal of Financial Management* 27(2), 1–33 (in Korean).

Kim, Keunsoo and Jinho Byun, 2010, Effect of Investor Sentiment on Market Response to Stock Split Announcement, *Asia-Pacific Journal of Financial Studies* 39, 687–719.

Kim, Seok-Chin and Hyun-Soo Byun, 1998, The Long-Run Performance of Seasoned Equity Offerings of Korean Firms, *Korean Journal of Finance* 16, 23–50 (in Korean).

Kim, S.-C. and H.-S. Byun, 2003, Long-Run Performance from Korean Equity Carve-Outs: Additional Evidence, *Korean Journal of Financial Management* 20(1), 331–339 (in Korean).

Kim, Su-In and Jinho Byun, 2016, Seasoned Equity Offerings and Trade of Largest Shareholders, *Asian Review of Financial Research* 29(1), 1–35.

Kim, Kyung-Soon, Jinwoo Park, Chune-Young Chung, and Jin-Hwon Lee, 2012, Is Stock Split a Manipulation Tool? Evidence from the Korean Stock Market, *Asia-Pacific Journal of Financial Studies* 41, 637–663.

Kim, Young-Kyoo, and Young-Hye Kim, 2000, Long-Term Performance of IPO Firms and Earnings Management, *Korean Journal of Financial Management* 17(2), 71–98 (in Korean).

Kim, Byung-Ki and Myung-Jae Kong, 2000, Long-term Stock Returns and Operation Performance after SEOs, *Korean Journal of Financial Management* 17(1), 13–44. (in Korean).

Lee, Jong-Ryong and Jin-Wook Kim, 2009, The Effect of Non-Trading Period on IPO Underpricing in Korean Stock Market, *Asian Review of Financial Research* 22(3), 1–34.

Lee, Tae-Hee, Chul-Kyoo Kim, and Byung-Moon Lim, 2000, A Study on Stock Prices after the Repurchase Tender Offers, *Korean Journal of Financial Management* 18(2), 193–213 (in Korean).

Lim, Byung-Gyoon, 1997, Short-Term and Long-Term Performance of IPOs and Operating Performance, *Korean Journal of Financial Management* 14(1), 253–271 (in Korean).

Lim, U. and S. K. Lee, 1995, Long-Run Performance of IPOs in Korean Market, *Journal of Korea Securities Association* 18, 333–369 (in Korean).

Loughran, T. and J. Ritter, 1995, The New Issues Puzzle, *Journal of Finance* 50(1), 23–51.

Loughran, T., J. Ritter, and K. Rydqvist, 2004, Initial Public Offerings: International Insights, *Pacific-Basin Finance Journal* 2, 165–199.

Nam, Myung-Soo, 2000, Information Effect of Stock Splits, *Korean Journal of Financial Studies* 6, 193–201 (in Korean).

Park, Joohyun, Sungwoo Suh, and Gyuyoung Hwang, 2004, An Empirical Study on the Information Contents of Stock Splits, *Dasehan Journal of Business* 45, 1625–1651 (in Korean).

Park, Kyung-Suh, Eunjung Lee, and Inmoo Lee, 2003, Determinants of Dividend Policy of Korea Firms, *Korean Journal of Finance* 16(2), 195–229 (in Korean).

Park, Rae-Soo and Bo-Sung Shin, 2007, Conflicts of Interest Among Securities Firms Running Asset Management Businesses, *Korean Journal of Finance* 20(3), 127–153 (in Korean).

Ritter, J., 1991, The Long-run Performance of Initial Public Offerings, *Journal of Finance* 46(1), 3–27.

Shim, Dong-Suk and Chang-Ho Ahn, 2005, Earning Management and Stock Price Reaction of Seasoned Equity Offerings, *Korean Accounting Information Review* 23(3), 47–74 (in Korean).

Shin, Min-Sik, Seok-Chin Kim, and Seok-Yoon Lee, 2002, Long-term Performance of Share Repurchase Firms, *Korean Journal of Financial Studies* 8(1), 117–156 (in Korean).

Yi, Ka-Youn and Kyung-In Park, 2012, An Empirical Study of Stock Splits Effect in Korean Stock Market, *Dasehan Journal of Business* 25(3), 1303–1320 (in Korean).

Chapter 6

Industry Analysis

This chapter examines the sales revenue, profitability, valuation, and financial risk of listed companies in the Korean stock market at both the sector and industry level by using the most recent data, including data from 2015. We also analyze individual industries according to their market share, profitability, valuation (M/B ratio), and financial risk.

We use the financial statements of all firms listed on KOSPI and KOSDAQ, covering 1980–2015. The Korea Listed Firms Association (KLCA) provides financial information of all listed firms, including delisted firms. Since 2011, Korean firms have been required to report their Korea International Financial Reporting Standard (K-IFRS) financial statement. Under K-IFRS, a parent firm is required to issue a consolidated financial statement as the primary. Because the consolidated financial statement provides earnings based on equity method, it is believed that the consolidated financial statement contains more useful information for stock valuation than a non-consolidated financial statement. However, the Korea Generally Accepted Accounting Principles (K-GAAP) financial statement, which is non-consolidated, was mandatory before 2011, while K-IFRS was subordinated. The K-IFRS financial statement therefore is frequently missing for some firms before 2011, while non-consolidated financial statements are available from 1981 to 2015. For continuity of data analyses, we mainly use non-consolidated financial data, but we also provide an industry analysis based on consolidated financial statements for 2011–2015.

According to Park *et al.* (2014), non-consolidated earnings are more related to stock valuation than consolidated earnings even during K-IFRS mandatory period when information about consolidated earnings is mandatory for all listed companies. Furthermore, a parent's subsidiaries may not belong to the main industry of the parent firm. For example, the Hyundai Motor firm owns financial business-related firms, such as Hyundai Capital and Hyundai Credit Card. As a result, the consolidated financial statement of Hyundai Motor firm should include information about these subsidiaries, although they are not directly related to the motor vehicle industry. Thus, the consolidated financial data may not accurately reflect an industry's financial situation.

We classify the listed firms based on Korea Standard Industrial Classification (KSIC), which basically complies with International Standard Industrial Classification. We divide all industries into three sectors: the primary, secondary, and tertiary sectors. The primary sector includes agriculture, forestry, fishing, and mining and quarrying, all of which make direct use of natural resources. The secondary sector includes manufacturing industries, construction, electricity, and gas and water industries. The tertiary sector produces services and is also known as the service sector.

According to the Key Indicators of Major Industries (2015) published by the Korea Institute of Industrial Economics & Trade, the primary sector's value-added was about KRW 34.2 trillion in 2014 on the basis of national account. It accounts for 2.5% of the value-added of all industries in 2014. The value-added of the secondary sector was about KRW 515.3 trillion, which accounts for 38.0% of total value-added in 2014. The tertiary sector had KRW 804.8 trillion of value-added, which accounts for 59.4%. Figure 6.1 shows the proportion of the tertiary sector's value-added in 2014 across major countries. Although the proportion of the tertiary sector's value-added in Korea is higher than in China, it is much lower than in the US and European countries. Thus, the manufacturing sector is still dominant in Korea, particularly for listed firms.

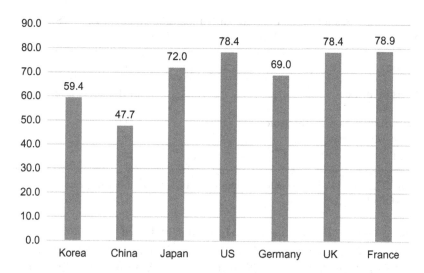

Figure 6.1. Proportion (%) of Tertiary Sector's Value Added as of 2014
Source: Key Indicators of Major Industries (2015).

6.1. Sector Analysis

6.1.1. *Number of Listed Firms*

Table 6.1 presents the number of all listed firms in the primary sector as of 2015. Numbers in parentheses indicate the number of firms ever listed on the Korea Exchange (KRX).[1] For example, the total number of firms in the agricultural industry ever listed on the KOSDAQ market is only two, one of which was delisted. There are many reasons for delisting: bankruptcy, transferring from one stock market to the other, merger and acquisition, and failure to maintain listing requirements.

The secondary sector in Table 6.2 includes manufacturing industries, construction, electricity, gas, steam, and air conditioning supply industries. The secondary sector has 1,264 listed firms as of 2015,

---

[1]The KRX was created through the integration of KOSPI, KOSDAQ, and Korea Futures Exchange under the Korea Stock and Futures Exchange Act. The KRX currently has three stock market divisions: KOSPI, KOSDAQ, and Korea New Exchange (KONEX).

Table 6.1. Primary Sector Standard Industrial Classification (SIC) and Number of Listed Firms in KOSPI and KOSDAQ Markets as of 2015

Sector	SIC Code	KOSPI (N)	KOSDAQ (N)
A: Agriculture	01	0 (0)	1 (2)
A: Fishing	03	5 (5)	0 (1)
B: Mining of Non-Metal Minerals, except Fuel	07	1 (1)	1 (1)
Total	N.A.	6 (6)	2 (4)

Note: The number in parentheses indicates the total number of firms ever listed on KOSPI or KOSDAQ.

among which 490 firms are listed on the KOSPI market and 774 on the KOSDAQ market. The number of firms ever listed is 744 in the KOSPI market and 1,106 in the KOSDAQ market. Thus, about 34% of firms were delisted from KOSPI, and 30% were delisted from KOSDAQ. In particular, a substantial percentage of publicly traded firms in the textile, apparel, and electronics industries were delisted.

The firms listed on KOSDAQ outnumber those on KOSPI, particularly in the electronics industry and the other machinery and equipment industries. The KOSDAQ market was originally developed to provide capital to young, small, and high-technology firms. IT is one of the industries that fits well with the purpose of the KOSDAQ market. However, after the IT bubble burst in the early 2000s, many firms listed on KOSDAQ moved to the KOSPI market, likely because of the discount effect of KOSDAQ. The electronics industry has 270 firms listed in the KRX market (KOSPI and KOSDAQ), which is the largest in the secondary sector.

The tertiary sector is composed of 28 industries, including the financial industry. The tertiary sector has 533 firms listed on either the KOSPI market or the KOSDAQ market as of 2015. Among those firms, 224 firms are listed on KOSPI, while 309 firms are listed on KOSDAQ. The wholesale and commission business industry has 96 firms, which is the largest number in the tertiary sector. The next largest is the publishing service industry, which has 87 firms.

Table 6.4 shows the number of listed firms in the financial industry. About 63% of firms in the financial industry were delisted

Table 6.2. Secondary Sector's SIC and Number of Listed Firms in KOSPI and KOSDAQ Markets as of 2015

Industry	SIC Code	KOSPI (N)	KOSDAQ (N)
Food	10	29 (30)	16 (20)
Beverage	11	5 (11)	6 (7)
Tobacco	12	1 (1)	0 (0)
Textile, excluding Apparel	13	10 (34)	5 (13)
Wearing Apparel, Clothing Accessories, Fur Articles	14	16 (29)	7 (19)
Leather, Luggage, and Footwear	15	5 (12)	0 (2)
Wood Products, except Furniture	16	3 (4)	1 (1)
Pulp, Paper, and Paper Products	17	20 (30)	8 (9)
Printing and Reproduction of Recorded Media	18	0 (0)	4 (6)
Refined Petroleum, Coke, and Hard-Coal	19	4 (5)	0 (0)
Chemical and Chemical Products	20	68 (89)	46 (61)
Pharmaceuticals, Medical Chemicals	21	40 (48)	65 (76)
Rubber and Plastic	22	19 (23)	23 (29)
Other Non-metallic Minerals	23	23 (31)	11 (13)
Basic Metal Products	24	44 (55)	30 (47)
Fabricated Metal Products, except Machinery & Furniture	25	11 (17)	33 (44)
Electronic Products	26	38 (94)	232 (371)
Medical, Precision, and Optical Instruments	27	4 (7)	41 (51)
Electrical Equipment	28	16 (26)	41 (61)
Other Machinery and Equipment	29	32 (43)	112 (151)
Motor Vehicles, Trailers, and Semitrailers	30	43 (52)	45 (59)
Other Transport Equipment	31	8 (10)	13 (14)
Furniture	32	6 (10)	3 (3)
Other Manufactured Products	33	1 (4)	6 (8)
Electricity, Gas, Steam, and Air Conditioning Supply	35	11 (12)	2 (2)
General Construction	41	28 (63)	12 (21)
Special Construction	42	4 (4)	12 (18)
Total		490 (744)	774 (1,106)

Note: The number in parentheses indicates the total number of firms ever listed on KOSPI or KOSDAQ.

Table 6.3. Tertiary Sector's SIC and Number of Listed Firms in KOSPI and KOSDAQ Markets as of 2015

	Industry	SIC Code	KOSPI (N)	KOSDAQ (N)
E:	Waste Collection, Disposal, and Materials Recovery	38	0 (0)	4 (4)
E:	Remediation and Other Waste Management Service	39	0 (0)	1 (1)
G:	Sales of Motor Vehicles and Parts	45	0 (3)	1 (1)
G:	Wholesale and Commission Business	46	44 (77)	52(89)
G:	Retail Business	47	18 (22)	9 (20)
H:	Land Transport and Transport via Pipelines	49	10 (11)	3 (3)
H:	Water Transport	50	6 (8)	0 (0)
H:	Air Transport	51	3 (3)	0 (1)
H:	Storage and Transport Support Service	52	3 (3)	0 (2)
I:	Accommodation and Food Service	56	1 (1)	1 (3)
J:	Publishing Service	58	3 (4)	84 (114)
J:	Motion Pictures, Video, and TV Program Production/ Sound Recording, Music Publishing Service	59	3 (5)	18 (30)
J:	Broadcasting	60	3 (3)	8 (13)
J:	Telecommunication	61	3 (6)	8 (14)
J:	Computer Programming and Consultancy Service	62	7 (16)	24 (53)
J:	Information Service	63	8 (8)	19 (28)
K:	Financial and Insurance Activities	64	50 (131)	7 (23)
I:	Real Estimate Service	68	2 (2)	3 (4)
I:	Renting and Leasing	69	2 (2)	0 (0)
M:	Research and Development	70	0 (0)	15 (15)
M:	Professional Service (Law, Patent, Accounting)	71	60 (64)	10 (11)
M:	Architectural, Engineering, and Technical Service	72	6 (7)	8 (11)
M:	Other Professional, Scientific, and Technical Service	73	0 (1)	6 (9)
N:	Business Support Service	75	5 (6)	13 (21)

(*Continued*)

Table 6.3. (*Continued*)

Industry		SIC Code	KOSPI (*N*)	KOSDAQ (*N*)
P:	Education Service	85	2 (2)	10 (14)
R:	Creative Arts and Recreation Related Service	90	0 (0)	2 (4)
R:	Sports and Amusement Business	91	4 (5)	3 (5)
S:	Other Personal Service	96	1 (1)	0 (1)
Total			224 (391)	309 (494)

Note: The number in parentheses indicates the total number of firms ever listed on KOSPI or KOSDAQ.

Table 6.4. Finance Sector SIC and Number of Listed Firms in KOSPI and KOSDAQ Markets

K: Financial and Insurance Activities	SIC Code	KOSPI (*N*)	KOSDAQ (*N*)
Commercial Banking	6412	12 (38)	0 (2)
Mutual Saving Banking	6413	0 (8)	1 (7)
Credit Granting	6491	3 (1)	5 (5)
Other Finance Service (Merchant Banking)	6499	1 (29)	0 (0)
Insurance	651	13 (16)	0 (0)
Securities Brokerage	6612	21 (32)	1 (4)
Total		50 (131)	7 (23)

Note: The number in parentheses indicates the total number of firms ever listed on KOSPI or KOSDAQ.

from the KRX market. During the Asian financial crisis, many commercial banks were financially distressed. Some were merged or went bankrupt. As shown in Table 6.4, out of 38 commercial banks ever listed on the KOSPI market, only 12 commercial banks were listed as of 2015. Likewise, most merchant banking corporations, which mainly provided short-term loan services to corporations, went bankrupt during the Asian financial crisis. As of 2015, only one merchant banking corporation remains in the KOSPI market. Many mutual saving banks, which were founded to provide financial services to retail customers and small firms with low credit, were also delisted after 2011 because they suffered from substantial losses of both real estate project financing and poor risk management.

6.1.2. *Sales Revenues*

Figure 6.2 shows the non-consolidated sales revenues of the secondary and tertiary sectors and their sales market share from 1981 to 2015. The left vertical line shows sales revenue in terms of KRW trillion, while the right vertical line shows the market share in terms of percentage. We exclude the primary sector's sales revenue because it accounts for less than 0.5% of the total revenue of all three sectors over the entire sample period. We eliminate financial firms as well as listed firms without available financial data.[2]

As of 2015, the total sales revenue of all listed firms in the primary sector was KRW 1.6 trillion, and the market share of the primary sector was only 0.13% of the total revenue (KRW 1,233 trillion) of all listed firms in the three sectors. Although the secondary

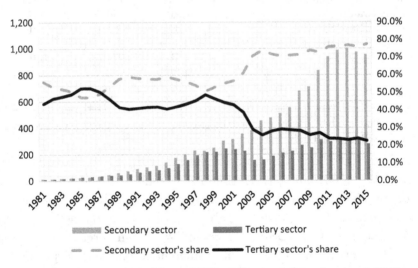

Figure 6.2. Sales Revenue (Unit: KRW Trillion) of Secondary and Tertiary Sectors and Their Market Shares (%) from 1981 to 2015

---

[2]For example, 19 firms are excluded out of 1,264 firms in the secondary sector because they lack data in 2015.

sector's market share was higher than the tertiary sector's in most years, their difference was less than 10 percentage points before 1989. The tertiary sector's revenue proportion was higher than 50%, especially in 1985 and 1986. However, the difference in the sales revenue between the secondary and the tertiary sectors has increased since the Asian financial crisis. As of 2015, the tertiary sector's sales revenue was less than 30% of the secondary sector's. The annual geometric growth rate of sales is 7.4% for the secondary sector from 2000 to 2015, but it is only 1.5% for the tertiary sector.

Korean economic growth has been heavily driven by the export of manufactured products, but the service sector's sales growth is more likely to have depended on domestic demand, which has been weakened since the Asian financial crisis. This may be one reason for the much lower sales growth in the tertiary sector. The low growth rate of revenue in the tertiary sector may reduce employment capacity of the Korean economy because the tertiary sector is an important source of job creation. According to Key Indicators of Major Industries (2015), KRW 1 billion of output in the service sector requires the employment of 7.7 persons, while the same amount of output in the manufacturing sector only requires 1.74 persons as of 2013.[3] As such, the sluggish growth of the tertiary sector may contribute to low employment growth, which results in weak growth of domestic demand. The low growth of domestic demand limits the tertiary sector's development. Such a vicious circle may overshadow Korean economic development.

The sales revenue of the secondary sector reached a peak of KRW 1,002.3 trillion in 2013 and thereafter declined to KRW 953.5 trillion in 2015, a 5.8% drop. The service sector's revenue rose to a record high of KRW 310.6 trillion in 2012. Afterward, it fluctuated but eventually decreased to KRW 286.9 trillion in 2015, an approximately

---

[3]According to the International Federation of Robotics, as of 2015, Korea led the world in terms of robot density, which indicates the number of multipurpose industrial robots (all types) per 10,000 employees in the manufacturing sector. The robot density of Korea was 531, whereas the robot densities of Japan and Germany were 305 and 301, respectively. High robot density can partially explain why employment capacity sharply decreases in Korea.

7.6% fall during the latest 3 years. A fall in sales revenue is historically rare for the entire period of 1981–2015 in Korea. The revenue of the secondary sector slightly decreased from KRW 230.2 trillion in 1997 to KRW 227.3 trillion in 1998 when the Asian financial crisis shocked the Korean economy. Except for the Asian financial crisis and the latest 2 years, the secondary sector did not experience a fall in sales for listed firms.

Except for the latest years, the service sector's revenue has only dropped twice. The service sector's sales revenue fell by 7.2% in 2009 when the global financial crisis took place and by 36% from 2000 to 2003 when the business of trading companies dramatically declined in Korea. General trading companies in Korea had been a main source of trading exports and imports under the export-oriented policy of Korea. Their role, however, has substantially decreased as the manufacturing firms began to trade by themselves in 2000. The sharp decrease in the service sector's sales in the early 2000s is mainly because manufacturing firms no longer relied on the general trading companies for export and import of manufactured products.

Figure 6.3 reports annual sales growth for seven sub-periods from 1981 to 2015. The annual sales growth of the secondary and tertiary

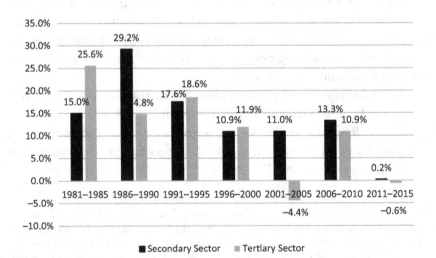

Figure 6.3. Annual Sales Growth (%) of Secondary and Tertiary Sectors for Seven Sub-periods

sectors is above 15% until 1995 and decreases to just above 10% during 1996–2010, except for the years 2001–2005. However, the annual sales growth of the secondary sector is close to 0.2% and that of the tertiary sector is −0.6% for 2011–2015. In fact, both sectors have negative sales growth after 2013. Such decreases in sales revenue in both the secondary and the tertiary sectors had never occurred previously in Korean stock markets.

6.1.3. *Profitability and Equity Valuation*

Figure 6.4 presents the operating margin and the M/B ratio of the secondary sector from 1981 to 2015. The left-hand side of the vertical line indicates the operating margin of the secondary sector, which was between 8% and 10% until 1995, except for 1984, and thereafter fluctuated between 5.9% and 9.7% from 1996 to 2004. After reaching 9.7% in 2004, the operating margin tends to decline. For example, the operating margin was in the range of 5% to 6% for 2006–2010

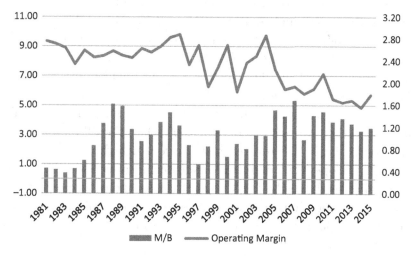

Figure 6.4.   Operating Margin and M/B Ratio of Secondary Sector from 1981 to 2015

Notes: Operating margin (%) is calculated as the total operating income of the secondary sector divided by its total sales revenue. The M/B ratio is calculated by the total capitalization value of the tertiary sector at the end of year *t* divided by its total equity value in year *t* when the fiscal year ends.

but only in the range of 4% to 5% for 2011–2015. Considering the low sales growth of 2011–2015, the operating margin of the secondary sector appears to substantially decrease.

The M/B ratio of the secondary sector is the ratio of the total market capitalization of all listed firms in the secondary sector to their total book value of equity. The market capitalization is measured at the end of each year, and the book value of equity is assumed to be available at the end of the year when the fiscal year ends. For example, if the fiscal year ends in June, 2001, the book value of equity is assumed to be available in December, 2001. The M/B ratio provides implications about either future growth earnings or risk. For example, a high M/B ratio indicates either high growth of earnings or low risk (low expected returns) in the future. Figure 6.4 shows that the annual M/B ratios of the secondary sector are initially very low in the early 1980s: The ratios are below 0.5, although the operating margins are between 7% and 9%. The M/B ratio of the secondary sector continued to rise from 0.46 in 1981 to 1.62 in 1988, when Korea hosted the Seoul Olympics. The M/B ratio of 1.62 in 1988, is the second highest from 1981 to 2015. After 1988, it sharply decreased, falling to 0.95 by 1991, although the operating margin is 8% or above for 1988–1991. The M/B ratio of the secondary sector plummeted to 0.53 in 1997 when the Asian financial crisis shocked the Korean economy. However, it bounced back to 1.15 in 1999 when the IT boom irrationally boosted the global stock markets. The M/B ratio then dropped to 0.67 in 2000 when the IT bubble burst. Afterward, the M/B ratio reached the record high of 1.69 in 2007, although the operating margin tends to decline after 2004. The global financial crisis drove the M/B ratio of the secondary sector down to 0.98 in 2008, but it immediately rose to 1.41 in 2009. As the sales growth and operating margin gradually decline after 2010, the M/B ratio decreases as well.

The operating margin and equity valuation of the tertiary sector are much more volatile than those of the secondary sector: The operating margin of the tertiary sector is, on average, 3 percentage points lower than that of the secondary sector. On the contrary, the M/B ratio of the tertiary sector is usually higher than that

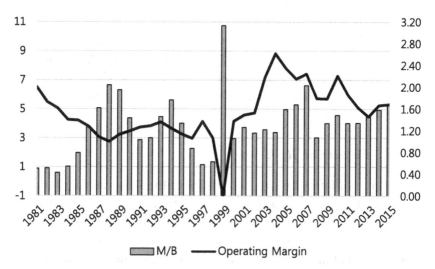

Figure 6.5. Operating Margin and M/B Ratio of Tertiary Sector from 1981 to 2015

Notes: Operating margin (%) is calculated as the total operating income of the tertiary sector divided by its total sales revenue. The M/B ratio is calculated as the total capitalization value of the tertiary sector at the end of year t divided by its total equity value in year t when the fiscal year ends.

of the secondary sector. Because the tertiary sector's assets are fundamentally different from those of the secondary sector, it may be difficult to directly compare the M/B ratios between two sectors.

Although the operating margin of the tertiary sector continued to decline from 1981 to 1988, according to Figure 6.5, its M/B ratio continued to rise. The opposite movement of operating margins and M/B ratios makes it difficult to justify if operating margins can proxy for future profitability. The opposite movement prominently occurs between the Asian financial crisis and the peak of the IT boom. The operating margin of the tertiary sector plummeted to −1.0% in 1999, its lowest point from 1981 to 2015. In 1999, however, the M/B ratio of the tertiary sector was 3.0, which is historically the highest in the Korean stock market. The extremely optimistic view of future IT might have driven the high equity valuation of the IT-based service industry during the IT boom period.

When the operating margin of the tertiary sector reaches the peak of 9.7% in 2004, its M/B ratio does not appear to be high at all. As the operating margin begins to decline after 2004, the M/B ratio rises until the global financial crisis hits the Korean economy. Opposite movement between M/B ratios and operating margin has not been found after that point.

6.1.4. *Financial Risk*

According to Figure 6.6, the debt ratios of the secondary and tertiary sectors, defined as their total debt to total asset ratio, continued to decline from 1981 to 2015. Their debt ratios were extremely high in the early 1980s, in particular for several reasons. First, because M/B ratios were below 0.5 in the early 1980s, firms had no incentive to issue equities at low value. Second, these firms aggressively pursued leverage effects during 1980–1990 for their high equity profitability. Third, moral hazard was common before the Asian financial crisis: Most big firms did not recognize the importance of risk management

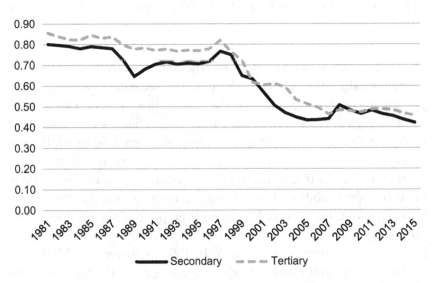

Figure 6.6.   Debt Ratio of Secondary and Tertiary Sectors from 1981 to 2015

Notes: The debt ratio is the ratio of the total debt value of all listed firms in the secondary (tertiary) sector to their total asset value.

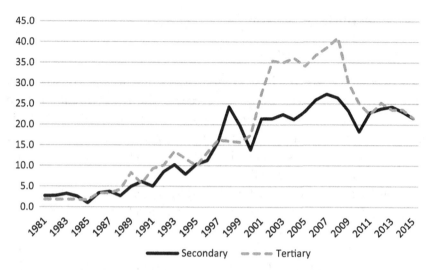

Figure 6.7. Percentage of Firms with Negative Operating Income in the Secondary and Tertiary Sector from 1981 to 2015

and believed that the Korean government could have banks provide additional financial loans to save them from bankruptcy. Because the Asian financial crisis broke their belief in the government's support and the government discouraged firms from having high debt ratios after the crisis, firms continued to reduce their debt ratios, as shown in Figure 6.6 and put more weight on equity issues instead of debt.

Because both secondary and tertiary sectors have had low debt ratios recently, they do not appear to have serious financial risk. However, the proportion of firms with negative operating income in the tertiary sector sharply increased between 2002 and 2008, as seen in Figure 6.7. The proportion of firms with negative operating income was above 35% in the tertiary sector from 2002 to 2008, while it was only around 16% during the Asian financial crisis. Although the proportion decreased by 21.6% in 2015, it is still higher than during the Asian financial crisis. The proportion of firms with negative operating income in the secondary sector gradually increases until 2007 but is much lower than in the tertiary sector for 2002–2008. However, the proportion of firms with negative operating income in both the secondary and tertiary sectors becomes similar after 2010.

6.2.   Secondary Sector

6.2.1.   *Sales Revenue and Growth*

The secondary sector has 27 industries, including construction and energy industries. Table 6.5 presents the sales revenue of the secondary sector in 2015 and growth rates from 2006 to 2015; it lists all industries in the secondary sector in descending order of non-consolidated sales revenue in 2015. Table 6.5 shows consolidated sales revenue in 2015 as well.

The largest industry in terms of sales revenue is the electronics industry. In 2015, the sales revenue of the electronics industry was KRW 251.2 trillion, which accounts for 26.3% of total sales in the secondary sector. The motor vehicle industry has the second largest sales revenue, and the electricity and gas industry is in third place in terms of non-consolidated sales revenue. These three biggest industries account for about 50% of sales revenue in the secondary sector. However, the electricity and gas industry is different from other industries in that it is highly regulated and has mainly domestic demand. The chemical and chemical products industry is the third largest in terms of consolidated sales revenue. Only seven industries exceed 5% of the secondary sector's total sales revenue: electronics, motor vehicles, gas and electricity, chemical, basic metal products, general construction, and other transport equipment industries.

According to Table 6.5, the major industries of the secondary sector experienced a sharp decrease in sales revenue growth for 2011-2015, compared to the period of 2006–2010. The sales growth of the electronics industry decreased from 13.0% for 2006–2010 to 3.1% for 2011–2015. The sales growth of the chemical and chemical products industry also fell from 14.8% for 2006–2010 to 0.3% for 2011–2015. The basic metal products industry, the fifth largest industry, had −2.7% sales growth for 2011–2015, down from 13.3% for 2006–2010. Among the top five industries, only the motor vehicles industry experienced an increase, from 7.5% for 2006–2010 to 8.5% for 2011–2015. Its sales growth, however, was only 3.2% for 2011–2015 based on consolidated sales revenue. The electrical

Table 6.5.　Sales Revenue of the Secondary Sector in 2015 and Growth Rate (%) from 2006 to 2015

Industry	Number of Firms	Sales* Revenue (KRW Trillion)	Market Share (%)	Sales Revenue (KRW Trillion)	Annual Sales Growth (%)		
					2006–2010	2011–2015	2011–2015*
Electronics	268	359.1	26.28	251.2	13.0	3.1	4.1
Motor Vehicles	87	231.9	16.95	132.4	7.5	8.5	3.2
Electricity and Gas	13	98.5	11.48	96.3	12.4	6.1	6.3
Chemical and Chem. Products	113	157.1	8.20	88.8	14.8	0.3	1.2
Basic Metal Products	74	112.2	7.20	71.1	13.3	−2.7	−1.3
General Construction	40	81.2	6.10	64.9	8.8	0.0	0.4
Other Transport Equipment	21	83.4	5.94	58.1	20.4	−0.1	0.3
Other Machinery Equipment	143	51.6	3.77	31.6	13.5	0.9	0.7
Food	43	47.5	3.48	30.0	12.2	6.9	10.6
Electrical Equipment	57	26.7	1.82	20.0	6.0	3.1	4.2
Refined Petroleum	4	18.7	1.56	18.7	13.8	1.5	1.3
Pharmaceuticals	101	17.0	1.37	15.3	12.1	7.2	8.0
Rubber and Plastic	42	21.3	1.25	14.6	19.5	7.5	11.7
Other Non-metallic Mineral	32	13.3	0.97	10.2	13.7	4.9	2.5

(*Continued*)

Table 6.5. (Continued)

Industry	Number of Firms	Sales* Revenue (KRW Trillion)	Market Share (%)	Sales Revenue (KRW Trillion)	Annual Sales Growth (%)		
					2006–2010	2011–2015	2011–2015*
Pulp and Paper	28	9.2	0.67	7.4	9.8	0.3	-0.7
Wearing Apparel and Accessories	22	8.2	0.60	7.1	14.1	3.9	5.4
Fabricated Metal Products	43	7.4	0.54	7.1	18.9	9.9	9.3
Beverage	11	5.2	0.38	4.7	20.6	6.4	2.2
Medical, Precision, and Optical Inst.	43	3.9	0.30	3.2	17.7	13.3	14.7
Special Construction	16	3.2	0.29	3.0	32.3	6.5	4.9
Tobacco	1	4.2	0.24	2.8	2.7	2.6	3.9
Textile	15	3.2	0.24	2.0	5.1	-2.1	0.1
Furniture	9	1.7	0.13	1.6	3.1	5.3	5.4
Wood Products	4	1.7	0.12	1.2	3.5	16.7	9.6
Other Manufactured Products	7	0.8	0.06	0.7	4.8	14.6	12.1
Leather, Luggage and Footwear	4	0.4	0.04	0.4	-7.0	-2.1	-1.9
Printing and Recorded Media	4	0.5	0.03	0.4	8.4	11.5	-2.0

Note: *indicates sales revenue and sales growth rate from the consolidated financial statement.

equipment, refined petroleum, pulp and paper, textile, and leather (luggage and footwear) industries suffered either extremely low or negative sales growth during 2011–2015. The sales revenue growth of many industries fell by more than half. In sum, major Korean industries in the secondary sector have recently experienced low sales growth.

Table 6.5 also shows that the sales growth of some industries continued to be high or higher for 2011–2015 than for 2006–2010. However, these industries account for only a small portion of sales revenue in the secondary sector. For example, wood products and other manufactured goods have much higher growth for 2011–2015 than for 2006–2010, but their sales revenue is relatively small among the industries in the secondary sector, accounting for less than 0.2% of the total market share in the secondary market. Although the sales growth of medical, precision, and optical instruments decreased from 2006–2010 to 2011–2015, its sales growth still exceeded 13% for 2011–2015.

We investigate the biggest four industries in more detail, except highly regulated electricity and gas industry. These industries also have a higher number of listed firms. Thus, we examine the four major firms of these industries. Table 6.6 reports the consolidated sales revenue of the four major firms and Others in the electronics industry, which comprises the firms excluding the four major firms. As can be seen from Table 6.6, a few firms dominate the market share of sales in the electronics industry. Samsung Electronics accounted for 55.8% of the market share, according to consolidated financial statements as of 2015. The market share of LG Electronics is 15.7%. The four largest firms, including LG Display and SK Hynix, account for 84.7% of the market share. Only six firms exceed KRW 1 trillion of sales out of 268 firms. The total sales of the electronics industry reached a peak in 2013 and thereafter gradually declined.

Table 6.7 shows the consolidated sales revenue of the motor industry, which is the second largest industry. The market share of Hyundai Motor company was 39.7% as of 2015. KIA Motor, Hyundai Mobis, and Hyundai Wia are ranked as the second, third, and fourth largest firms, respectively, and are all affiliated firms of

Table 6.6.   Consolidated Sales Revenue of Electronics Industry from 2011 to 2015 (KRW Trillion)

Firm	2011	2012	2013	2014	2015
Samsung Electronics	165.0	201.1	228.7	206.2	200.7
	(54.7)	(58.1)	(59.0)	(56.6)	(55.8)
LG Electronics	54.3	51.0	58.1	59.0	56.5
	(18.0)	(14.7)	(15.0)	(16.2)	(15.7)
LG Display	24.3	29.4	27.0	26.5	28.4
	(8.0)	(8.5)	(7.0)	(7.3)	(7.9)
SK Hynix	10.4	10.2	14.2	17.1	18.8
	(3.4)	(2.9)	(3.7)	(4.7)	(5.2)
Others	47.9	54.5	59.9	55.3	55.2
	(15.9)	(15.7)	(15.4)	(15.2)	(15.3)
Total	301.9	346.1	387.9	364.2	359.5

Notes: The number in parentheses indicates a firm's market share. "Others" indicates all firms excluding the four firms shown in the table.

Table 6.7.   Consolidated Sales Revenue of Motor Industry from 2011 to 2015 (KRW Trillion)

Firm	2011	2012	2013	2014	2015
Hyundai Motor	77.8	84.5	87.3	89.3	92.0
	(42.6)	(41.6)	(40.8)	(40.7)	(39.7)
Kia Motor	43.2	47.2	47.6	47.1	49.5
	(23.7)	(23.3)	(22.2)	(21.5)	(21.4)
Hyundai Mobis	26.3	30.8	34.2	36.2	36.0
	(14.4)	(15.2)	(16.0)	(16.5)	(15.5)
Hyundai Wia	6.4	7.0	7.1	7.6	7.9
	(3.5)	(3.5)	(3.3)	(3.5)	(3.4)
Others	28.9	33.6	37.9	39.4	46.4
	(15.8)	(16.6)	(17.7)	(17.9)	(20.0)
Total	182.6	203.1	214.1	219.5	231.8

Notes: The number in parentheses indicates a firm's market share. "Others" include all firms except the four firms shown in the table.

Hyundai Motor company. The main business of Hyundai Mobis is manufacturing automobile parts, such as safety and brake systems. Hyundai Wia focuses on key automotive parts such as engines and modules. These four firms accounted for 80% of the market share as of 2015. Nine firms exceeded KRW 1 trillion of sales revenue out of 86 firms in the motor vehicles industry. According to Table 6.7, other firms excluding these four have gradually increased their market share in the motor vehicles industry. The sales revenue of the motor vehicles industry also reached a peak in 2013 and gradually declined afterward.

The chemical and chemical products industry covers industrial chemicals and diverse chemical products formed from chemical reactions, such as detergents and cosmetics. However, the consolidated sales revenue does not accurately reflect the sales revenue of the chemical industry. Hanwha has been the largest firm in the industry since 2013. It has four types of main business: explosive, defense, trade, and machine. As such, not all of Hanwha's sales are related to the chemical industry. The second largest firm is LG Chem, which manufactures not only basic materials and chemicals but also IT and electronics materials, such as LCD polarizers. Hyosung is a holding company; its main business areas are industrial materials, chemicals, textile and ITC, construction, and trading. As such, only part of Hyosung's sales belongs to the chemical and chemical products industry. According to Hyosung's business report (2015), sales revenue of chemical products is only 12.5% of the firm's main business sales. Lotte Chemical is a firm that focuses on petrochemistry.

According to Table 6.8, Hanwha's sales revenue accounted for 26.4% of total sales in the chemical industry as of 2015. LG Chem and Lotte Chemical have gradually decreased their market share. Compared to the electronics and motor vehicles industries, the major firms' market share is low in the chemical and chemical products industry. However, because the chemical industry covers diverse products, it may be difficult to directly compare these firms. The chemical industry's sales revenue also has gradually declined after 2013.

According to Table 6.9, the sales revenue of the basic steel industry tended to decrease from 2011 to 2015. Such a decrease is mainly due to stronger global competition caused by over-supply of steel in the world as well as the global economic recession. POSCO,

Table 6.8. Consolidated Sales Revenue of Chemical and Chemical Products Industry from 2011 to 2015 (KRW Trillion)

Firm	2011	2012	2013	2014	2015
Hanwha	12.2	11.5	38.7	37.5	41.4
	(8.4)	(7.9)	(22.4)	(22.9)	(26.3)
LG Chem	22.7	23.3	23.1	22.6	20.2
	(15.6)	(16.0)	(13.4)	(13.8)	(12.9)
Hyosung	11.3	12.6	12.6	12.2	12.5
	(7.8)	(8.7)	(7.3)	(7.4)	(7.9)
Lotte Chemical	15.7	15.9	16.4	14.9	11.7
	(10.8)	(10.9)	(9.5)	(9.1)	(7.5)
Others	83.2	82.1	81.7	76.4	71.3
	(57.3)	(56.5)	(47.3)	(46.7)	(45.4)
Total	145.1	145.4	172.6	163.5	157.1

Notes: The number in parentheses indicates a firm's market share. "Others" indicate all firms excluding the four firms shown in the table.

Table 6.9. Consolidated Sales Revenue of Basic Steel Industry from 2011 to 2015 (KRW Trillion)

Firm	2011	2012	2013	2014	2015
POSCO	68.9	63.6	61.9	65.1	58.2
	(48.9)	(47.7)	(50.0)	(51.2)	(51.8)
Hyundai Steel	15.3	14.1	13.5	16.8	16.1
	(10.8)	(10.6)	(10.9)	(13.2)	(14.4)
Dongkuk Steel	8.8	7.9	6.7	6.1	5.7
	(6.3)	(5.9)	(5.4)	(4.8)	(5.1)
Korea Zinc	5.6	5.5	4.8	4.9	4.8
	(3.9)	(4.1)	(3.9)	(3.9)	(4.3)
Others	42.4	42.3	36.9	34.2	27.4
	(30.1)	(31.7)	(29.8)	(26.9)	(24.4)
Total	141.0	133.4	123.8	127.1	112.2

Notes: The number in parentheses indicates a firm's market share. "Others" indicates all firms excluding the four firms shown in the table.

Dongkuk Steel, and Korea Zinc suffered a decrease in sales revenue from 2011 to 2015. Although POSCO's sales growth is −4.1% for the same period, its market share increased from 48.9% in 2011 to 58.2% in 2015; this increase indicates that most firms in the basic steel industry have experienced severe decreases in sales revenue. Dongkuk Steel and Others in particular had substantial decreases in sales growth. For example, the geometric average annual growth of Others, which comprises all firms excluding the four major firms, was −11.5% during 2011–2015.

6.2.2. *Profitability*

We examine the profitability of all the industries in the secondary sector in descending order of profitability. Table 6.10 lists the top 10 most profitable industries in decending order of ROE for 2011–2015 based on non-consolidated financial statements. The tobacco, special construction, refined petroleum, and printing and recorded media industries have only a small number of listed firms. The profitabilities of these industries are mainly discussed here, and further analyses of the other industries will be provided, including the four major firms of each industry.

The tobacco industry has a single listed firm, KT&G. Although there are many foreign tobacco products in Korea, KT&G enjoys high profitability because of its dominant market share in Korea and an increase in exports. Its average ROE decreased from 21.69% for 2006–2010 to 14.69% for 2011–2015, although the operating margin moderately rose for the same period. The third most profitable industry is the special construction industry: Its profitability performance sharply increased during 2011–2015, and its operating margin was 8.38% per year for 2011–2015, which is even higher than 4.93% for 2006–2010. The annual sales growth of special construction, however, was 6.5% for 2011–2015, as shown in Table 6.5, while it was 32.3% for 2006–2010. The high profitability of this industry is mainly due to KEPCO KPS, which was listed on the KOSPI in December 2007. KEPCO KPS, of which KEPCO has more than 50% ownership, provides powerplant services such as maintenance services for hydro, thermal, and nuclear power plants to ensure a stable supply of electricity. KEPCO KPS accounted for approximately 69.6% of total earnings from the special construction industry as of 2015. The operating margins and ROE fell to 4.47% and 2.12%, respectively, for 2011–2015 if KEPCO KPS is excluded.

Table 6.10. Profitability (%) of 10 Most Profitable Industries in the Secondary Sector from 2006 to 2015

Industry	Period	Margin (%)	ROE (%)	ROA (%)
Tobacco	2006–2010	34.50	21.69	17.60
	2011–2015	38.40	14.69	12.14
	2011–2015*	28.62	14.50	11.00
Motor Vehicles	2006–2010	5.50	11.32	6.49
	2011–2015	7.47	12.19	7.91
	2011–2015*	7.45	14.80	6.62
Special Construction	2006–2010	4.93	−2.48	−1.09
	2011–2015	8.38	10.53	6.77
	2011–2015*	8.61	10.90	6.69
Refined Petroleum	2006–2010	5.14	17.34	7.18
	2011–2015	2.64	9.50	4.18
	2011–2015*	2.64	9.52	4.18
Electronics	2006–2010	5.99	9.20	5.96
	2011–2015	7.68	9.38	6.33
	2011–2015*	9.19	11.73	7.23
Rubber and Plastic	2006–2010	4.59	−3.43	−1.32
	2011–2015	6.94	7.03	3.71
	2011–2015*	8.06	8.30	3.61
Chemical and Chemical Products	2006–2010	7.92	11.13	6.19
	2011–2015	6.13	6.80	3.92
	2011–2015*	5.21	6.29	2.57
Printing and Recorded Media	2006–2010	3.81	−8.99	−2.41
	2011–2015	12.17	6.57	4.70
	2011–2015*	5.97	5.52	3.36
Pharmaceutical	2006–2010	10.71	7.49	4.84
	2011–2015	8.46	6.23	3.98
	2011–2015*	8.47	6.29	3.94
Other Manufactured Products	2006–2010	0.83	−1.88	−1.14
	2011–2015	4.66	6.01	3.81
	2011–2015*	7.12	7.89	4.75

Notes: Margin is the operating margin, defined as the total operating income of an industry divided by its total sales. ROE is the ratio of the total net income of an industry to its total equity book value. ROA is the ratio of the total net income to the total asset value. *indicates profitability measured by using consolidated financial statements.

The fourth most profitable industry, the refined petroleum industry, has only four listed firms. S-oil is the largest firm; its earnings are almost 90% of total earnings from the refined petroleum industry as of 2015. However, Shell in Korea, Michang Oil, and Kukdong Oil and Chem, which mainly produces lubricants, tend to have higher profitability ratios than S-oil.

The printing and recorded media industry is one of the smallest industries in terms of sales revenue in the secondary sector. There are four listed firms in the industry, but their businesses are very different. Loen is the most profitable firm; it distributes music via the digital music platform called Melon. The other three firms's earnings were negative for 2011–2015.

Other manufactured products industry includes jewelries; accessories; musical instruments; toys, games, and other playthings; and so on. The biggest firm in this industry is Samick, which produces musical instruments such as pianos. Samick accounted for 21.3% of total consolidated sales revenues in the industry as of 2015. The next biggest firm is Romanson, which manufactures watches and other accessories. The third biggest firm is Spigen, which was listed on KOSDAQ in 2014; its main products are mobile accessories. Spigen's consolidated sales revenue accounted for approximately 20% of total sales revenue in the other manufactured products industry as of 2015. Spigen, however, is the most profitable firm in the industry. Its operating income was about 58.5% of total operating income generated by the industry, and its ROE was 23.9% in 2015.

The electronics, motor vehicles, and chemical industries are the three largest industries in Korea when the electricity and gas industry is excluded. The profitabilies of these industries are still high compared to most other industries. The rubber and plastic and the pharmaceutical industries are also important, not only in terms of their sales revenue but also in their number of listed firms. Thus, we will examine the profitabilies of major firms in these industries, which have been selected based on their proportion of the total operating income generated by each industry.

The motor vehicle industry is the second most profitable industry in the secondary sector. According to Table 6.10, all profitability

Table 6.11. Consolidated Operating Margin and ROE of Motor Vehicles Industry from 2011 to 2015

Firm	2011 MG	2011 ROE	2012 MG	2012 ROE	2013 MG	2013 ROE	2014 MG	2014 ROE	2015 MG	2015 ROE
Hyundai Motor	10.3	14.6	10.0	14.2	9.5	12.4	8.5	10.8	6.9	10.9
Hyundai Mobis	10.0	15.5	9.4	16.8	8.6	13.6	8.5	12.5	8.1	9.3
Kia Motor	8.1	13.8	7.5	14.3	6.7	15.3	5.5	12.6	4.8	12.0
Hyundai Wia	5.0	15.8	7.7	21.1	7.5	17.9	6.9	15.1	6.4	11.3
Others	3.5	6.2	3.8	6.4	4.3	7.3	3.5	6.1	3.7	6.2

Notes: MG indicates the operating margin, defined as operation income divided by sales. ROE is net income divided by book value of equity. "Others" comprise all firms excluding the four firms shown in the table. The ROE and operating margin of Others are calculated based on a summation of the related financial variables, such as net income, equity value, operating income, and sales revenue.

ratios of the motor vehicles industry, such as operating margin, ROE, and ROA, increased for 2011–2015 compared to 2006–2010. The average sales growth of the motor vehicles industry also increased for the same period, as shown in Table 6.5. However, Table 6.7 reports that the sales revenue of the motor vehicles industry decreased in both 2014 and 2015, which indicates that all major industries of the secondary sector recently experienced poor sales revenue growth in Korea.

Table 6.11 lists four firms in the motor vehicles industry in descending order of operating income in 2015. These four firms are also the biggest in terms of sales revenue, although the order of second and third biggest firms are reversed. The operating income of Hyundai Motor accounted for 45.8% of the total operating income in the motor vehicles industry as of 2015, which is higher than its sales share of 39.7%. Hyundai Motor had gradual decreases in operating margin, from 10.3% in 2011 to 6.0% in 2015, but its ROE fell less than its operating margin — to 10.9% in 2015 from 14.6% in 2011. Although the secondary sector's sales tend to decline after 2013, Hyundai Motor firm maintains its competitivess in terms of sales revenue and profitability. Hyundai Mobis has a similar pattern, likely because Hyundai Mobis's business relies on Hundai Motor's.

Although Kia Motor is in the same business as Hyundai Motor, Kia's ROE and operating margin are different from those of Hyundai Motor. It's operating margin is consistently lower than that of Hyundai Motor, while its ROE continues to be higher. Hyundai Wia has a similar pattern; Kia Motor and Hyundai Wia are the two most profitable companies in terms of ROE. Others comprises all firms excluding the four major firms in the motor vehicles industry. Although the profitability of Others is much lower than the four major firms, it is still reasonably high compared to the profitability of other industries.

The electronics industry is the fifth most profitable industry, as shown in Table 6.10, although it is the biggest industry. The operating income of Samsung Electronics accounted for 73.1% of total operating income in the electronics industry as of 2015, which is much higher than its 54.7% of the market share. Table 6.12 shows that the operating margin of Samsung Electronics reaches its peak in 2013, when its sales revenue was the highest. Its profitability does not appear to be significantly influenced by the decrease in sales after 2013. Samsung Electronics' operating margin and ROE in 2015 were 13.2% and 9.0%, respectively. The most impressive company, however, is SK Hynix, the main products of which are

Table 6.12. Consolidated Operating Margin and ROE of Electronics Industry from 2011 to 2015

Firm	2011		2012		2013		2014		2015	
	MG	ROE	MG	ROE	MG	ROE	MG	ROE	MG	ROE
Samsung Elect.	9.4	11.3	14.4	16.4	16.1	14.7	12.1	11.0	13.2	9.0
SK Hynix	1.0	1.6	−2.2	−4.9	23.9	21.2	29.8	21.3	28.4	19.4
LG Display	−3.1	−10.2	3.1	0.3	4.3	1.0	5.1	9.2	5.7	8.5
LG Electronics	0.6	−2.6	2.2	−3.5	2.2	−1.9	3.1	−1.6	2.1	−4.0
Others	2.3	0.6	3.7	1.9	3.2	1.4	2.2	0.8	2.8	1.7

Notes: MG indicates the operating margin, defined as operation income divided by sales. ROE is net income divided by the book value of equity. "Others" comprise all firms excluding the four firms shown in the table. The ROE and operating margin of Others are calculated based on the summation of the related financial variables, such as net income, equity value, operating income, and sales revenue.

semiconductors, such as DRAM, NAND, and MCP (Multi-chip Package). The operating income of SK Hynix accounted for about 15% of the industry's total operating income in 2015. Its operating margin and ROE were −2.2% and −4.9% in 2012, respectively; afterward, its profitability sharply increases. The operating margins were close to 30% in both 2014 and 2015.

LG Display has the third largest operating income in the electronics industry. Table 6.12 shows that its profitability gradually improves: Its operating margin and ROE were 5.7% and 8.5% in 2015, respectively. In contrast, LG Electronics, although it is the second biggest firm in terms of sales revenue, suffers from low profitability: Its ROE continues to be negative from 2011 to 2015. The electronics industry, excluding Samsung, SK Hynix, and LG Display, appears to struggle with low profitability: The ROE of Others is below 2% for 5 years, as shown in Table 6.12.

The rubber and plastic industry is the sixth most profitable industry, as shown in Table 6.10. Except for LG Hausys, the major business products of firms in the rubber and plastic industry are tires. Hankook Tire was split into Hankook Tire and Hankook Tire World Wide in 2012. Because Hankook Tire World Wide is the holding firm, Hankook Tire's financial statements before 2012 were transferred to Hankook Tire World Wide. Hankook Tire accounted for 47.3% of total operating income in the rubber and plastic industry as of 2015. According to Table 6.13, Hankook Tire achieved excellent profitability for 2012–2015; its average operating margin and ROE were 13.8% and 9.6%, respectively. Nexen Tire also shows high profitability ratios. The profitability ratios of Kumho Tire, however, are low in 2015 especially. Its operating margin was 4.5%, which is much lower than that of its competitors, and its ROE was −3.4% in 2015. LG Hausys belongs to the plastic industry and produces intermediate goods for interior, building, automotive, and IT and Electronics. It accounted for 8.0% of total operating income in the rubber and plastic industry as of 2015, and its operating margin and ROE were 5.4% and 7.6% in 2015, respectively. The rubber and plastic industry has high profitability, likely because it achieved high sales growth of 11.7% per year for 2011–2015.

Table 6.13. Consolidated Operating Margin and ROE of Rubber and Plastic Industry from 2011 to 2015

	2011		2012		2013		2014		2015	
Firm	MG	ROE	MG	ROE	MG	ROE	MG	ROE	MG	ROE
Hankook Tire			13.3	5.6	14.6	14.9	15.4	11.7	13.8	9.6
Nexen Tire	7.8	16.2	10.4	18.8	10.2	14.4	11.9	12.9	12.2	12.6
LG Hausys	2.8	5.5	2.3	5.7	4.3	8.7	5.2	6.8	5.4	7.6
Kumho Tire	4.9	15.3	9.2	11.9	9.4	5.2	10.4	8.7	4.5	−3.4
Others	5.5	4.0	5.6	5.9	5.2	2.9	3.8	2.8	6.6	5.9

Notes: MG indicates the operating margin, defined as operation income divided by sales. ROE is net income divided by the book value of equity. "Others" comprises all firms excluding the four firms shown in the table. The ROE and operating margin of Others are calculated based on the summation of the related financial variables, such as net income, equity value, operating income, and sales revenue.

Table 6.14. Consolidated Operating Margin and ROE of Chemical Industry from 2011 to 2015

	2011		2012		2013		2014		2015	
Firm	MG	ROE	MG	ROE	MG	ROE	MG	ROE	MG	ROE
LG Chem	12.4	22.3	8.2	14.1	7.5	10.6	5.8	7.1	9.0	9.7
Lotte Chem	9.4	14.7	2.3	5.6	3.0	5.3	2.4	3.4	13.8	11.6
Hyosung	2.4	3.8	1.5	6.3	3.9	−12.5	4.9	6.8	7.6	10.6
Amore Pacific	14.6	15.0	12.8	11.7	11.9	10.5	14.6	12.4	16.2	16.1
Others	6.9	10.3	4.0	4.8	3.0	1.3	3.0	2.1	4.2	3.7

Notes: MG indicates the operating margin, defined as operation income divided by sales. ROE is net income divided by the book value of equity. "Others" comprise all firms excluding the four firms shown in the table. The ROE and operating margin of Others are calculated based on the summation of the related financial variables, such as net income, equity value, operating income, and sales revenue.

The chemical and chemical products industry is the third largest industry in terms of consolidated sales revenue and the seventh most profitable industry in terms of ROE for 2011–2015. Although Hanwha accounted for 26.3% of sales revenue in the industry, its operating income was not high enough to be listed among the four major firms in terms of operating income as of 2015. According to Table 6.14, LG Chem maintains high profitability ratios, although its sales revenue

Table 6.15. Consolidated Operating Margin and ROE of Pharmaceutical Industry from 2011 to 2015

Firm	2011		2012		2013		2014		2015	
	MG	ROE	MG	ROE	MG	ROE	MG	ROE	MG	ROE
Celltrion	64.0	18.8	55.8	16.3	44.1	9.5	42.8	10.2	42.9	11.5
Hanmi	3.5	−2.7	7.1	2.2	8.5	7.6	4.5	3.5	16.1	23.7
Green Cross	11.1	8.7	9.2	8.1	8.9	8.3	9.9	7.0	8.7	11.5
Yuhan	7.8	7.6	4.5	6.0	6.6	6.1	7.3	6.7	7.6	8.4
Others	7.7	5.9	6.3	3.6	7.3	6.9	6.6	3.6	7.7	5.4

Notes: MG indicates the operating margin, defined as operation income divided by sales. ROE is net income divided by the book value of equity. "Others" comprise all firms excluding the four firms shown in the table. The ROE and operating margin of Others are calculated based on the summation of the related financial variables, such as net income, equity value, operating income, and sales revenue.

has moderately decreased since 2012. Lotte Chem, whose main business is petrochemistry, struggled with low profitability in both 2012 and 2013. It, however, achieved high profitability ratios of 13.8% operating margin and 11.6% ROE in 2015. Hyosung's performance has improved since 2013. Amore Pacific, the main business of which is cosmetics, has high profitability: Its operating margin and ROE continue to be well above 10% from 2011 to 2015 and are above 10% in 2015.

The pharmaceutical industry has the fourth largest number of listed firms in the secondary sector, and no firm has more than 10% of market share in the industry. The market share of Hanmi, which has the largest sales revenue, is 7.7% in 2015. Celltrion, a biologics firm that was the first in the world to develop an antibody biosimilar, has become a highly profitable firm since its foundation in 2002. Celltrion accounts for 3.5% of the market share and has the largest operating income. Celltrion accounted for 15.7% of total operating income in the pharmaceutical industry as of 2015. Its operating margin decreased from 64.0% in 2011 to 42.9% in 2015, which is still extremely high. However, its ROE is relatively low compared to its operating margin, around 10%. Hami accounted for 12.9% of the total operating income of the pharmaceutical industry in 2015. Its

ROE bounced from 3.5% in 2014 to 23.7% in 2015. Green Cross and Yuhan have also achieved high profitability ratios. The profitability of Others also appears to be high, compared to other industries; their operating margin and ROE are 7.7% and 5.4% in 2015, respectively.

Table 6.16 shows the profitability ratios of 10 moderately profitable industries, the top 11 to top 20 in terms of ROE, during 2011–2015. The electricity and gas industry and the basic metal products industry, the third and fifth largest industries in Korea, respectively, belong to this group. The ROEs of these 10 moderately profitable industries are between 1% and 6% for 2011–2015. In particular, most of these industries tend to have lower profitability ratios for 2011–2015 than for 2006–2010.

The furniture and wood products industries have few listed firms, and their sales revenue is also small when compared to other moderately profitable industries. Thus, we explain profitability of these two industries at the industry level. For the other industries, we analyze the major listed firms.

The furniture industry is the 12th most profitable industry in the secondary sector and the 23rd largest in terms of sales revenue, as shown in Table 6.5. Hyundai Livart is the leading company in the furniture industry. Its profitability ratios recently improved, and its ROE was 12.8% in 2015, compared to 3.4% in 2011. However, the operating margin of Ace Bed has been much higher than that of Hyundai Livart. The operating margin of Ace Bed decreased from 22.6% in 2011 to 17.8% in 2015. When we exclude the four leading firms, the furniture industry has suffered from losses in operating income and net income, except for 2011. Its ROE was −11.8% in 2015.

There are only four listed firms in the wood products industry, which ranked 24th in sales revenue as of 2015. As its sales revenue grew to 16.7% for 2011–2015 from 3.5% for 2006–2010 as shown in Table 6.5, its profitability ratios moderately increased. However, its ROE in terms of consolidated net income was only 1.48% for 2011–2015. Dong Hwa, which accounted for 38.9% of total sales in the industry as of 2015, has improved profitability. It had an operating margin of 11.7% and an ROE of 5.9% in 2015.

Table 6.16.   Profitability (%) of 10 Moderately Profitable Industries from 2006 to 2015

Industry	Period	Margin	ROE	ROA
Wearing Apparel and Accessories	2006–2010	6.94	6.68	4.13
	2011–2015	4.86	5.56	3.48
	2011–2015*	4.65	5.34	3.15
Furniture	2006–2010	6.47	9.90	6.67
	2011–2015	4.48	5.32	3.83
	2011–2015*	4.49	5.47	3.92
Medical, Precision, Optical Instruments	2006–2010	4.90	−4.31	−2.39
	2011–2015	8.81	5.18	3.20
	2011–2015*	7.11	4.65	2.68
Food	2006–2010	5.29	8.27	4.83
	2011–2015	4.42	5.03	2.81
	2011–2015*	4.56	5.21	2.45
Basic Metal Products	2006–2010	10.83	11.66	7.25
	2011–2015	6.67	4.92	3.00
	2011–2015*	5.29	4.45	2.24
Beverages	2006–2010	10.17	5.93	3.81
	2011–2015	8.69	4.55	2.45
	2011–2015*	8.16	6.04	3.13
Electrical Equipment	2006–2010	2.90	−0.05	−0.02
	2011–2015	2.54	3.04	1.84
	2011–2015*	2.63	2.82	1.56
Other Non-Metallic Minerals	2006–2010	1.83	−2.61	−1.22
	2011–2015	6.07	2.68	1.92
	2011–2015*	5.80	3.08	1.95
Electricity and Gas	2006–2010	0.44	1.26	0.82
	2011–2015	1.38	1.80	0.81
	2011–2015*	4.69	2.74	0.97
Wood Products	2006–2010	2.97	−1.47	−0.69
	2011–2015	3.28	1.59	0.80
	2011–2015*	4.41	1.48	0.68

Notes: Margin is the operating margin. Defined as the total operating income of an industry divided by its total sales. ROE is the ratio of the total net income of an industry to its total equity book value. ROA is the ratio of total net income to total asset value. *indicates profitability measured by using consolidated financial statements.

The wearing apparel and accessories industry is 11th in profitability in the secondary sector. According to Table 6.16, its operating margin decreased from 6.94% for 2006–2010 to 4.86% for 2011–2015. The leading firms in this industry are Hansae and LF, which accounted for 19.4% and 19.2%, respectively, of total sales revenue as of 2015. Hansae is an OEM–ODM company that has overseas corporations in Asia and Latin America. Its customers are famous apparel retailers, such as GAP and Old Navy. Table 6.17 shows that the ROEs of Hansae continue to be around 20% for 2011–2015, while its operating margins are between 5% and 9%. LF, formerly called LG fashion, manufactures its own brand of apparel and accessories. The profitability of LF is close to or above the industry's overall profitability. Although there are 23 listed firms in this industry, the market share of Others, excluding the four major firms, is only 1.4%. The profitability ratios of Others also recently approached zero or even negative values.

The medical, precision, and optical instruments industry (including watches and clocks) is rapidly growing, as shown in Table 6.5. The industry has 43 listed firms as of 2015. Its profitability improved from 2006–2010 to 2011–2015. According to Table 6.18, KCTech is the leading company; it manufactures semiconductor equipment,

Table 6.17. Consolidated Operating Margin and ROE of Wearing Apparel and Accessories Industry from 2011 to 2015

Firm	2011		2012		2013		2014		2015	
	MG	ROE	MG	ROE	MG	ROE	MG	ROE	MG	ROE
Hansae	7.3	27.1	5.6	21.5	4.8	18.7	7.1	20.0	9.0	22.0
LF	9.1	12.9	5.3	8.9	5.7	8.9	6.6	9.1	4.7	5.4
Hansome	21.2	13.1	14.3	9.4	10.7	6.8	8.7	6.4	10.7	9.4
BYC	17.9	8.9	15.4	7.7	13.8	5.9	15.8	5.2	11.6	3.7
Others	3.2	3.0	1.6	−0.8	2.3	1.5	1.2	−0.1	0.4	−1.0

Notes: MG indicates the operating margin, defined as operation income divided by sales. ROE is net income divided by the book value of equity. "Others" comprise all firms excluding the four firms shown in the table. The ROE and operating margin of Others are calculated based on the summation of the related financial variables, such as net income, equity value, operating income, and sales revenue.

Table 6.18.   Consolidated Operating Margin and ROE of Medical, Precision, and Optical Instruments Industry from 2011 to 2015

Firm	2011 MG	2011 ROE	2012 MG	2012 ROE	2013 MG	2013 ROE	2014 MG	2014 ROE	2015 MG	2015 ROE
KCTech	5.0	7.1	5.2	5.4	10.9	10.2	8.7	10.5	12.3	14.2
Vatech	0.1	7.4	6.8	1.7	8.9	5.7	16.2	8.2	18.9	11.6
Austem	9.6	14.0	10.1	17.3	8.7	15.6	12.1	15.5	13.1	23.1
Dio	18.4	1.0	16.9	−4.1	−1.2	−20.0	8.4	0.7	28.3	9.3
Others	6.2	0.3	6.5	2.6	9.0	8.9	4.6	2.8	4.6	3.6

Notes: MG indicates the operating margin, defined as operation income divided by sales. ROE is net income divided by the book value of equity. "Others" comprise all firms excluding the four firms shown in the table. The ROE and operating margin of Others are calculated based on the summation of the related financial variables, such as net income, equity value, operating income, and sales revenue.

such as the chemical–mechanical polishing system required for semiconductors. KCTech accounted for 19% of the total operating income of the industry as of 2015. Vatech, the firm with the second largest operating income in the industry, is a manufacturer of medical imaging systems and dental instruments. Austem and Dio's main products are implants. Austem is highly profitable; its ROE was 23.1% in 2015. The operating margin and ROE of the industry excluding these four firms were 4.6% and 3.6%, respectively, in 2015. Others, however, show poor performance, as in other industries.

According to Table 6.16, the ROE of the food industry decreased by more than 3% point from 2006–2010 to 2011–2015. Its operating margin also decreased from 5.29% for 2006–2010 to 4.42% for 2011–2015. CJ Cheil Jedang accounted for 32.1% of the operating income in the food industry as of 2015. The profitability ratios of CJ Cheil Jedang moderately declined during 2011–2015, as shown in Table 6.19. In 2015, its operating margin was 5.8%, which is lower than the operating margins of Orinon, Lotte Confectionery, and Ottogi.

The basic metal industry is the fifth largest industry in the secondary sector. However, the basic steel industry has −1.3% of annual growth in terms of consolidated sales revenue, as shown in

Table 6.19.   Consolidated Operating Margin and ROE of Food Industry from 2011 to 2015

Firm	2011 MG	2011 ROE	2012 MG	2012 ROE	2013 MG	2013 ROE	2014 MG	2014 ROE	2015 MG	2015 ROE
CJ Cheil Jedang	7.0	6.5	6.2	6.6	3.2	7.2	5.0	4.3	5.8	5.2
Orion	11.1	6.3	11.1	0.8	10.4	1.5	11.3	0.6	12.6	1.8
Lotte Confectionery	9.3	5.0	6.2	3.7	4.6	2.5	5.2	1.0	6.4	1.3
Ottogi	5.3	11.8	6.4	10.8	6.1	11.9	6.5	12.4	7.1	12.1
Others	3.4	5.4	3.3	6.0	3.2	5.6	3.4	4.9	3.6	5.2

Notes: MG indicates the operating margin, defined as operation income divided by sales. ROE is net income divided by the book value of equity. "Others" comprise all firms excluding the four firms shown in the table. The ROE and operating margin of Others are calculated based on the summation of the related financial variables, such as net income, equity value, operating income, and sales revenue.

Table 6.5. POSCO accounted for 51.8% of total sales in the basic steel industry as of 2015. Table 6.20 shows that the operating margin of POSCO gradually decreased from 7.9% in 2011 to 4.1% in 2015. Although POSCO is the biggest firm in the basic metal industry, its profitability is lower than other major firms, such as Hyundai Steel, Korea Zinc, and SeAH Besteel. The profitability ratios of Korea Zinc are fairly above 10%, except for ROE in 2015. The industry excluding the four major firms had low profitability ratios. Its ROEs were −4.6% in 2014 and −0.5% in 2015.

The beverage industry is ranked 18th in terms of sales revenue for 2011–2015, as shown in Table 6.5. The profitability of the beverages industry slightly decreased from 2006–2010 to 2011–2015. Table 6.16 reports that its operating margin was 8.69% for 2011–2015, which is about 1.5 percentage points lower than for 2006–2010. The leading company is Lotte Chilsung, which accounted for 34.4% of the consolidated operating income in the beverage industry as of 2015. According to Table 6.21, the operating margin and ROE of Lotte Chilsung were 6.2% and 3.7% in 2015, respectively, lower than those of the beverage industry. Hite Jinro, with its main business products of liquor and beer, is the second largest company in terms of consolidated operating income, although it does not show

Table 6.20. Consolidated Operating Margin and ROE of Basic Metal Industry from 2011 to 2015

	2011		2012		2013		2014		2015	
Firm	MG	ROE	MG	ROE	MG	ROE	MG	ROE	MG	ROE
POSCO	7.9	8.5	5.7	6.4	4.8	3.7	4.9	2.7	4.1	3.1
Hyundai Steel	8.4	8.1	6.2	8.1	5.6	5.2	8.9	5.5	9.1	5.2
Korea Zinc	17.4	20.5	13.8	15.6	12.4	11.2	13.8	10.1	14.1	9.9
SeAH Besteel	12.2	17.6	7.8	8.8	6.8	7.3	8.0	8.2	8.8	7.6
Others	3.6	3.6	2.9	2.7	2.6	9.4	1.7	−4.6	2.7	−0.5

Notes: MG indicates the operating margin, defined as operation income divided by sales. ROE is net income divided by the book value of equity. "Others" comprise all firms excluding the four firms shown in the table. The ROE and operating margin of Others are calculated based on the summation of the related financial variables, such as net income, equity value, operating income, and sales revenue.

Table 6.21. Consolidated Operating Margin and ROE of Beverages Industry from 2011 to 2015

	2011		2012		2013		2014		2015	
Firm	MG	ROE	MG	ROE	MG	ROE	MG	ROE	MG	ROE
Lotte Chilsung	8.4	2.4	6.8	3.9	7.8	3.8	4.5	1.2	6.2	3.7
Hite Jinro	9.1	4.3	8.2	9.1	8.5	6.0	5.0	2.3	7.0	3.5
Muhak	22.0	18.2	21.2	12.2	24.9	15.8	28.1	19.6	22.2	6.8
JD	13.5	9.5	16.1	31.3	22.5	25.2	9.2	7.5	9.8	9.6
Others	4.6	69.3	6.3	1.3	6.0	4.6	9.5	6.3	9.9	6.8

Notes: MG indicates the operating margin, defined as operation income divided by sales. ROE is net income divided by the book value of equity. "Others" comprise all firms excluding the four firms shown in the table. The ROE and operating margin of Others are calculated based on the summation of the related financial variables, such as net income, equity value, operating income, and sales revenue.

outstanding profitability. Its margin and ROE are slightly lower than those of the industry overall. Muhak is the third largest firm and mainly produces liquor in regional areas. Its profitability ratio is much higher than Lotte Chilsung and Hite Jinro. The operating margin and ROE of Muhak were 22.2%, and 6.8%, respectively, in 2015.

Table 6.5 shows that the electrical equipment industry is the 10th largest industry in the secondary sector for 2011–2015. The sales growth of the electrical equipment industry decreased from 6.0% for 2006–2010 to 3.1% for 2011–2015. However, Table 6.16 reports that its profitability ratios slightly improved for the same period, although they are still low compared to the industries mentioned above. LSIS is the biggest company in the electrical equipment industry, accounting for 8.9% of sales revenue as of 2015. LSIS is a manufacturer of intermediate goods for green business, electronic power, and automation. Table 6.22 shows that its profitability ratios are a little higher than those of the industry overall, although its ROE has tended to slightly decline recently. The profitability ratios of Sebang Global Battery, KET, and Atlas BX are better than those of LSIS. The electrical equipment industry has 57 listed firms as of 2015. The total market share of the four major firms was less than 20%, but their share of operating income was more than 58% in 2015. Others in the electrical industry, excluding these four firms, suffer from low profitability.

Table 6.22.   Consolidated Operating Margin and ROE of Electrical Equipment Industry from 2011 to 2015

Firm	2011		2012		2013		2014		2015	
	MG	ROE	MG	ROE	MG	ROE	MG	ROE	MG	ROE
LSIS	6.3	7.9	6.9	12.4	7.4	12.3	6.9	9.8	7.0	7.1
Sebang G. B.	13.8	21.5	14.6	16.7	9.3	10.8	8.5	8.8	10.0	10.3
KET	8.9	8.0	9.8	6.0	9.3	8.0	13.9	17.7	13.7	17.8
AtlasBX	12.7	19.0	15.2	17.8	12.8	15.2	11.3	11.2	12.5	11.5
Others	1.3	0.6	1.3	8.1	−0.1	−3.9	2.1	−1.1	1.3	2.3

Notes: MG indicates the operating margin, defined as operation income divided by sales. ROE is net income divided by the book value of equity. "Others" comprise all firms excluding the four firms shown in the table. The ROE and operating margin of Others are calculated based on the summation of the related financial variables, such as net income, equity value, operating income, and sales revenue.

Table 6.23.   Consolidated Operating Margin and ROE of Other Non-Metallic Mineral Industry from 2011 to 2015

Firm	2011		2012		2013		2014		2015	
	MG	ROE	MG	ROE	MG	ROE	MG	ROE	MG	ROE
SaangYong Cement	3.6	−4.3	7.2	1.3	6.7	1.5	8.0	7.2	10.5	4.3
Hanil Cement	3.4	1.1	7.2	−6.0	11.0	5.7	9.6	6.5	8.8	2.5
IS Dongseo	6.7	3.5	5.7	2.7	8.2	5.9	10.0	11.4	12.1	18.2
POSCO Chemtech	10.1	28.2	7.1	19.7	14.3	1.8	12.9	7.0	12.9	5.5
Others	2.3	−4.0	3.0	−4.6	4.3	−23.5	6.5	26.8	6.1	12.8

Notes: MG indicates the operating margin, defined as operation income divided by sales. ROE is net income divided by the book value of equity. "Others" comprise all firms excluding the four firms shown in the table. The ROE and operating margin of Others are calculated based on the summation of the related financial variables, such as net income, equity value, operating income, and sales revenue.

The profitability of other non-metallic mineral industry improved for 2011–2015, although its sales growth decreased from 13.7% for 2006–2010 to 4.9% for 2011–2015, as shown in Table 6.5. The main business of three biggest firms is cement; therefore, their performance relies on construction and infrastructure business. Saang Yong Cement accounted for 15.7% of the total sales of the non-metallic industry as of 2015. Its operating margin tended to improve from 2011 to 2015, as shown in Table 6.23. Likewise, the operating margin rates of Hanil, IS Dongseo, and POSCO Chemtech also tended to improve after 2012, although their ROEs fluctuate greatly. Others have a similar pattern, but their ROEs are extremely volatile at −23.5% in 2013 but 26.8% in 2014.

The electricity and gas industry is the third largest industry in terms of non-consolidated sales revenue in the secondary sector. Its profitability tends to be very low because its retail prices are heavily regulated. The leading company is KEPCO, which has continued to increase its sales revenue by generating more electricity from new electric power facilities. Its recent profitability has sharply increased because of low fuel costs. KEPCO and Korea Gas Safety accounted for 59.9% and 26.4% of total sales revenue, respectively, as

Table 6.24. Consolidated Operating Margin and ROE of Electricity and Gas Industry from 2011 to 2015

Firm	2011 MG	2011 ROE	2012 MG	2012 ROE	2013 MG	2013 ROE	2014 MG	2014 ROE	2015 MG	2015 ROE
KEPCO	−7.9	−1.7	−7.8	2.8	0.6	10.1	2.4	19.2	19.1	−7.9
Korea Gas Safety	2.8	3.6	6.3	3.9	−3.1	2.9	1.0	3.9	0.6	2.8
Korea District Heating	1.1	8.7	9.9	8.0	7.1	3.6	4.1	10.5	6.7	1.1
Samchully	3.1	1.2	3.5	1.4	3.7	0.7	1.2	2.4	1.8	3.1
Others	6.7	1.9	7.6	1.8	7.0	1.6	7.5	1.2	4.4	6.7

Notes: MG indicates the operating margin, defined as operation income divided by sales. ROE is net income divided by the book value of equity. "Others" comprise all firms excluding the four firms shown in the table. The ROE and operating margin of Others are calculated based on the summation of the related financial variables, such as net income, equity value, operating income, and sales revenue.

of 2015. As such, both companies dominated the market share of the electricity and gas industry. In general, the industry's profitability is not impressive, but it has tended to improve recently, as shown in Table 6.24. Korea Distric Heating had stable earnings compared to other firms. In contrast, gas firms such as Korea Gas Safety and Samchully had low profitability ratios.

Table 6.25 displays the profitability ratios of the seven least profitable industries in the secondary sector. Most of these industries had less than 1% of ROE for the entire sample period of 2006–2015. The general construction and other transport equipment industries are ranked sixth and seventh in the secondary sector. They faced very low sales growth for 2011–2015, as shown in Table 6.5. In fact, all industries shown in Table 6.25 have negative or negligible sales growth rates for 2011–2015, except for the fabricated metal industry. The general construction, other transport equipment, and other machinery equipment industries are the top 10 biggest industries in Korea. Thus, we will investigate the profitabilities of their major firms with additional information. However, the other four industries will be reviewed here.

Table 6.25. Profitability (%) of the Seven Least Profitable Industries from 2006 to 2015

Industry	Period	Margin	ROE	ROA
Pulp and Paper	2006–2010	4.02	−0.20	0.09
	2011–2015	3.49	1.19	0.61
	2011–2015*	3.81	0.73	0.31
Other Machinery and Equipment	2006–2010	6.92	4.31	2.13
	2011–2015	4.36	0.55	0.20
	2011–2015*	4.88	1.00	0.42
Textiles	2006–2010	1.90	0.51	0.30
	2011–2015	1.65	0.03	0.03
	2011–2015*	2.41	0.45	0.26
Fabricated Metal	2006–2010	6.42	2.88	1.74
	2011–2015	3.50	−0.74	−0.21
	2011–2015*	3.14	−0.80	−0.24
Leather, Luggage, and Footwear	2006–2010	1.77	−5.34	−3.54
	2011–2015	−1.22	−1.47	−0.95
	2011–2015*	−1.00	−1.27	−0.80
Other Transport Equipment	2006–2010	8.04	18.77	5.09
	2011–2015	−0.73	−7.66	−2.15
	2011–2015*	−0.33	−6.49	−1.51
General Construction	2006–2010	5.32	5.06	2.05
	2011–2015	0.39	−8.35	−2.66
	2011–2015*	0.93	−7.44	−2.23

Notes. Margin is the operating margin, defined as the total operating income of an industry divided by its total sales. ROE is the ratio of the total net income of an industry to its total equity book value. ROA is the ratio of the total net income to the total asset value. *indicates profitability measured by using consolidated financial statements.

The pulp and paper industry has 28 listed firms as of 2015. Moorim is the leading company and accounted for 12.5% of total sales and 34.2% of total operating income in the industry as of 2015. Its operating margin was around 5%, but its ROE was highly volatile at −9.6% in 2012 and −8.8% in 2014, respectively, while it was 7.5% in 2015. The other firms have very poor profitability ratios. In general, many listed firms appeared to be financially distressed.

The textile industry experienced negative sales growth for 2011–2015, according to Table 6.5. The textile industry's profitability was negligibly small, and its average ROE was only 0.03% for 2011–2015.

Dong-Il is the biggest company and accounted for 23.3% of total sales generated by the textile industry as of 2015. Although most firms suffered from low profitability, the operating margin of Kyungbang was 10.9% in 2015. In addition, Kyungbang's operating income was larger than that of Dong-Il.

The leather and luggage industry has only four listed firms as of 2015. Its average operating margin and ROE were slightly negative for the 10-year sample period. In addition, the industry suffered from negative operating income, which increased from −4.1 trillion KRW in 2012 to −19.6 trillion KRW in 2014. However, Samyang Tongsang and Chokwang, which accounted for 51.4% and 43.4% of total sales, respectively, had relatively good performance. For example, the operating margin of Samyang Tongsang was 5.6% and that of Chokwang was 4.1% in 2015. The two other firms suffered from poor performance.

As the average sales growth of the fabricated metal product industry fell by almost half between 2006–2010 and 2011–2015, its operating margin decreased as well, as seen in Table 6.25. LIG Next 1 became the leading firm in the industry when it was listed on the KOSPI market in October 2015. LIG Next 1 is a military defense manufacturer that produces precise guided munitions, surveillance, and other cutting-edge weapons. It accounted for 25.1% of the total sales revenue and 28.0% of total operating income in the fabricated metal industry as of 2015. Except for LIG Next 1, no firm dominated the market share in the industry. Sammok S-Form, with the second largest operating income in 2015, produces aluminum forms. LIG Next 1 had 5.9% of operating margin and 14.4% of ROE in 2015, while the operating margin of Sammok S-Form was 15.8% in 2015. The operating margins of YG-1, which manufactures tools for drilling and milling, and Hankuk Carbon were also above 12% in 2015. The profitability of this industry tended to improve in 2015. When the aforementioned four firms are excluded, the industry's operating margin was low in 2015.

The other machinery and equipment industry is the eighth largest industry, with 143 listed firms as of 2015. Its average sales growth significantly decreased from 13.5% for 2006–2010 to 0.9%

for 2011–2015, according to Table 6.5. Its operating margin and ROE also decreased to 4.36% and 0.55%, respectively, for 2011–2015. Table 6.26 shows the profitability ratios of four major firms in order of sales revenue. Doosan Heavy Industries & Construction (HIC) and Doosan Infracore accounted for 31.4% and 14.0% of the market share, respectively, as of 2015. However, the operating income proportion of Doosan HIC and Doosan Infracore in the other machinery and equipment industry is only 4.42% and 1.95%, respectively, in 2015. Thus, both firms suffer from seriously low profitability. Doosan HIC has diverse business areas, such as power and water plants, power generation, and shipbuilding components. Doosan Infracore is a manufacturer of construction equipments and diesel engines. As major firms in the other machinery and equipment industry, both firms experienced a serious downturn in performance. Hanon System, which is the third largest in terms of sales revenue, has fairly good profitability ratios, as shown in Table 6.26. Hanon System is a manufacturer of automotive thermal management and climate control systems, which are directly related to the motor vehicles industry. When the four major firms are excluded, the industry tends

Table 6.26. Consolidated Operating Margin and ROE of Other Machinery and Equipment Industry from 2011 to 2015

Firm	2011 MG	2011 ROE	2012 MG	2012 ROE	2013 MG	2013 ROE	2014 MG	2014 ROE	2015 MG	2015 ROE
Doosan HIC	5.9	4.7	6.2	−6.3	5.0	9.8	4.9	−1.0	0.4	−10.1
Doosan Infracore	8.0	18.6	4.4	−5.7	4.8	−4.7	5.9	1.8	0.4	−38.1
Hanon System	8.2	12.3	8.5	12.3	7.0	11.5	6.8	14.2	6.5	8.4
Hanwha Tech	3.0	14.6	5.3	7.0	4.2	5.2	0.3	−9.5	−2.3	5.5
Others	7.5	5.6	4.8	1.7	3.3	−11.2	4.4	1.1	5.1	3.6

Notes: MG indicates the operating margin, defined as operation income divided by sales. ROE is net income divided by the book value of equity. "Others" comprise all firms excluding the four firms shown in the table. The ROE and operating margin of Others are calculated based on the summation of the related financial variables, such as net income, equity value, operating income, and sales revenue.

to have better profitability ratios. The better performance may be due to the diverse business areas that this industry covers.

Table 6.5 reports that the other transport equipment industry, with 21 listed firms, is the seventh largest industry as of 2015. The average sales growth of other transport equipment significantly decreased from 20.4% for 2006–2010 to −0.1% for 2011–2015. Its profitability ratios were all negative during 2011–2015; its average operating margin was −0.73%. This industry has suffered from negative operating income since 2013. Its total operating income was KRW −1.1 trillion in 2013, −4.5 trillion in 2014, and −5.7 trillion in 2015. Because most of the major firms suffered from earnings losses, we rank major firms based on sales revenue as of 2015 in Table 6.27. Hyundai Heavy Industries is the leading firm and accounted for 55.4% of sales revenue as of 2015. The second biggest firm is DSME, which accounted for 18.0%. Most firms suffered from significant earnings losses, and the profitability of the other transport equipment industry worsened from 2011 to 2015 because of the global economic recession and oversupply of shipbuilding business. Table 6.27 shows

Table 6.27. Consolidated Operating Margin and ROE of Other Transport Equipment Industry from 2011 to 2015

	2011		2012		2013		2014		2015	
Firm	MG	ROE	MG	ROE	MG	ROE	MG	ROE	MG	ROE
Hyundai H. I.	8.4	13.2	3.6	7.3	1.5	2.9	−6.2	−12.7	−3.3	−12.5
DSME	7.6	16.4	3.5	3.0	−5.3	5.3	−4.8	−27.9	−19.6	−1,514.8
Samsung H. I.	8.1	18.8	8.3	14.2	6.2	11.3	1.4	2.1	−15.5	−30.6
Hyundai Mipo	8.2	7.1	2.1	3.5	−6.9	−6.0	−21.9	−38.4	1.4	1.5
Others	2.7	−0.5	−5.1	−28.9	−22.7	N.A.	2.7	2.1	2.1	−1.9

Notes: MG indicates the operating margin, defined as operation income divided by sales. ROE is net income divided by the book value of equity. "Others" comprise all firms excluding the four firms shown in the table. The ROE and operating margin of Others are calculated based on the summation of the related financial variables, such as net income, equity value, operating income, and sales revenue. The ROE of Others in 2013 is not calculated because of impaired capital (negative value of total equity) and negative net income.

Table 6.28.   Consolidated Operating Margin and ROE of General Construction
Industry from 2011 to 2015

Firm	2011 MG	2011 ROE	2012 MG	2012 ROE	2013 MG	2013 ROE	2014 MG	2014 ROE	2015 MG	2015 ROE
Hyundai E&C	6.2	11.7	5.7	7.7	5.7	7.7	5.5	6.3	5.2	5.3
GS E&C	4.4	10.9	1.7	3.1	−9.8	−31.0	0.5	−2.4	1.2	−1.0
Daewoo E&C	4.7	6.7	4.2	4.7	−2.8	−28.4	4.3	4.0	3.5	5.3
Daerim Const.	5.5	9.9	4.7	10.2	0.4	3.3	−2.9	−10.6	2.9	2.8
Others	−1.0	−16.6	−3.4	−34.8	−2.8	−26.5	−0.9	−16.5	1.1	−16.7

Notes: MG indicates the operating margin, defined as operation income divided by
sales. ROE is net income divided by the book value of equity. "Others" comprise
all firms excluding the four firms shown in the table. The ROE and operating
margin of Others are calculated based on the summation of the related financial
variables, such as net income, equity value, operating income, and sales revenue.

that only Hyundai Mipo among the four major firms recovered
positive profitability ratios in 2015.

   The general construction industry is the least profitable in terms
of ROE and the sixth largest in terms of non-consolidated sales
revenue as of 2015. Table 6.25 shows that the operating margin of
the construction industry was 0.39% for 2011–2015, which decreased
from 5.32% for 2006–2010. Its ROE was −8.35% for 2011–2015,
which is the lowest in the secondary sector. There are 40 listed
firms in the general construction industry. Hyundai Engineering and
Construction (Hyundai E&C) is the leading firm and accounted
for 23.5% of total sales revenue in the industry as of 2015. The
profitability ratios of Hyundai E&C exceed those of the industry
overall. Although its profitability slightly decreases over time, its
margin and ROE are above 5% as shown in Table 6.28. GS E&C,
the second largest firm, has faced low profitability since 2013. When
the four major firms were excluded, the industry struggled with
extremely low or negative profitability. Thus, the major construction
firms have maintained reasonable profitability in contrast to the other
firms in the transport equipment industry.

6.2.3.   *Financial Risk*

The financial risk of the secondary sector does not appear to be substantial because the leverage ratio of the secondary sector tends to decrease. However, the profitability of the secondary sector gradually decreased over time. As such, individual industries in the secondary sector may have different financial risk. In particular, the industries with poor profitability may be in financial distress.

6.2.3.1.   *Interest coverage ratio*

The interest coverage ratio is one of the most important measurements for examining the financial soundness of an organization. The interest coverage ratio is the ratio of EBIT (earnings before interest and taxes) to interest expenses; it shows the capacity of an organization to bear its interest expenses out of its earnings. Because the leverage ratios of industries vary due to the different characteristics of their assets and business, interest expenses vary as well. As such, appropriate interest coverage should be different across industries. In practice, however, the appropriate interest coverage ratio needs be at least 3 or higher.

Table 6.29 presents the interest coverage ratios of the secondary sector from 2011 to 2015 in ascending order of the ratio as of 2015. The industries with low interest coverage ratios tend to have poor profitability. The other transport equipment industry has had negative interest coverage ratios since 2013, and its ratios have worsened since that point. Three consecutive years of negative EBITs indicate that the industry is in deep financial distress. The pulp and paper industry had the second lowest interest coverage ratio in 2015 at −0.38, and its interest coverage ratio was consistently low from 2011 to 2015. The low profitability and interest coverage ratios may imply that many firms in this industry have difficulty in paying their debt obligations. The other machinery equipment industry also continued to have low and worsening interest coverage ratio. Major firms like Doosan HIC and Doosan Infracore in particular had negative net income in 2015, as shown in Table 6.26.

The general construction industry, the least profitable industry, has a very low interest coverage ratio as well, although the interest

Table 6.29. Interest Coverage Ratios of Secondary Sector from 2011 to 2015

	2011	2012	2013	2014	2015
Other Transport Equipment	11.31	3.76	−5.52	−8.06	−13.45
Pulp and Paper	1.34	2.62	1.78	1.32	−0.38
Other Machinery Equipment	3.91	1.83	0.85	1.35	0.02
General Construction	0.90	−0.28	−1.61	0.30	0.95
Textile	1.48	0.65	3.37	1.37	1.65
Basic Metal Products	4.95	3.91	3.38	2.27	2.19
Electrical Equipment	2.50	6.64	1.10	3.66	3.35
Wood Products	1.35	1.27	1.31	2.70	3.60
Fabricated Metal	0.26	1.38	1.21	2.17	4.05
Food	5.38	4.35	3.66	3.76	4.69
Beverage	4.60	4.00	5.60	3.68	4.79
Other Non-metallic Mineral	1.11	0.79	−0.50	6.36	5.14
Chemical and Chemical Products	7.76	4.41	3.16	3.58	5.76
Rubber and Plastic	2.20	3.43	5.41	5.71	5.98
Wearing Apparel and Accessories	8.08	5.19	5.23	5.75	6.14
Leather, Luggage, and Footwear	1.29	0.81	−1.17	0.77	6.43
Medical, Precision, Optical Inst.	2.06	2.52	5.85	3.76	6.78
Electricity and Gas	0.42	0.08	1.07	2.50	7.62
Pharmaceuticals	6.69	5.48	7.66	6.07	9.40
Other Manufactured	2.13	3.43	6.65	11.48	11.64
Electronics	8.38	15.40	21.81	18.93	17.65
Motor Vehicles	20.06	24.08	28.57	27.66	23.96
Refined Petroleum	27.42	10.02	9.30	−6.19	25.88
Printing and Recorded Media	22.21	−4.13	6.48	18.08	30.16
Special Construction	10.06	10.94	13.91	18.98	32.38
Furniture	13.35	7.00	6.11	22.87	33.57
Tobacco	275.29	101.08	75.79	106.76	150.17

Notes: Interest coverage ratio is defined as EBIT/Interest Expenses. EBIT and interest expenses are obtained from consolidated financial statements.

coverage ratio has slightly improved since 2013. Because its EBIT does not cover interest expenses, the general construction industry itself may be in financial distress. The industry, excluding the four major firms, has negative profitability ratios from 2011 to 2015 as shown in Table 6.28, indicating that financial risk may be very high. The textile industry also has poor profitability and low interest coverage ratios. The interest coverage ratio of the basic metal products industry continuously decreased. However, the interest coverage ratios of the other industries appear to be high enough to cover interest expenses.

6.2.3.2. *Debt ratio (debt/asset)*

Table 6.30 presents the debt ratios and percentage of firms with negative operating income for each industry in 2015. We provide two debt ratios. The first is the ratio of total book value of an industry's debt to the total book value of its assets. The second, indicated by an asterisk, is the ratio of the total debt value to the debt value plus the market value of equity.

In the general construction industry, the firms with negative operating income tend to have higher debt ratios than those with positive operating income; 30% of 40 firms had negative operating income in 2015. The debt ratio measured with the market value of equity for firms with negative operating income is 0.89, which is much higher than the debt ratio for firms with positive operating income. Thus, many financially distressed firms seem to have suffered from low profitability and high debt ratios in the general construction industry.

The other transport equipment industry has faced serious financial risk as well: 42.9% of firms in the industry have negative operating income, and their debt ratios are much higher than those with positive operating income. Considering the negative interest coverage ratio of the other transport equipment industry, its high debt ratio implies that the industry is in deep financial risk.

The pulp and paper industry has the third highest debt ratio as measured by the market value of assets as of 2015. Although 32.1% of firms in the pulp and paper industry had negative operating income in 2015, their debt ratios are similar to those with positive operating income. Because the debt ratio of the pulp and paper industry is relatively high with low profitability, the industry in general is vulnerable to financial risk.

The textile industry, regarded as typical of declining industries in Korea, has 31.3% of firms with negative operating income. The debt ratios of these firms are higher than those of firms with positive

Table 6.30. Debt Ratio of Industries and Percentage of Firms with Negative Operating Income in 2015

Industry	OI ≥ 0		OI <0		Percentage of Firms with OI <0	Number of Firms
	Debt Ratio	Debt Ratio*	Debt Ratio	Debt Ratio*		
General Construction	0.67	0.76	0.80	0.89	30.0	40
Other Transport Equipment	0.72	0.51	0.76	0.85	42.9	21
Pulp and Paper	0.56	0.68	0.56	0.66	32.1	28
Textile	0.40	0.54	0.58	0.63	31.3	16
Food	0.53	0.40	0.65	0.61	9.3	43
Chemical and Chem. Products	0.71	0.62	0.55	0.60	17.7	113
Electricity and Gas	0.64	0.79	0.44	0.57	15.4	13
Motor Vehicles	0.54	0.63	0.66	0.57	7.0	86
Fabricated Metal Products	0.47	0.37	0.62	0.56	14.0	43
Other Machinery Equipment	0.64	0.61	0.53	0.52	15.4	143
Basic Metal Products	0.46	0.64	0.41	0.49	25.7	74
Rubber and Plastic	0.54	0.47	0.41	0.45	16.7	42
Electrical Equipment	0.47	0.36	0.33	0.41	23.2	56
Electronics	0.33	0.33	0.54	0.40	34.3	268
Furniture	0.21	0.15	0.44	0.29	44.4	9
Leather, Luggage, and Footwear	0.24	0.21	0.60	0.28	25.0	4
Medical, Precision, and Optical	0.38	0.18	0.53	0.28	25.6	43
Wearing Apparel and Accessories	0.40	0.32	0.48	0.27	31.8	22
Special Construction	0.34	0.15	0.50	0.18	25.0	16
Printing and Recorded Media	0.39	0.08	0.31	0.17	50.0	4
Other Non-metallic Mineral	0.46	0.48	0.23	0.15	3.1	32
Beverage	0.49	0.41	0.12	0.09	18.2	11

(*Continued*)

Table 6.30. (*Continued*)

Industry	OI ≥0		OI <0		Percentage of Firms with OI <0	Number of Firms
	Debt Ratio	Debt Ratio*	Debt Ratio	Debt Ratio*		
Pharmaceuticals	0.37	0.15	0.37	0.08	15.8	101
Other Manufactured Products	0.36	0.25	0.18	0.05	14.3	7
Tobacco	0.28	0.14	N.A	N.A.	0.0	1
Wood Products	0.54	0.59	N.A	N.A.	0.0	4
Refined Petroleum	0.49	0.36	N.A	N.A.	0.0	4

Notes: Debt ratio is the ratio of the total debt of an industry to its total assets. *indicates the ratio of the total debt of an industry to its total assets, which are defined as the book value of debt plus the market value of equity. OI ≥0 indicates firms with non-negative operating income.

operating income. Because the textile industry has low profitability and a low interest coverage ratio, some of the industry seem to have high financial risk.

The food industry also has high debt ratios, but only 9.3% of firms in the industry have negative operating income. The food industry tends to have a stable operating income because it is less vulnerable to the business cycle. This stable income may allow the industry to have high debt ratios. The food industry is among the moderately profitable industries, as shown in Table 6.16, and its interest coverage ratio was 4.65 in 2015. As such, only a small number of firms in the food industry may be financially distressed.

Although the basic metal products industry has a low interest coverage ratio of 2.19 in 2015, it still has acceptable debt ratios, as shown in Table 6.30. However, 25.7% of firms have negative operating income. Because this industry has very low profitability ratios except among the four leading firms, as Table 6.20 indicates, there may be marginal firms that have struggled in paying interest expenses.

It is interesting to note that the electronics industry has 34.3% of firms with negative operating income. Although the industry is among the top 10 profitable industries, firms except for the four major firms have low profitability ratios, as shown in Table 6.12.

Thus, many firms in the electronics industry may have suffered from low profitability and financial difficulties.

In general, the industries with low profitability tend to have higher debt ratios and a greater number of financially distressed firms. In particular, the other transport equipment industry and the general construction industry seem to have high financial risk in terms of high debt ratios, low profitability, and low interest coverage ratios.

6.2.4. *Valuation*

M/B and price–earnings (P/E) ratios are typically employed to examine stock valuation. However, the P/E ratio can be misleading in some cases. For example, the P/E ratio of the textile industry was 501.4 in 2014, which may be misinterpreted as an extremely high valuation. However, the consolidated net income of this industry was only KRW 3.25 trillion in 2014. Because the net income was too small as a denominator, the P/E ratio was extremely high. Industries with poor profitability in particular frequently have extremely high P/E ratios. As such, we provide M/B ratios using the consolidated book value of equity to examine stock valuation.

Figure 6.8 presents the M/B ratios of the top 10 most profitable industries, as defined in Table 6.10. Although the profitability of the motor vehicles industry slightly decreased from 2006–2010 to 2011–2015, it still achieved good performance. Nevertheless, its M/B ratio was very low. On the other hand, the printing and recorded media has the highest M/B ratio. The electronics industry has the second lowest M/B ratio; although its sales growth tended to decrease after 2013, it maintained high profitability ratios, as shown in Table 6.10 and Table 6.12. As such, the electronics industry seems to be relatively undervalued. The pharmaceutical industry has the second highest M/B ratio, but its profitability ratios do not appear to be excellent compared to other industries, as shown in Table 6.10. The pharmaceutical industry, however, has stable and high sales growth. The high valuation of the pharmaceutical industry may reflect the promising prospect of biotech and stable sales growth.

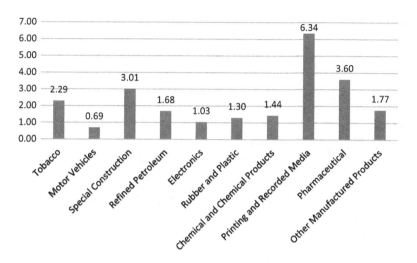

Figure 6.8. M/B Ratios of Top 10 Most Profitable Industries in 2015

Note: The M/B ratio is calculated as the total market value of equity divided by the total consolidated book value of equity in an industry.

Figure 6.9 shows 5 years of M/B ratios for the four industries with the first and second highest (lowest) M/B ratios of 2015 among the top 10 most profitable industries. The M/B ratio of the printing and recorded media industry has sharply increased after 2013. This industry has only four listed firms, and Loen is the only profitable firm among them in 2015. In general, the printing and recorded media industry appears to be fast growing in terms of non-consolidated sales revenue but not in terms of consolidated sales revenue, as shown in Table 6.5. In addition, its profitability ratios were not outstanding for 2011–2015 in terms of its consolidated income statement, according to Table 6.10. It is difficult to justify a high valuation of printing and recorded media based on its financial information.

The motor vehicles industry is exactly the opposite. Its annual sales growth and profitability ratios slightly increased between 2006–2010 and 2011–2015, but its M/B ratios have gradually decreased to 0.69. Such low valuation does not appear to match the performance of the motor vehicles industry. However, because the valuation of a firm is based on future cash flows, such a low valuation does not necessarily imply undervaluation.

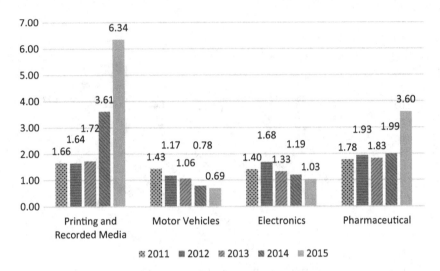

Figure 6.9.   M/B Ratios of Printing and Recorded Media, Motor Vehicles, Electronics, Pharmaceutical Industries from 2011 to 2015

Note: The M/B ratio is calculated as the total market value of equity divided by the total consolidated book value of equity in an industry.

The electronics industry reached an M/B ratio of 1.68 in 2012 and gradually decreased to 1.03 in 2015. Although the annual sales growth of this industry sharply decreased between 2006–2010 and 2011–2015, its ROE and ROA were higher than those of the printing and recorded media and the pharmaceutical industry. Its low valuation may be difficult to justify, although more than 30% of firms suffered from negative operating income.

The M/B ratio of the pharmaceutical industry dramatically increased from 1.88 in 2014 to 3.6 in 2015. The annual sales growth of the pharmaceutical industry decreased from 12.1% for 2006–2010 to 7.2% for 2011–2015, although the annual growth for 2011–2015 is relatively high compared to other manufacturing industries. The profitability ratios of major firms in the industry appear to be excellent, but except for Hanmi, they have no tendency to increase. As such, the profitability of the pharmaceutical industry does not explain the recent increase in the M/B ratio. However, as the proportion of the aged population has rapidly increased in Korea, we may expect strong demand in the pharmaceutical industry in

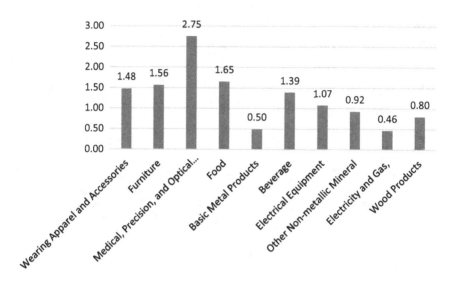

Figure 6.10.   M/B Ratios of Moderately Profitable Industries in 2015

Note: The M/B ratio is calculated as the total market value of equity divided by the total consolidated book value of equity in an industry.

addition to the promising prospect of biotech. These factors may partially explain the industry's high valuation.

Figure 6.10 shows the M/B ratios of 10 moderately profitable industries in 2015, as defined in Table 6.16. The medical, precision, and optical instruments industry has an M/B ratio of 2.75, which is highest among the moderately profitable industries. The profitability ratios of the four major firms in the medical, precision, and optical instruments industry gradually increased from 2011 to 2015. For example, the operating margin of KCTech increased from 5.0% in 2011 to 12.3% in 2015. Similarly, the M/B ratio of this industry continued to increase from 1.36 in 2011 to 2.75 in 2015. The electricity and gas industry and the basic metal industry have the lowest and second lowest M/B ratios, respectively. Although the electricity and gas industry has maintained high annual sales growth, its profitability ratios have been low. Because the price of electricity and gas is controlled by the Korean government, market expectations about the industry's profitability may be low. The M/B ratios of the basic metal industry continued to decrease from 0.84 in 2011

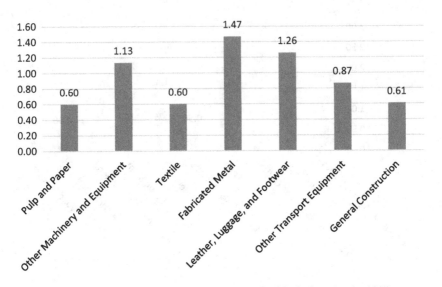

Figure 6.11.   M/B Ratios of Least Profitable Industries in 2015

Note: The M/B ratio is calculated as the total market value of equity divided by the total consolidated book value of equity in an industry.

to 0.50 in 2015. The slight decrease in its profitability ratios during 2011–2015, as shown in Table 6.20, may not be enough to justify the substantial decrease in its M/B ratios. The global oversupply of the basic metal products, however, may exacerbate the gloomy expectations about the industry's profitability.

Figure 6.11 shows the M/B ratios of the least profitable industries in 2015, as described in Table 6.25. The pulp and paper industry and the textile industry had the lowest M/B ratio at 0.6 among seven least profitable industries, which was still higher than that of the basic metal industry in Figure 6.10. The M/B ratio of the pulp and paper industry was 0.37 in 2011, while that of the textile industry was 0.32 in 2012. The general construction industry had the third lowest M/B ratio at 0.61. The general construction industry had consistently negative ROE and ROA for 2011–2015; the M/B ratio of this industry continued to decrease from 0.83 in 2011 to 0.61 in 2015. The fabricated metal industry had the highest M/B ratio among seven industries at 1.47. As we discussed in Table 6.25, the profitability of the fabricated metal industry has tended to improve recently, which may result in relatively high valuation of this industry among the least profitable industries. The M/B ratio of the other transport equipment industry decreased from 1.12 in 2011 to 0.87 in 2015. Its ROE, ROA, and operating margin have been negative since 2013. Although its profitability seriously deteriorated, its valuation appears to be not as low as that of the other least profitable industries.

6.3. Tertiary Sector

6.3.1. *Sales Revenue and Growth*

The tertiary sector has 27 industries, excluding the financial industry. The tertiary sector, however, has fewer listed firms than the secondary sector; 13 industries in the tertiary sector have fewer than 10 listed firms. Table 6.31 lists the industries in the tertiary sector in order of non-consolidated sales revenue in 2015.

Table 6.31 reports that the professional service industry has KRW 187.0 trillion of consolidated sales revenue in 2015, which is the largest in the tertiary sector. However, most listed firms in the professional service industry are holding firms that are more likely to belong to the secondary sector. Thus, the professional service industry may not be classified as any specific industry in the tertiary sector.

According to Table 6.31, the wholesale and commission industry is the largest in the tertiary sector aside from the professional service sector in terms of consolidated sales revenue. This industry had KRW 90.9 trillion of consolidated sales revenue in 2015, which is much less than the KRW 359.1 trillion of the electronics industry, the largest industry of the secondary sector. The wholesale and commission industry accounted for 16.07% of total sales revenue in the tertiary sector as of 2015. However, its annual sales growth decreased from 13.0% for 2006–2010 to –3.6% for 2011–2015. Its annual sales growth was also negative in terms of consolidated sales revenue for 2011–2015.

The retail business industry is the second largest industry; its sales revenue accounts for 12.78% of the total sales revenue. Although

Table 6.31. Sales Revenue of the Tertiary Sector as of 2015 and Growth Rate (%) from 2006 to 2015

Industry	Number of Firms	Sales* Revenue (KRW Trillion)	Market* Share (%)	Sales Revenue (KRW Trillion)	Annual Sales Growth (%)		
					2006–2010	2011–2015	2011–2015*
Wholesale Business	94	90.9	16.07	63.4	13.0	-3.6	-5.0
Retail Business	27	72.3	12.78	53.6	29.0	12.1	11.5
Telecommunication	11	51.3	9.06	41.3	5.5	-1.3	1.3
Air Transport	3	17.9	3.17	17.1	10.6	0.8	0.9
Water Transport	6	16.8	2.98	16.4	38.6	-8.7	-9.6
Storage and Transport	3	15.5	2.74	12.6	90.9	13.7	14.1
Land Transport	13	11.2	1.98	9.2	10.4	11.9	9.9
Professional Service	70	187.0	33.05	8.8	6.1	-26.4	-3.0
Computer Programming	30	50.1	8.86	8.6	17.4	15.6	75.9
Architecture Engineering	14	10.1	1.79	8.2	32.1	3.5	6.5
Information Service	27	9.4	1.66	6.4	4.2	62.3	86.5
Broadcasting	11	7.7	1.37	6.3	9.2	20.1	20.3
Publishing Service	85	6.8	1.71	4.7	23.0	10.2	15.0
Business Support Service	18	4.2	0.74	3.7	25.1	25.5	21.9
Sports and Amusement	7	3.0	0.53	2.8	15.0	2.5	3.4
Motion Picture and Music Production	20	2.87	0.51	2.2	9.0	16.3	16.0

(*Continued*)

Table 6.31. (*Continued*)

Industry	Number of Firms	Sales* Revenue (KRW Trillion)	Market* Share (%)	Sales Revenue (KRW Trillion)	Annual Sales Growth (%)		
					2006–2010	2011–2015	2011–2015*
Other Personal Service	1	2.32	0.41	2.2	4.6	−9.0	−0.6
Education Service	10	2.33	0.41	1.9	18.6	−3.4	−0.5
Accommodation and Food	2	0.94	0.17	0.9	18.3	7.7	7.9
Renting and Leasing	2	1.69	0.3	0.7	NA	24.5	78.1
Other Professional Service	6	0.35	0.06	0.3	4.6	−9.0	−7.5
Real Estate Service	5	0.34	0.06	0.3	−0.9	187.4	44.1
Waste Recycle Service	4	0.24	0.04	0.2	51.7	−0.49	1.9
Research and Development	13	0.19	0.03	0.2	58.0	53.88	53.9
Sales of Motor Vehicles	1	0.07	0.01	0.1	−15.7	−20.4	−20.8
Creative Arts and Recreation	2	0.4	0.01	0.04	−4.6	222.9	248.8
Remediation Service	1	0.1	0.00	0.01	27.0	−14.6	−9.7

Notes: *indicates sales revenue and sales growth from consolidated financial statements.

the annual sales growth of the retail business industry decreased by more than half between 2006–2010 and 2011–2015, it still remained high. The annual sales growth for 2011–2015 was 12.1%. Among the five largest industries of the tertiary sector, the retail business industry has rapidly increased in terms of sales revenue. The annual sales growth of the other four industries were either very low or negative for 2011–2015, even lower than those in the secondary sector, as shown in Table 6.5.

According to Figure 6.2, the sales revenue of the tertiary sector increased less than that of the secondary sector. This is mainly due to the low sales growth of the biggest industries in the tertiary sector. However, several industries in the tertiary sector, such as the computer programming industry, the information service industry, and the broadcasting industry, rapidly increased in terms of sales growth from 2006 to 2015.

6.3.2. *Profitability*

Table 6.32 lists the top 10 most profitable industries in descending order of ROE during 2011–2015 based on non-consolidated financial statements. In general, the profitability ratios of the top 10 industries in the tertiary sector are higher than those in the secondary sector. The most profitable industry is the other personal service industry. This industry has only one listed firm, Coway, which provides rental service for air and water purifiers. Although its annual sales growth was negative for 2011–2015, as shown in Table 6.31, its profitability ratios increased between 2006–2010 and 2011–2015.

The information service industry is one of the most rapidly growing and profitable industries. Its annual sales growth rate and ROE were 62.3% and 13.61%, respectively, for 2011–2015. The operating margin was 14.57% for 2011–2015. The leading firm is Naver, which provides a web-based searching service similar to Google. Although the profitability ratios of Naver tended to decrease from 2011 to 2015, its operating margin and ROE were 23.4% and 27.0% in 2015, respectively, which are much higher than in other industries.

Table 6.32. Profitability Ratios (%) of 10 Most Profitable Industries from 2006 to 2015

Industry	Period	Margin	ROE	ROA
Other Personal Service	2006–2010	13.47	21.28	11.46
	2011–2015	17.38	23.04	13.83
	2011–2015*	16.01	22.48	13.01
Information Service	2006–2010	19.59	14.59	10.46
	2011–2015	20.57	22.39	16.71
	2011–2015*	4.79	17.20	8.04
Storage and Transport	2006–2010	3.93	13.67	7.88
	2011–2015	4.10	15.70	7.75
	2011–2015*	4.79	17.20	8.04
Sports and Amusement	2006–2010	28.00	14.15	10.23
	2011–2015	28.44	13.61	10.23
	2011–2015*	27.34	13.39	9.78
Renting and Leasing	2006–2010	N.A.	N.A.	N.A.
	2011–2015	9.70	9.07	2.30
	2011–2015*	8.88	8.66	2.07
Business Support Service	2006–2010	9.47	1.57	1.01
	2011–2015	8.69	8.69	5.29
	2011–2015*	8.37	8.42	4.90
Broadcasting	2006–2010	11.74	8.70	5.30
	2011–2015	9.48	8.65	5.24
	2011–2015*	9.36	9.49	5.21
Publishing	2006–2010	10.70	−1.54	−1.01
	2011–2015	15.88	8.06	6.07
	2011–2015*	11.91	8.17	5.61
Education	2006–2010	10.97	10.97	7.59
	2011–2015	6.52	7.42	5.40
	2011–2015*	6.34	7.36	5.08
Retail Business	2006–2010	8.80	9.41	5.40
	2011–2015	6.70	7.21	4.05
	2011–2015*	5.91	7.16	3.49

Notes: Margin is the operating margin, defined as the total operating income of an industry divided by its total sales. ROE is the ratio of the total net income of an industry to its total equity book value. ROA is the ratio of the total net income to the total asset value. *indicates profitability measured by using consolidated financial statements.

The storage and transport industry is the third most profitable industry. It accounted for 2.74% of total sales revenue in the tertiary industry as of 2015, although the industry is the sixth biggest in terms of sales revenue in 2015, as shown in Table 6.31. The industry has only three listed firms: Hyundai Glovis, Korea Airport Service (KAS), and Hansol Logistics. The main business of all these firms is logistics. The ROE of the storage and transport industry was 15.7% but its operating margin was only 4.7% for 2011–2015.

The sports and amusement industry is the fourth most profitable industry. This industry maintained high profitability ratios from 2006 to 2015, but its annual sales growth sharply decreased from 90.9% for 2006–2010 to 13.7% for 2011–2015.

The renting and leasing industry has only two listed firms: AJ Rentacar and AJ networks. AJ Rentacar provides car rental service, and AJ networks provides a rental service for IT devices, lifting equipment, and pallets for logistics. These kinds of businesses are new in Korea. The annual sales growth of this industry was 24.5% during 2011–2015. Its operating margin and ROE were 9.70% and 9.07%, respectively, during the same period, and its ROA was 2.30%.

The business support service industry has 18 listed firms, which provide diverse services including security, tourism, and IT business solutions. S1 is the leading firm; its main business is security service for airports, plants, buildings, and households. The business support service industry has been rapidly expanding: The annual sales growth was above 25% both for 2006–2010 and 2011–2015. The industry accounted for 3.71% of total sales revenue in the tertiary sector as of 2015. The operating margin and ROE were a little higher than 8.0% for 2011–2015.

The broadcasting industry, which accounted for 1.37% of total revenue in the tertiary sector as of 2015, is also a profitable industry. Although the profitability ratios of this industry slightly decreased, its operating margin and ROE were 9.48% and 8.65%, respectively, for 2011–2015. Its annual sales growth increased from 9.2% for 2011–2015 to 20.1% for 2011–2015.

The publishing service industry includes diverse services, such as internet, mobile game business, and electronic transaction services.

There are 85 listed firms in the industry. The sales growth of the publishing service industry decreased by more than 50% between 2006–2010 and 2011–2015. However, its sales growth of 10.2% for 2011–2015 is still high compared to the average sales growth of industries in the tertiary sector. Digital gaming is the main business of the leading firms in the publishing service industry. NCSOFT, NHN Entertainment, and Com2us are the first, third, and fourth biggest firms, respectively, and accounted for 12.12%, 8.4%, and 5.7% of total industry revenue in 2015, respectively. The second biggest firm is KG Inisis, which is mainly an electronic transaction service. NCSOFT is a highly profitable firm in the publishing service industry: Its operating margin was 28.3% in 2015, whereas NHN Entertainment's was −8.4%. Excluding the four major firms, the operating margin and ROE of the other listed firms were 8.9% and 15.6%, respectively, in 2015. In general, the publishing service is a profitable and rapidly expanding industry.

The education service industry, the ninth most profitable industry, accounted for 1.94% of total sales revenue in the tertiary sector as of 2015. Its sales growth decreased from 18.61% for 2006–2011 to −3.37% for 2011–2015. Likewise, the profitability ratios of the education industry have decreased as well. The operating margin and ROE decreased to 6.58% and 7.53%, respectively, for 2011–2015 from the same 10.97% for 2006–2010. Daekyo is the biggest firm and accounted for almost 34.9% of total sales revenue in the education service industry as of 2015.

The retail business industry is the 10th most profitable industry and accounted for 12.78% of total sales revenue in the tertiary sector as of 2015. Although its sales growth decreased from 29.0% for 2006–2010 to 12.1% for 2011–2015, its profitability ratios decreased only by a little over 2 percentage points between these two periods. The biggest firm is Lotte Shopping, which accounted for 40.29% of total revenue in the retail business industry in 2015. Its margin and ROE were 2.93% and −1.96%, respectively, in 2015. The four biggest firms, Lotte Shopping, E-mart, GS Retail, and BGF Retail, had lower profitability ratios than the remaining 27 listed firm in 2015.

Table 6.33 presents the profitability ratios of 10 moderately profitable industries in descending order of ROE for 2011–2015. The telecommunication industry is a mature industry in Korea. Its sales growth has decreased from 5.5% for 2006–2010 to −1.3% for 2011–2015. The profitability ratios likewise substantially declined between these two periods. The operating margin of this industry decreased from 11.57% for 2006–2010 to 7.02% for 2011–2015. The industry has 15 listed firms. The major firms are KT, SK Telecom, and LG U+, which account for 44.6%, 33.4%, and 21.1% of the total revenue, respectively. Although major firms dominate the market share in the industry, their profitability does not appear to be superior to that of other small firms. For example, the operating margin of KT was 5.8% in 2015, whereas the operating margin of other firms excluding the four biggest was 8.84%.

The motion picture and music publishing industry is an expanding industry. Its sales growth increased from 9.0% for 2006–2010 to 16.3% for 2011–2015. The profitability ratios also improved, according to Table 6.33. CJ CGV is the leading firm in the industry and accounts for 41.6% of total sales revenue. Its main business is motion picture project services. The second biggest firm is SM Entertainment, the main business of which is production and distribution of music, as well as managing and training music groups. SM Entertainment accounts for 11.3% of total revenue in the motion picture and music publishing industry as of 2015.

Because the professional service industry consists of holding firms with diverse businesses, it is difficult to classify this industry into specific business categories. The biggest firm is SK Innovation, the main business of which is natural resource exploration, such as oil and new sources of energy. CJ, which is the second biggest firm in the industry, is a holding firm with businesses that include food, logistics, bio and engineering, and construction. Doosan and GS are the third and fourth biggest firms and are also holding firms. The annual sales growth of the professional industry was −3.0% for 2011–2015 based on consolidated financial statements, as shown in Table 6.33. Its operating margin and ROE were a little above 5% for 2011–2015.

Table 6.33. Profitability Ratios (%) of 10 Moderately Profitable Industries from 2006 to 2015

Industry	Period	Margin	ROE	ROA
Telecommunication	2006–2010	11.57	9.79	5.15
	2011–2015	7.02	5.71	2.71
	2011–2015*	6.54	6.74	2.93
Motion Picture and Music Production	2006–2010	−0.03	−16.53	−8.45
	2011–2015	9.48	5.69	3.24
	2011–2015*	7.09	4.53	2.47
Professional Service	2006–2010	8.43	10.10	6.03
	2011–2015	25.40	5.40	4.26
	2011–2015*	5.05	5.38	2.63
Computer Programming	2006–2010	−0.63	−18.53	−9.76
	2011–2015	3.46	5.32	4.29
	2011–2015*	2.83	0.81	0.79
Other Professional Service	2006–2010	−0.50	−7.66	−3.45
	2011–2015	7.00	5.03	2.91
	2011–2015*	7.05	4.99	2.67
Real Estate Service	2006–2010	−20.07	−6.10	−4.71
	2011–2015	15.03	3.71	2.89
	2011–2015*	4.75	2.63	1.88
Wholesale Business	2006–2010	2.03	3.88	1.78
	2011–2015	1.69	2.32	1.00
	2011–2015*	1.81	2.57	1.02
Accommodation and Food Service	2006–2010	5.20	7.71	4.96
	2011–2015	2.08	2.28	1.72
	2011–2015*	1.84	2.27	1.68
Land Transport	2006–2010	3.89	0.20	0.35
	2011–2015	3.22	1.72	0.96
	2011–2015*	3.52	2.80	1.38
Waste Recycling Business	2006–2010	10.37	2.07	1.39
	2011–2015	4.79	−3.75	−2.02
	2011–2015*	4.45	−3.89	−2.03

Notes: Margin is the operating margin, defined as the total operating income of an industry divided by its total sales. ROE is the ratio of the total net income of an industry to its total equity book value. ROA is the ratio of the total net income to the total asset value. *indicates profitability measured by using consolidated financial statements.

The other professional service industry has only six listed firms, which have diverse main businesses. The leading firm is Aurora, which provides toy designs in the global gift industry. As of 2015, Aurora accounted for 34.7% of total sales revenue in the other professional service industry. The second biggest firm is Macrogen, which provides genome research services to create information-based, drug and diagnostic tools. Macrogen accounts for 22.6% of total sales revenue as of 2015. The ROEs of these two firms were 11.1% and 5.2% in 2015, respectively. However, the industry faced negative sales growth of −9.01% for 2011–2015.

The wholesale business industry experienced negative sales growth for 2011–2015. Its profitability ratios have been low and slightly decreased between 2006–2010 and 2011–2015. The wholesale business industry has 94 listed firms. The four biggest in terms of sales revenue are SK Networks, Posco Daewoo, LG International, and E1. SK Networks accounted for 22.4% of total revenue in the industry as of 2015. The market share of the four major firms was about 61.5% in the industry. The profitability of these major firms was lower than that of the other 90 firms. When the operating margin is defined as the total operating income of the other firms divided by their total sales, the operating margin of the other firms was 3.88%, which was higher than that of any major firm.

The land transport industry had high and stable annual sales growth, above 10% from 2006 to 2015. CJ Korea Express is the biggest firm and accounted for 45.1% of total sales revenue as of 2015. The second biggest firm is Hanjin, with a market share of 14.5%. There is no outstanding firm with high profitability. Most firms in the land transport industry had low operating margins below 5%.

Table 6.34 shows the profitability ratios of the seven least profitable industries in the tertiary sector. The market shares of the research and development, creative arts and recreation, remediation service, and sales of motor vehicles industries were less than 0.1%, and the number of listed firms is also very small. We do not provide analyses of major firms for these industries.

The air transport industry has only three listed firms: Korean Air, Asian Airline, and Jeju Air. The market shares of Korean airline and

Table 6.34. Profitability Ratios (%) of Seven Least Profitable Industries from 2006 to 2015

Industry	Period	Margin	ROE	ROA
Research and Development	2006–2010	−34.37	−6.94	−4.95
	2011–2015	−16.00	−7.74	−5.21
	2011–2015*	−16.46	−7.85	−5.28
Air Transport	2006–2010	4.11	−10.34	−1.48
	2011–2015	2.80	−7.96	−0.84
	2011–2015*	3.14	−7.60	−0.82
Architecture Engineering	2006–2010	6.26	17.44	7.23
	2011–2015	0.90	−16.32	−1.56
	2011–2015*	−0.85	−11.26	−0.86
Creative Arts and Recreation	2006–2010	−104.65	−105.09	−69.17
	2011–2015	−11.74	−47.25	−38.53
	2011–2015*	−14.23	−61.06	−37.97
Water Transport	2006–2010	3.19	5.38	2.34
	2011–2015	−2.32	−47.43	−5.97
	2011–2015*	−1.81	−43.21	−5.56
Remediation Service	2006–2010	0.96	−29.05	−12.93
	2011–2015	−6.86	−57.30	−25.71
	2011–2015*	−7.08	−60.72	−21.31
Sales of Motor Vehicles	2006–2010	−17.74	−155.69	−8.77
	2011–2015	−4.80	N.A.	−14.18
	2011–2015*	−6.11	−344.28	−9.25

Notes: Margin is the operating margin, defined as the total operating income of an industry divided by its total sales. ROE is the ratio of the total net income of an industry to its total equity book value. ROA is the ratio of the total net income to the total asset value. *indicates profitability measured by using consolidated financial statements.

Asian airline were 64.3% and 32.2% in 2015, respectively. The annual sales growth of the air transport industry decreased from 10.6% for 2006–2010 to 0.8% for 2011–2015. Although the average operating margins of this industry were positive for both 2006–2010 and 2011–2015, its ROEs were negative for the same periods. For example, the operating margin of Korean airline was 7.6%, but its ROE was −17.8% in 2015. Likewise, the operating margin of Asiana airline was 1.7%, while its ROE was −23.9% in 2015.

The architecture engineering industry accounted for 1.79% of total sales revenue in the tertiary sector in 2015, as Table 6.31

indicates. The annual sales growth of this industry sharply decreased from 32.1% for 2006–2010 to 3.5% for 2011–2015. Similarly, the profitability ratios substantially declined, according to Table 6.34. The operating margin of this industry decreased from 6.26% for 2006–2010 to 0.90% for 2011–2015. Its ROE decreased from 17.44% for 2006–2010 to −16.32% for 2011–2015. The biggest firm is Samsung Engineering, which has businesses that include engineering services such as upstream and downstream hydrocarbon facilities, power plants, water and waste treatments plants, and industrial production facilities. Samsung Engineering accounted for 63.5% of total revenue in 2015. Its operating margin was −22.6% in 2015, which lowered the operating margin of the industry.

6.3.3. *Financial Risk*

Table 6.35 presents the interest coverage ratios of the tertiary sector. The tertiary sector has seven industries that do not make enough EBIT to cover interest expenses, whereas the secondary sector has four industries. However, more industries with low interest coverage ratios in the tertiary sector do not necessarily mean that the tertiary sector faces more serious financial difficulties. The tertiary sector has several industries with an extremely small number and size of firms. For example, the sales of motor vehicles and parts industry, which has only one listed firm, had an interest coverage ratio of −3.45 in 2015. In this case, higher financial risk exists at the level of an individual firm rather than at an industrial level.

According to Table 6.35, the industries with poor profitability tend to have interest coverage ratios of less than one. All seven least profitable industries shown in Table 6.34 had low interest coverage ratios. The architectural engineering service and the accommodation and food service industries have recently faced a dramatic decrease in interest coverage ratio. The research and development, air transport, water transport, and remediation service industries continued to have low interest coverage ratios from 2011 to 2015. However, an interest coverage ratio might sharply drop because of abnormally poor short-term profitability. As such, we also need to closely look at the debt ratios of industries.

Table 6.35. Interest Coverage Ratios of Tertiary Sector from 2011 to 2015

	2011	2012	2013	2014	2015
Architectural Engineering Services	24.79	16.29	−11.71	4.66	−29.74
Creative Arts and Recreation	NA	NA	NA	−112.74	−11.13
Accommodation and Food Service	17.18	17.35	6.81	−1.32	−5.30
Research and Development	−8.26	−2.69	0.15	−1.23	−4.83
Sales of Motor Vehicles and Parts	0.87	0.43	−7.91	3.32	−3.45
Air Transport	0.61	1.70	0.18	0.66	−0.09
Water Transport	−2.02	−1.35	−1.69	0.84	0.03
Remediation Service	−7.65	−3.01	−4.18	−6.28	1.75
Renting and Leasing	*N.A.*	1.78	2.05	2.09	1.98
Waste Recycling Business	2.78	0.71	0.84	−3.00	2.53
Other Professional Service	4.36	2.55	2.45	7.89	3.11
Wholesale and Commission Business	4.26	3.09	0.02	4.95	3.11
Land Transport and Pipeline Transport	2.09	2.51	1.23	2.84	3.79
Professional Service	6.51	3.62	2.90	2.94	3.97
Telecommunication	4.90	3.50	3.10	2.39	4.79
Retail Business	7.58	6.79	5.58	5.22	5.01
Motion Picture Production and Music Publishing	3.96	6.38	3.78	3.07	6.52
Broadcasting	8.40	8.79	8.36	4.69	7.91
Real Estate Service	1.62	−1.58	22.12	9.44	9.30
Business Support Service	10.83	10.04	20.29	13.30	10.31
Storage and Transport Support	27.72	25.95	32.44	26.44	12.79
Computer Programming and Consultancy	1.09	3.02	−6.48	8.88	18.55
Publishing Service	8.76	9.31	10.17	20.35	18.57
Education Service	19.21	12.13	15.57	20.01	19.29
Information Service	58.04	65.20	46.32	83.18	85.80
Sports and Amusement Business	84.45	42.34	52.60	60.14	92.45
Other Personal Service	9.25	5.82	18.57	29.83	105.74

Note: Interest coverage ratio is defined as EBIT/Interest Expenses. EBIT and interest expenses are obtained from consolidated financial statements the.

Table 6.36 shows the debt ratios of industries in the tertiary sector and the percentage of firms with negative operating income in 2015. The debt ratio marked with an asterisk is calculated as total debt divided by total debt plus the market value of equity, whereas the debt ratio without an asterisk is defined as the ratio of

Table 6.36. Debt Ratio of Industries and Percentage of Firms with Negative Operating Income in 2015

Industry	OI ≥0 Debt Ratio	OI ≥0 Debt Ratio*	OI <0 Debt Ratio	OI <0 Debt Ratio*	Percentage of Firms with OI <0	Number of Firms
Water Transport	0.71	0.74	0.95	0.86	16.67	6
Professional Service	0.52	0.55	0.68	0.80	4.29	70
Land Transport and Pipeline Transport	0.53	0.50	0.78	0.76	7.69	13
Architectural Engineering Services	0.48	0.34	1.05	0.67	14.29	14
Retail Business	0.51	0.54	0.81	0.66	14.81	27
Wholesale and Commission Business	0.62	0.56	0.62	0.48	31.18	93
Real Estate Service	0.49	0.34	0.56	0.40	40.00	5
Accommodation	0.43	0.24	0.69	0.34	50.00	2
Computer Programming and Consultancy	0.56	0.61	0.52	0.34	32.26	31
Other Professional Service	0.51	0.27	0.29	0.25	66.67	6
Motion Picture Production and Music Publishing	0.45	0.20	0.35	0.24	35.00	20
Publishing Service	0.31	0.14	0.23	0.19	30.23	86
Education Service	0.30	0.26	0.47	0.19	10.00	10
Business Support Service	0.44	0.19	0.53	0.18	22.22	18
Sales of Motor Vehicles and Parts	NA	NA	0.77	0.16	100.00	1
Broadcasting	0.41	0.35	0.40	0.12	9.09	11
Information Service	0.53	0.21	0.35	0.12	11.54	26
Research and Development	0.11	0.01	0.40	0.11	69.23	13
Waste Recycling Business	0.47	0.39	N.A.	N.A.	N.A.	4
Remediation Service	0.44	0.32	N.A.	N.A.	N.A.	1
Air Transport	0.89	0.88	N.A.	N.A.	N.A.	3
Storage and Transport Support	0.57	0.38	N.A.	N.A.	N.A.	3

(*Continued*)

Table 6.36. (*Continued*)

Industry	OI ≥0		OI <0		Percentage of Firms with OI <0	Number of Firms
	Debt Ratio	Debt Ratio*	Debt Ratio	Debt Ratio*		
Telecommunication	0.54	0.55	N.A.	N.A.	N.A.	11
Renting and Leasing	0.77	0.75	N.A.	N.A.	N.A.	2
Creative Arts and Recreation	0.32	0.18	N.A.	N.A.	N.A.	2
Sports and Amusement Business	0.27	0.14	N.A.	N.A.	N.A.	7
Other Personal Service	0.30	0.08	N.A.	N.A.	N.A.	1

Notes: Debt ratio is the ratio of the total debt of an industry to its total assets. *indicates the ratio of the total debt of an industry to its total assets which are defined as the book value of debt plus the market value of equity. OI ≥0 indicates firms with non-negative operating income.

debt to the book value of the asset. The debt ratio of industries is divided into categories of non-negative operating income or negative operating income. If an industry faces serious financial risk, the firms with negative operating income may face more serious financial risk, such as a high debt ratio, than firms with positive operating income. Table 6.36 lists industries in descending order of the debt ratio* of firms with negative operating income.

According to Table 6.36, the water transport, professional service, land transport service, architectural engineering service, and retail business industries had higher debt ratios than industries with positive operating income. These five industries appear to have higher financial risk, especially for listed firms with negative operating income. For example, the debt ratio of firms with negative operating income in the water transport industry was 0.95 in 2015, which is much higher than 0.71 for firms with positive operating income. Given the poor profitability and low interest coverage ratio of the water transport industry, the listed firms with negative operating income are more likely to have serious financial risk.

6.3.4.   *Valuation*

Figure 6.12 presents the M/B ratios of the top 10 most profitable industries of the tertiary sector in 2015. The valuation of the industries in terms of M/B ratios varies. The other personal service industry, which is the most profitable, has the highest M/B ratio at 5.24 but it has only one listed firm. The information service industry, the second most profitable, has the second highest M/B ratio at 4.23. This industry, with 70 listed firms, has been rapidly expanding and was profitable for 2011–2015, as we discussed earlier. The industry with the third highest valuation of 3.55 is the business support industry, which has also been rapidly expanding. Its annual sales growth was 25.5% for 2011–2015, as shown in Table 6.31. This industry is the sixth most profitable industry in the tertiary section, according to Table 6.32.

The retail business industry, which is the 10th most profitable industry, has the lowest M/B ratio, 0.89, among the top 10 most profitable industries. Although the sales growth of the retail business industry decreased by half between 2006–2010 and 2011–2015, its

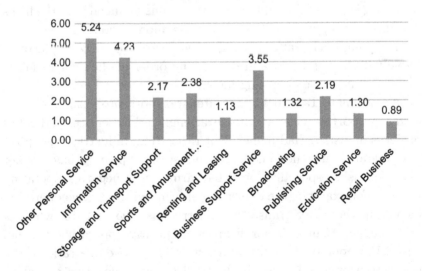

Figure 6.12.   M/B Ratios of Top 10 Most Profitable Industries in 2015

Note: The M/B ratio is calculated as the total market value of equity divided by the total consolidated book value of equity in an industry.

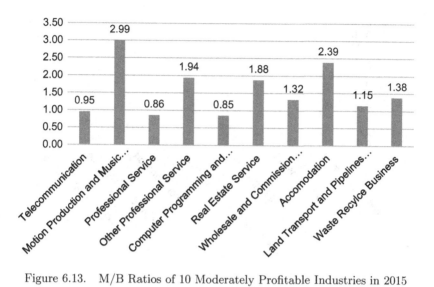

Figure 6.13. M/B Ratios of 10 Moderately Profitable Industries in 2015
Note: The M/B ratio is calculated as the total market value of equity divided by the total consolidated book value of equity in an industry.

annual sales growth, on average, was 12.1% for 2011–2015. Given its high profitability and high sales growth, the low M/B ratio of this industry may be questionable. Its profitability ratios, however, tended to decrease. For example, its operating margin decreased from 8.46% in 2011 to 4.18% in 2015.

The 10 moderately profitable industries, on average, have lower M/B ratios than the 10 most profitable industries. The motion picture production and music publishing industry has the highest M/B ratio at 2.99. The sales revenue of this industry expanded from 9.0% for 2006–2010 to 16.3% for 2011–2015, as shown in Table 6.31. The accommodation industry, which has only two listed firms, has the second highest M/B ratio at 2.38. Its profitability ratios continued to decrease from 2011 to 2015. For example, the operating margin was −0.08% in 2014 and −0.17% in 2015.

The valuation of the seven least profitable industries in the tertiary sector is puzzling. The sales of motor vehicles industry and the research and development industry have the two highest M/B ratios among the 27 industries in the tertiary sector. The M/B ratios

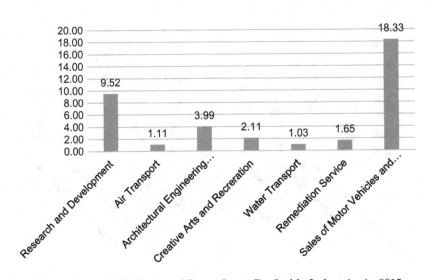

Figure 6.14.   M/B Ratios of Seven Least Profitable Industries in 2015

Note: The M/B ratio is calculated as the total market value of equity divided by the total consolidated book value of equity in an industry.

of all seven industries are above 1, according to Figure 6.14. The sales of motor vehicles industry, which has only one listed firm, New Pride Corporation, continued to have negative profitability ratios. For example, the operating margin was −17.74% for 2006–2010 and −4.8% for 2011–2015. The annual sales growth of New Pride Corporation was also −20.4% for 2011–2015. Its sales growth and profitability fail to justify the extremely high valuation of this firm.

On the other hand, the research and development industry, with 13 listed firms, had extremely high annual sales growth, according to Table 6.31. The annual sales growth of this industry was 58.0% for 2006–2011 and 53.9% for 2011–2015. However, its operating margin and ROE were negative for both 2006–2010 and 2011–2015. Although the operating margin improved between these two periods, it was −16.0% for 2011–2015, as shown in Table 6.34. In general, the valuation of the least profitable industries does not appear to be justified by their financial information. These industries may be overvalued. However, it is possible that the future prospects of these industries may be much better than indicated by past financial information.

References

Korea Instutute for Industrial Economics & Trade, 2015, Key Indicators of Major Industries (in Korean). Retrieved from http://www.kiet.re.kr/kiet_web/? sub_num=73&state=view&idx=52128.

Park, Jong-Il, S., Choi, and H. Nam, 2014, The Effect of Mandatory Adoption of K-IFRS on Relative Value Revlevance of Earnings: An Comparative Analysis of Consolidated, Separate, and Individual Financial Statements, Academic Conference Papers of Korean Accounting Association 2, 1424–1455 (In Korean).

Index